The Standard of Review in WTO Dispute Settlement

The Standard of Review in WTO Dispute Settlement

Critique and Development

Ross Becroft

Principal, Gross & Becroft Lawyers and Sessional Academic, Melbourne Law School, Australia

Edward Elgar

Cheltenham, UK • Northampton, MA, USA

Published by
Edward Elgar Publishing Limited
The Lypiatts
15 Lansdown Road
Cheltenham
Glos GL50 2JA
UK

Edward Elgar Publishing, Inc.
William Pratt House
9 Dewey Court
Northampton
Massachusetts 01060
USA

A catalogue record for this book
is available from the British Library

Library of Congress Control Number: 2012930615

MIX
Paper from
responsible sources
FSC® C018575

ISBN 978 1 78100 223 0

Printed and bound by MPG Books Group, UK

Contents

Preface

This book deals with the question of what kind of standard of review WTO panels should apply when reviewing whether a WTO member has complied with its obligations under the WTO Agreements. The key conceptual issue is the degree of deference (if any) that WTO panels ought to apply to measures of WTO members. This is important because it may affect the allocation of power between international organizations and States. In the case of the WTO, this question is particularly relevant because many measures derive from domestic administrative or judicial processes, and WTO panels are often not merely examining whether domestic laws or decisions made by domestic governments comply with WTO obligations.

I argue that the WTO should adopt a flexible standard of review that would vary depending upon the type of measure being examined. It is contended that panels should, as a general proposition, apply a highly intensive and non-deferential factual standard of review when examining domestic measures. If, however, WTO members have separately retained certain jurisdictional competencies to deal with particular disciplines, such as in the case of anti-dumping and countervailing measures, then a more deferential standard of review should apply. This approach constitutes a completely new conceptual framework, but it would not always vary the standard of review that is presently applied.

In this book, I examine existing WTO jurisprudence and literature on this issue, and I also conduct a brief survey of standards of review within selected domestic and international legal systems. From this analysis, I contend that the WTO standard of review should be based on three major considerations: the promotion of key objectives of WTO dispute settlement, enhancing adjudicative legitimacy, and procedural effectiveness. I conclude that a new flexible standard of review as proposed would best satisfy these considerations in an overall sense. That is, this test provides the best balance of these sometimes competing issues. I then go on to articulate the theoretical elements of this new standard, and then discuss how this standard may be applied to several WTO Agreements where its application may be contentious.

I conclude that this new standard of review would be a significant enhancement to the WTO dispute settlement system. It would provide for a more balanced and consistent interpretation of the WTO Agreements. Further, this standard, and the underlying principles, may provide the foundations for developing similar standards in other international dispute bodies in the future. This work ultimately concerns the nature and scope of judicial review in international trade law, treaty interpretation, and constitutional questions about the level of intrusion by international bodies in domestic affairs.

The genesis of this book was the idea that the standard of review exercised by WTO panels may affect the way in which the WTO Agreements are interpreted and applied. This legal concept may then result in more or less strict adherence to WTO commitments. Therefore, the standard of review is an influential mechanism that has the potential to mediate the legal relationship the WTO and its membership, being predominantly sovereign States. It is my view that the reform of the standard of review as advocated in this work will develop and strengthen the WTO and the international trading system.

Ross Becroft
Melbourne
May 2012

Acknowledgements

This book was researched and written between 2004 and 2012 whilst I was working in private legal practice.

I would like to thank Andrew Mitchell at the Melbourne Law School for his outstanding guidance and friendship.

Most importantly, I must acknowledge the dedication and support of my wife Candice and children Lara and Elliot, which is so valuable and unlauded in projects of this kind.

Abbreviations

GENERAL ABBREVIATIONS

AAT	Administrative Appeals Tribunal
ADJR Act	Administrative Decisions (Judicial Review) Act 1977 (Cth)
Agreement on Customs Valuation	Agreement on Implementation of Article VII of the GATT 1994
Anti-Dumping Agreement	Agreement on Implementation of Article VI of the GATT 1994
APA	Administrative Procedure Act
ATC	Agreement on Textiles and Clothing
BISD	Basic Instruments and Selected Documents
DSB	Dispute Settlement Body
DSU	Understanding on Rules and Procedures Governing the Settlement of Disputes (Dispute Settlement Understanding)
EC	European Communities
ECHR	European Court of Human Rights
ECJ	European Court of Justice
GATS	General Agreement on Trade in Services
GATT or GATT 1947	General Agreement on Tariffs and Trade
GATT 1994	General Agreement on Tariffs and Trade 1994, Annex 1A, Marrakesh Agreement Establishing the World Trade Organization
ICJ	International Court of Justice
ICSID	International Convention on the Settlement of Investment Disputes between States and Nationals of Other States
ITO	International Trade Organisation
ITO Charter	Charter for an International Trade Organization
Maastricht Treaty	Treaty on European Union
Marrakesh Agreement	Agreement Establishing the World Trade Organization

NAFTA	North American Free Trade Agreement
Safeguards Agreement	Agreement on Safeguards
SCM Agreement	Agreement on Subsidies and Countervailing Measures
SPS Agreement	Agreement on the Application of Sanitary and Phytosanitary Measures
TBT Agreement	Agreement on Technical Barriers to Trade
Trade Remedy Agreements	The Anti-Dumping Agreement, SCM Agreement and Safeguards Agreement
TRIPS Agreement	Agreement on Trade-Related Aspects of Intellectual Property Rights
TMB	Textile Monitoring Body
USITC	United States International Trade Commission
VCLT	Vienna Convention on the Law of Treaties
WTO	World Trade Organization
WTO Agreements	The Marrakesh Agreement and the documents contained in its four annexes
WTO Tribunals	WTO Arbitral Bodies, Panels and the Appellate Body

GATT REPORT ABBREVIATIONS

Korea-Resins	GATT Panel Report, *Panel on Korea-Anti-Dumping Duties on Imports of Polyacetal Resins from the United States*, ADP/92 and Corr.1, adopted 27 April 1993, BISD 40S/205
New Zealand-Finnish Transformers	GATT Panel Report, *New Zealand-Imports of Electrical Transformers from Finland*, L/5814, adopted 18 July 1985, BISD 32S/55
US-Fur Felt Hats	*Report on the Withdrawal by the United States of a Tariff Concession under Article XIX of the General Agreement on Tariffs and Trade*, GATT/CP/106, adopted 22 October 1951
US-Norwegian Salmon AD	GATT Panel Report, *Imposition of Anti-Dumping Duties on Imports of Fresh and Chilled Atlantic Salmon from Norway*, ADP/87, adopted 27 April 1994, BISD 41S/229

US-Section 337 Tariff Act	GATT Panel Report, *United States Section 337 of the Tariff Act of 1930*, L/6439, adopted 7 November 1989, BISD 36S/345
US-Swedish Steel	GATT Panel Report, *United States – Imposition of Anti-Dumping Duties on Imports of Seamless Stainless Steel Hollow Products from Sweden*, ADP/47, 20 August 1990, unadopted

WTO REPORT AND AWARD ABBREVIATIONS

Argentina-Footwear (EC)	Appellate Body Report, *Argentina-Safeguard Measures on Imports of Footwear*, WT/DS121/AB/R, adopted 12 January 2000, DSR 2000:I, 515
Argentina-Footwear (EC)	Appellate Body Report, *Argentina-Safeguard Measures on Imports of Footwear*, WT/DS121/AB/R, adopted 12 January 2000, DSR 2000:I, 515
Argentina-Footwear (EC)	Panel Report, *Argentina-Safeguard Measures on Imports of Footwear*, WT/DS121/R, adopted 12 January 2000, as modified by Appellate Body Report WT/DS121/AB/R, DSR 2000:II, 575
Argentina-Hides and Leather	Panel Report, *Argentina-Measures Affecting the Export of Bovine Hides and Import of Finished Leather*, WT/DS155/R and Corr.1, adopted 16 February 2001, DSR 2001:V, 1779
Argentina-Textiles and Apparel	Appellate Body Report, *Argentina-Measures Affecting Imports of Footwear, Textiles, Apparel and Other Items*, WT/DS56/AB/R and Corr.1, adopted 22 April 1998, DSR 1998:III, 1003
Argentina-Textiles and Apparel	Panel Report, *Argentina-Measures Affecting Imports of Footwear, Textiles, Apparel and Other Items*, WT/DS56/R, adopted 22 April 1998, as modified by Appellate Body Report WT/DS56/AB/R, DSR 1998:III, 1033

Australia-Apples	Appellate Body Report, *Australia-Measures Affecting the Importation of Apples from New Zealand*, WT/DS367/AB/R, adopted 17 December 2010
Australia-Apples	Panel Report, *Australia-Measures Affecting the Importation of Apples from New Zealand*, WT/DS367/R, adopted 17 December 2010, as modified by Appellate Body Report WT/DS367/AB/R
Australia-Salmon	Appellate Body Report, *Australia-Measures Affecting Importation of Salmon*, WT/DS18/AB/R, adopted 6 November 1998, DSR 1998:VIII, 3327
Australia-Salmon	Panel Report, *Australia-Measures Affecting Importation of Salmon*, WT/DS18/R and Corr.1, adopted 6 November 1998, as modified by Appellate Body Report WT/DS18/AB/R, DSR 1998:VIII, 3407
Brazil-Retreaded Tyres	Appellate Body Report, *Brazil-Measures Affecting Imports of Retreaded Tyres*, WT/DS332/AB/R, adopted 17 December 2007, DSR 2007:IV, 1527
Brazil-Retreaded Tyres	Panel Report, *Brazil-Measures Affecting Imports of Retreaded Tyres*, WT/DS332/R, adopted 17 December 2007, as modified by Appellate Body Report WT/DS332/AB/R, DSR 2007:V, 1649
Brazil-Retreaded Tyres (Article 21.3(c))	Award of the Arbitrator, *Brazil-Measures Affecting Imports of Retreaded Tyres-Arbitration under Article 21.3(c) of the DSU*, WT/DS332/16, 29 August 2008
Canada-Aircraft	Appellate Body Report, *Canada-Measures Affecting the Export of Civilian Aircraft*, WT/DS70/AB/R, adopted 20 August 1999, DSR 1999:III, 1377
Canada-Autos	Appellate Body Report, *Canada-Certain Measures Affecting the Automotive Industry*, WT/DS139/AB/R, WT/DS142/AB/R, adopted 19 June 2000, DSR 2000:VI, 2985

Canada-Autos — Panel Report, *Canada-Certain Measures Affecting the Automotive Industry*, WT/DS139/R, WT/DS142/R, adopted 19 June 2000, as modified by Appellate Body Report WT/DS139/AB/R, WT/DS142/AB/R, DSR 2000:VII, 3043

Canada-Continued Suspension — Appellate Body Report, *Canada-Continued Suspension of Obligations in the EC-Hormones Dispute*, WT/DS321/AB/R, adopted 14 November 2008

Canada-Continued of Suspension — Panel Report, *Canada-Continued Suspension Obligations in the EC-Hormones Dispute*, WT/DS321/R, adopted 14 November 2008, as modified by Appellate Body Report WT/DS321/AB/R

Canada-Periodicals — Appellate Body Report, *Canada-Certain Measures Concerning Periodicals*, WT/DS31/AB/R, adopted 30 July 1997, DSR 1997:I, 449

Canada-Periodicals — Panel Report, *Canada-Certain Measures Concerning Periodicals*, WT/DS31/R and Corr.1, adopted 30 July 1997, as modified by Appellate Body Report WT/DS31/AB/R, DSR 1997:I, 481

Chile-Alcoholic Beverages — Appellate Body Report, *Chile-Taxes on Alcoholic Beverages*, WT/DS87/AB/R, WT/DS110/AB/R, adopted 12 January 2000, DSR 2000:I, 281

Chile-Alcoholic Beverages — Panel Report, *Chile-Taxes on Alcoholic Beverages*, WT/DS87/R, WT/DS110/R, adopted 12 January 2000, as modified by Appellate Body Report WT/DS87/AB/R, WT/DS110/AB/R, DSR 2000:I, 303

Chile-Price Band System — Panel Report, *Chile-Price Band System and Safeguard Measures Relating to Certain Agricultural Products*, WT/DS207/R, adopted 23 October 2002, as modified by Appellate Body Report WT/DS207AB/R, DSR 2002:VIII, 3127

China-Auto Parts	Appellate Body Reports, *China-Measures Affecting Imports of Automobile Parts*, WT/DS339/AB/R, WT/DS340/AB/R, WT/DS342/AB/R, adopted 12 January 2009
China-Auto Parts	Panel Reports, *China-Measures Affecting Imports of Automobile Parts*, WT/DS339/R, WT/DS340/R, WT/DS342/R and Add.1 and Add.2, adopted 12 January 2009, as upheld (WT/DS339/R), and as modified (WT/DS340/R, WT/DS342/R) by Appellate Body Reports WT/DS339/AB/R, WT/DS340/AB/R, WT/DS342/AB/R
China-Publications and Audiovisual Products	Appellate Body Report, *China-Measures Affecting Trading Rights and Distribution Services for Certain Publications and Audiovisual Entertainment Products*, WT/DS363/AB/R, adopted 19 January 2010
China-Publications and Audiovisual Products	Panel Report, *China-Measures Affecting Trading Rights and Distribution Services for Certain Publications and Audiovisual Entertainment Products*, WT/DS363/R and Corr.1, adopted 19 January 2010, as modified by Appellate Body Report WT/DS363/AB/R
Colombia-Ports of Entry	Panel Report, *Colombia-Indicative Prices and Restrictions on Ports of Entry*, WT/DS366/R and Corr.1, adopted 20 May 2009
Colombia-Ports of Entry (Article 21.3(c))	Award of the Arbitrator, *Colombia-Indicative Prices and Restrictions on Ports of Entry-Arbitration under Article 21.3(c) of the DSU*, WT/DS366/13, 2 October 2009
Dominican Republic-Import and Sale of Cigarettes	Appellate Body Report, *Dominican Republic-Measures Affecting the Importation and Internal Sale of Cigarettes*, WT/DS302/AB/R, adopted 19 May 2005, DSR 2005:XV, 7367
Dominican Republic-Import and Sale of Cigarettes	Panel Report, *Dominican Republic-Measures Affecting the Importation and Internal Sale of*

	Cigarettes, WT/DS302/R, adopted 19 May 2005, as modified by Appellate Body Report WT/DS302/AB/R, DSR 2005:XV, 7425
EC-Approval and Marketing	Panel Report, *European Communities-Measures of Biotech Products Affecting the Approval and Marketing of Biotech Products*, WT/DS291/R, WT/DS292/R, WT/DS293/R, Add.1 to Add.9, and Corr.1, adopted 21 November 2006, DSR 2006:III-VIII
EC-Asbestos	Appellate Body Report, *European Communities-Measures Affecting Asbestos and Asbestos-Containing Products*, WT/DS135/AB/R, adopted 5 April 2001, DSR 2001:VII, 3243
EC-Asbestos	Panel Report, *European Communities-Measures Affecting Asbestos and Asbestos-Containing Products*, WT/DS135/R and Add.1, adopted 5 April 2001, as modified by Appellate Body Report WT/DS135/AB/R, DSR 2001:VIII, 3305
EC-Bananas III (Article 21.5-US)	Panel Report, *European Communities-Regime for the Importation, Sale and Distribution of Bananas-Recourse to Article 21.5 of the DSU by the United States*, WT/DS27/RW/USA and Corr.1, adopted 22 December 2008, upheld by Appellate Body Report WT/DS27/AB/RW/USA
EC-Bed Linen	Appellate Body Report, *European Communities-Anti-Dumping Duties on Imports of Cotton-Type Bed Linen from India*, WT/DS141/AB/R, adopted 12 March 2001, DSR 2001:V, 2049
EC-Chicken Cuts (Brazil)	Panel Report, *European Communities-Customs Classification of Frozen Boneless Chicken Cuts, Complaint by Brazil*, WT/DS269/R, adopted 27 September 2005, as modified by Appellate Body Report WT/DS269/AB/R, WT/DS286/AB/R, DSR 2005:XIX, 9295

EC-Chicken Cuts (Thailand)	Panel Report, *European Communities-Customs Classification of Frozen Boneless Chicken Cuts, Complaint by Thailand*, WT/DS286/R, adopted 27 September 2005, as modified by Appellate Body Report WT/DS269/AB/R, WT/DS286/AB/R, DSR 2005:XX, 9721
EC-Computer Equipment	Appellate Body Report, *European Communities-Customs Classification of Certain Computer Equipment*, WT/DS62/AB/R, WT/DS67/AB/R, WT/DS68/AB/R, adopted 22 June 1998, DSR 1998:V, 1851
EC-Computer Equipment	Panel Report, *European Communities-Customs Classification of Certain Computer Equipment*, WT/DS62/R, WT/DS67/R, WT/DS68/R, adopted 22 June 1998, as modified by Appellate Body Report WT/DS62/AB/R, WT/DS67/AB/R, WT/DS68/AB/R, DSR 1998:V, 1891
EC-Hormones	Appellate Body Report, *EC Measures Concerning Meat and Meat Products (Hormones)*, WT/DS26/AB/R, WT/DS48/AB/R, adopted 13 February 1998, DSR 1998:I, 135
EC-Hormones (Canada)	Panel Report, *EC Measures Concerning Meat and Meat Products (Hormones), Complaint by Canada*, WT/DS48/R/CAN, adopted 13 February 1998, as modified by Appellate Body Report WT/DS26/AB/R, WT/DS48/ AB/R, DSR 1998:II, 235
EC-Hormones (US)	Panel Report, *EC Measures Concerning Meat and Meat Products (Hormones), Complaint by the United States*, WT/DS26/R/USA, adopted 13 February 1998, as modified by Appellate Body Report WT/DS26/AB/R, WT/DS48/AB/R, DSR 1998:III, 699
EC-Hormones (Article 21.3(c))	Award of the Arbitrator, *EC Measures Concerning Meat and Meat Products (Hormones)-Arbitration under Article 21.3(c)*

	of the DSU, WT/DS26/15, WT/DS48/13, 29 May 1998, DSR 1998:V, 1833
EC-Hormones (Canada) (Article 22.6-EC)	Decision by the Arbitrators, *European Communities-Measures Concerning Meat and Meat Products (Hormones), Original Complaint by Canada – Recourse to Arbitration by the European Communities under Article 22.6 of the DSU*, WT/DS48/ARB, 12 July 1999, DSR 1999:III, 1135
EC-Hormones (US) (Article 22.6-EC)	Decision by the Arbitrators, *European Communities-Measures Concerning Meat and Meat Products (Hormones), Original Complaint by the United States-Recourse to Arbitration by the European Communities under Article 22.6 of the DSU*, T/DS26/ARB, 12 July 1999, DSR 1999:III, 1105
EC-Poultry	Appellate Body Report, *European Communities-Measures Affecting the Importation of Certain Poultry Products*, WT/DS69/AB/R, adopted 23 July 1998, DSR 1998:V, 2031
EC-Sardines	Appellate Body Report, *European Communities-Trade Description of Sardines*, WT/DS231/AB/R, adopted 23 October 2002, DSR 2002:VIII, 3359
EC-Sardines	Panel Report, *European Communities-Trade Description of Sardines*, WT/DS231/R and Corr.1, adopted 23 October 2002, as modified by Appellate Body Report WT/DS231/AB/R, DSR 2002:VIII, 3451
EC-Selected Customs Matters	Appellate Body Report, *European Communities-Selected Customs Matters*, WT/DS315/AB/R, adopted 11 December 2006, DSR 2006:IX, 3791
EC-Selected Customs Matters	Panel Report, *European Communities-Selected Customs Matters*, WT/DS315/R, adopted 11 December 2006, as modified by Appellate Body Report WT/DS315/AB/R, DSR 2006: IX-X, 3915

Egypt-Steel Rebar	Panel Report, *Egypt-Definitive Anti-Dumping Measures on Steel Rebar from Turkey*, WT/DS211/R, adopted 1 October 2002, DSR 2002:VII, 2667
Guatemala-Cement I	Appellate Body Report, *Guatemala-Anti-Dumping Investigation Regarding Portland Cement from Mexico*, WT/DS60/AB/R, adopted 25 November 1998, DSR 1998:IX, 3767
Guatemala-Cement I	Panel Report, *Guatemala-Anti-Dumping Investigation Regarding Portland Cement from Mexico*, WT/DS60/R, adopted 25 November 1998, as modified by Appellate Body Report WT/DS60/AB/R, DSR 1998:IX, 3797
Guatemala-Cement II	Panel Report, *Guatemala-Definitive Anti-Dumping Measures on Grey Portland Cement from Mexico*, WT/DS156/R, adopted 17 November 2000, DSR 2000:XI, 5295
India-Additional Import Duties	Appellate Body Report, *India-Additional and Extra-Additional Duties on Imports from the United States*, WT/DS360/AB/R, adopted 17 November 2008
India-Additional Import Duties	Panel Report, *India-Additional and Extra-Additional Duties on Imports from the United States*, WT/DS360/R, adopted 17 November 2008, reversed by Appellate Body Report WT/DS360/AB/R
India-Patents (US) Protection	Appellate Body Report, *India-Patent for Pharmaceutical and Agricultural Chemical Products*, WT/DS50/AB/R, adopted 16 January 1998, DSR 1998:I, 9
Indonesia-Autos	Panel Report, *Indonesia-Certain Measures Affecting the Automobile Industry*, WT/DS54/R, WT/DS55/R, WT/DS59/R, WT/DS64/R and Corr.1 and 2, adopted 23 July 1998, and Corr. 3 and 4, DSR 1998:VI, 2201

Japan-Agricultural Products II	Panel Report, *Japan-Measures Affecting Agricultural Products*, WT/DS76/R, adopted 19 March 1999, as modified by Appellate Body Report WT/DS76/AB/R, DSR 1999:I, 315
Japan-Alcoholic Beverages II	Appellate Body Report, *Japan-Taxes on Alcoholic Beverages*, WT/DS8/AB/R, WT/DS10/AB/R, WT/DS11/AB/R, adopted 1 November 1996, DSR 1996:I, 97
Japan-Apples	Appellate Body Report, *Japan-Measures Affecting the Importation of Apples*, WT/DS245/AB/R, adopted 10 December 2003, DSR 2003:IX, 4391
Japan-Apples	Panel Report, *Japan-Measures Affecting the Importation of Apples*, WT/DS245/R, adopted 10 December 2003, as upheld by Appellate Body Report WT/DS245/AB/R, DSR 2003:IX, 4481
Japan-DRAMs (Korea)	Appellate Body Report, *Japan-Countervailing Duties on Dynamic Random Access Memories from Korea*, WT/DS336/AB/R and Corr.1, adopted 17 December 2007, DSR 2007:VII, 2703
Japan-DRAMs (Korea)	Panel Report, *Japan-Countervailing Duties on Dynamic Random Access Memories from Korea*, WT/DS336/R, adopted 17 December 2007, as modified by Appellate Body Report WT/DS336/AB/R, DSR 2007:VII, 2805
Japan-Film	Panel Report, *Japan-Measures Affecting Consumer Photographic Film and Paper*, WT/DS44/R, adopted 22 April 1998, DSR 1998:IV, 1179
Korea-Alcoholic Beverages	Appellate Body Report, *Korea-Taxes on Alcoholic Beverages*, WT/DS75/AB/R, WT/DS84/AB/R, adopted 17 February 1999, DSR 1999:I, 3

Korea-Alcoholic Beverages	Panel Report, *Korea-Taxes on Alcoholic Beverages*, WT/DS75/R, WT/DS84/R, adopted 17 February 1999, as modified by Appellate Body Report WT/DS75/AB/R, WT/DS84/AB/R, DSR 1999:I, 44
Korea-Various Measures on Beef	Appellate Body Report, *Korea-Measures Affecting Imports of Fresh, Chilled and Frozen Beef*, WT/DS161/AB/R, WT/DS169/AB/R, adopted 10 January 2001, DSR 2001:I, 5
Mexico-Anti-Dumping Measures on Rice	Panel Report, *Mexico-Definitive Anti-Dumping Measures on Beef and Rice, Complaint with Respect to Rice*, WT/DS295/R, adopted 20 December 2005, as modified by Appellate Body Report WT/DS295/AB/R, DSR 2005:XXIII, 11007
Mexico-Corn Syrup	Panel Report, *Mexico-Anti-Dumping Investigation of High Fructose Corn Syrup (HFCS) from the United States*, WT/DS132/R, adopted 24 February 2000, and Corr.1, DSR 2000:III, 1345
Mexico-Olive Oil	Panel Report, *Mexico-Definitive Countervailing Measures on Olive Oil from the European Communities*, WT/DS341/R, adopted 21 October 2008
Mexico-Taxes on Soft Drinks	Appellate Body Report, *Mexico-Tax Measures on Soft Drinks and Other Beverages*, WT/DS308/AB/R, adopted 24 March 2006, DSR 2006:I, 3
Mexico-Taxes on Soft Drinks	Panel Report, *Mexico-Tax Measures on Soft Drinks and Other Beverages*, WT/DS308/R, adopted 24 March 2006, as modified by Appellate Body Report WT/DS308/AB/R, DSR 2006:I, 43
Thailand-Cigarettes (Philippines) (Panel)	Panel Report, *Thailand-Customs and Fiscal Measures on Cigarettes from the Philippines*, WT/DS371/R, adopted 15 July 2011

Thailand-H-Beams	Appellate Body Report, *Thailand-Anti-Dumping Duties on Angles, Shapes and Sections of Iron or Non-Alloy Steel and H-Beams from Poland*, WT/DS122/AB/R, adopted 5 April 2001, DSR 2001:VII, 2701
Thailand-H-Beams	Panel Report, *Thailand-Anti-Dumping Duties on Angles, Shapes and Sections of Iron or Non-Alloy Steel and H-Beams from Poland*, WT/DS122/R, adopted 5 April 2001, as modified by Appellate Body Report WT/DS122/AB/R, DSR 2001:VII, 2741
US-1916 Act	Appellate Body Report, *United States-Anti-Dumping Act of 1916*, WT/DS136/AB/R, WT/DS162/AB/R, adopted 26 September 2000, DSR 2000:X, 4793
US-Anti-Dumping and Countervailing Duties (China)	Appellate Body Report, Definitive Anti-Dumping and Countervailing Duties on Certain Products from China, WT/DS379/AB/R, adopted 25 March 2011
US-Certain EC Products	Appellate Body Report, *United States-Import Measures on Certain Products from the European Communities*, WT/DS165/AB/R, adopted 10 January 2001, DSR 2001:I, 373
US-Continued Suspension	Appellate Body Report, *United States-Continued Suspension of Obligations in the EC-Hormones Dispute*, WT/DS320/AB/R, adopted 14 November 2008, DSR 2008:X, 3507
US-Continued Suspension	Panel Report, *United States-Continued Suspension of Obligations in the EC-Hormones Dispute*, WT/DS320/R, adopted 14 November 2008, as modified by Appellate Body Report WT/DS320/AB/R, DSR 2008:XI, 3891
US-Continued Zeroing	Appellate Body Report, *United States-Continued Existence and Application of Zeroing Methodology*, WT/DS350/AB/R, adopted 19 February 2009

US-Corrosion-Resistant Steel Sunset Review	Appellate Body Report, United States-Sunset Review of Anti-Dumping Duties on Corrosion-Resistant Carbon Steel Flat Products from Japan, WT/DS244/AB/R, adopted 9 January 2004, DSR 2004:I, 3
US-Cotton Yarn	Appellate Body Report, *United States-Transitional Safeguard Measure on Combed Cotton Yarn from Pakistan*, WT/DS192/AB/R, adopted 5 November 2001, DSR 2001:XII, 6027
US-Cotton Yarn	Panel Report, *United States-Transitional Safeguard Measure on Combed Cotton Yarn from Pakistan*, WT/DS192/R, adopted 5 November 2001, as modified by Appellate Body Report WT/DS192/AB/R, DSR 2001:XII, 6067
US-Countervailing Duty Investigation on DRAMS	Appellate Body Report, *United States-Countervailing Duty Investigation on Dynamic Random Access Memory Semiconductors (DRAMS) from Korea*, WT/DS296/AB/R, adopted 20 July 2005, DSR 2005:XVI, 8131
US-Countervailing Duty Investigation on DRAMS	Panel Report, *United States-Countervailing Duty Investigation on Dynamic Random Access Memory Semiconductors (DRAMS) from Korea*, WT/DS296/R, adopted 20 July 2005, as modified by Appellate Body Report WT/DS296/AB/R, DSR 2005:XVII, 8243
US-DRAMS	Panel Report, *United States-Anti-Dumping Duty on Dynamic Random Access Memory Semiconductors (DRAMS) of One Megabit or Above from Korea*, WT/DS99/R, adopted 19 March 1999, DSR 1999:II, 521
US-Gasoline	Appellate Body Report, *United States-Standards for Reformulated and Conventional Gasoline*, WT/DS2/AB/R, adopted 20 May 1996, DSR 1996:I, 3

US-Gasoline	Panel Report, *United States-Standards for Reformulated and Conventional Gasoline*, WT/DS2/R, adopted 20 May 1996, as modified by Appellate Body Report WT/DS2/AB/R, DSR 1996:I, 29
US-Hot-Rolled Steel	Appellate Body Report, *United States-Anti-Dumping Measures on Certain Hot-Rolled Steel Products from Japan*, WT/DS184/AB/R, adopted 23 August 2001, DSR 2001:X, 4697
US-Hot-Rolled Steel	Panel Report, *United States-Anti-Dumping Measures on Certain Hot-Rolled Steel Products from Japan*, WT/DS184/R, adopted 23 August 2001 modified by Appellate Body Report WT/DS184/AB/R, DSR 2001:X, 4769
US-Lamb	Appellate Body Report, *United States-Safeguard Measures on Imports of Fresh, Chilled or Frozen Lamb Meat from New Zealand and Australia*, WT/DS177/AB/R, WT/DS178/AB/R, adopted 16 May 2001, DSR 2001:IX, 4051
US-Lead and Bismuth II	Appellate Body Report, *United States-Imposition of Countervailing Duties on Certain Hot-Rolled Lead and Bismuth Carbon Steel Products Originating in the United Kingdom*, WT/DS138/AB/R, adopted 7 June 2000, DSR 2000:V, 2595
US-Oil Country Tubular Goods Sunset Reviews	*Appellate Body Report, United States-Sunset Reviews of Anti-Dumping Measures on Oil Country Tubular Goods from Argentina*, WT/DS268/AB/R, adopted 17 December 2004, DSR 2004:VII, 3257
US-Section 301 Trade Act	Panel Report, *United States-Sections 301-310 of the Trade Act of 1974*, WT/DS152/R, adopted 27 January 2000, DSR 2000:II, 815
US-Shrimp	Appellate Body Report, *United States-Import Prohibition of Certain Shrimp and Shrimp Products*, WT/DS58/AB/R, adopted 6 November 1998, DSR 1998:VII, 2755

US-Shrimp	Panel Report, *United States-Import Prohibition of Certain Shrimp and Shrimp Products*, WT/DS58/R and Corr.1, adopted 6 November 1998, as modified by Appellate Body Report WT/DS58/AB/R, DSR 1998:VII, 2821
US-Softwood Lumber IV (Article 21.5-Canada)	Panel Report, *United States-Final Countervailing Duty Determination with Respect to Certain Softwood Lumber from Canada-Recourse by Canada to Article 21.5 [of the DSU]*, WT/DS257/RW, adopted 20 December 2005, as upheld by Appellate Body Report WT/DS257/AB/RW, DSR 2005:XXIII, 11401
US-Softwood Lumber VI (Article 21.5-Canada)	Appellate Body Report, *United States-Investigation of the International Trade Commission in Softwood Lumber from Canada-Recourse to Article 21.5 of the DSU by Canada*, WT/DS277/AB/RW, adopted 9 May 2006, and Corr.1, DSR 2006:XI, 4761
US-Softwood Lumber VI (Article 21.5-Canada)	Panel Report, *United States-Investigation of the International Trade Commission in Softwood Lumber from Canada-Recourse to Article 21.5 of the DSU by Canada*, WT/DS277/RW, adopted 9 May 2006, as modified by Appellate Body Report WT/DS277/AB/RW, DSR 2006:XI, 4935
US-Stainless Steel (Mexico)	Appellate Body Report, *United States-Final Anti-Dumping Measures on Stainless Steel from Mexico*, WT/DS344/AB/R, adopted 20 May 2008, DSR 2008:II, 513
US-Stainless Steel (Mexico)	Panel Report, *United States-Final Anti-Dumping Measures on Stainless Steel from Mexico*, WT/DS344/R, adopted 20 May 2008, as modified by Appellate Body Report WT/DS344/AB/R, DSR 2008:II, 599
US-Steel Plate	Panel Report, *United States-Anti-Dumping and Countervailing Measures on Steel Plate from India*, WT/DS206/R and Corr.1, adopted 29 July 2002, DSR 2002:VI, 2073

US-Steel Safeguards	Appellate Body Report, *United States-Definitive Safeguard Measures on Imports of Certain Steel Products*, WT/DS248/AB/R, WT/DS249/AB/R, WT/DS251/AB/R, WT/DS252/AB/R, WT/DS253/AB/R, WT/DS254/AB/R, WT/DS258/AB/R, WT/DS259/AB/R, adopted 10 December 2003, DSR 2003:VII, 3117
US-Tuna II (Mexico)	Panel Report, *Measures Concerning the Importation, Marketing and Sale of Tuna and Tuna Products*, WT/DS 381/R, circulated 15 September 2011
US-Tyres (China)	Appellate Body Report, *United States-Measures Affecting Imports of Certain Passenger Vehicle and Light Truck Tyres from China*, WT/DS399/AB/R, circulated 5 September 2011
US-Tyres (China)	Panel Report, *United States-Measures Affecting Imports of Certain Passenger Vehicle and Light Truck Tyres from China*, WT/DS399/R, circulated 13 December 2010, as modified by Appellate Body Report, *United States-Measures Affecting Imports of Certain Passenger Vehicle and Light Truck Tyres from China*
US-Underwear	Panel Report, *United States-Restrictions on Imports of Cotton and Man-made Fibre Underwear*, WT/DS24/R, adopted 25 February 1997, as modified by Appellate Body Report WT/DS24/AB/R, DSR 1997:I, 31
US-Upland Cotton (Article 21.5-Brazil)	Appellate Body Report, *United States-Subsidies on Upland Cotton-Recourse to Article 21.5 of the DSU by Brazil*, WT/DS267/AB/RW, adopted 20 June 2008
US-Wheat Gluten	Appellate Body Report, *United States-Definitive Safeguard Measures on Imports of Wheat Gluten from the European Communities*, WT/DS166/AB/R, adopted 19 January 2001, DSR 2001:II, 717

US-Wheat Gluten	Panel Report, *United States-Definitive Safeguard Measures on Imports of Wheat Gluten from the European Communities*, WT/DS166/R, adopted 19 January 2001, as modified by Appellate Body Report WT/DS166/AB/R, DSR 2001:III, 779
US-Wool Shirts and Blouses	Panel Report, *United States-Measure Affecting Imports of Woven Wool Shirts and Blouses from India*, WT/DS33/R, adopted 23 May 1997, as upheld by Appellate Body Report WT/DS33/AB/R, DSR 1997:I, 343
US-Zeroing (Japan)	Appellate Body Report, *United States-Measures Relating to Zeroing and Sunset Reviews,* WT/DS322/AB/R, adopted 23 January 2007, DSR 2007:I, 3
US-Zeroing (Japan)	Panel Report, *United States-Measures Relating to Zeroing and Sunset Reviews*, WT/DS322/R, adopted 23 January 2007, as modified by Appellate Body Report WT/DS322/AB/R, DSR 2007:I, 97

Table of cases

Non-WTO

ECJ

ECtHR

Table of legislation

INTERNATIONAL INSTRUMENTS

WTO

Non-WTO

NATIONAL INSTRUMENTS

Australia

Canada

Mexico

United States

1. Introduction

> Justice must always question itself, just as society can exist only by means of the work it does on itself and on its institutions.[1]

1.1 THE IMPORTANCE OF WTO OVERSIGHT OF GOVERNMENT TRADE MEASURES

This book deals with standards of review in WTO dispute settlement. Under the present WTO system, disputes are resolved primarily through panel adjudication and a second tier review by the WTO Appellate Body. It is the role of panels, at the request of a member, to review measures of another member in order to determine if the measures are consistent with WTO obligations. When panels review matters in order to reach findings, they will inevitably do so with a particular level of scrutiny or oversight that is referred to as a standard of review. This book concerns the question of what is the appropriate standard of review that WTO panels should apply when examining domestic measures. It does not deal with the standard of review applied by the WTO Appellate Body, which hears appeals on the basis of errors of law.[2]

The question of what kind of standard of review a WTO panel should apply is important because it is part of the broader issue of determining the role of panels in the WTO dispute settlement system. If a standard is less intrusive in nature, then panels may not have a great deal of power to review domestic measures. The reverse is of course equally true. Accordingly, the standard of review may be seen as an element of procedure that has a number of substantive and institutional consequences. For example, it may affect the 'vertical' allocation of competency of decision-making between WTO panels and the membership, or it may affect the 'horizontal' relationship that panels have in relation to other parts of the WTO structure, such as the Ministerial Conference and the General Council in that these organs may loosely be said

[1] Michel Foucoult, 'Vous Etes Dangereux', *Liberation* No 639, 10 June 1983 (available at http://foucoult.info/documents/foucoult.entretienDangereux.fr.html, last accessed 31 March 2012.

[2] DSU, art 17.6.

to have legislative functions.[3] In recent times, the standard of review has also been cited as an issue that may affect the way in which the WTO Agreements are interpreted, and which may potentially affect how the WTO rules are applied.[4] It has therefore sometimes been associated with the idea of the WTO 'overreaching' its mandate, and feeds into the general issues of legitimacy, competency and sustainability of international institutions. In this book I will argue that the current standard of review applied is inadequate, and that a new standard of review should be formulated. The current objective assessment test articulated by the Appellate Body in the *EC-Hormones* case is not an adequate basis for a standard of review, and it has not been applied consistently.[5] I will contend that the Appellate Body should instead develop a new flexible standard of review. This approach has two components. The first involves the formulation of a general standard of review that would be applied in all disputes concerning member obligations under the WTO Agreements, subject to the particular exceptions discussed below. The general standard of review advocated in this book requires panels to conduct a full and unrestricted review of both issues of fact and law in relation to measures. This has similarities to what is often termed *de novo* review in many domestic legal systems.

The second aspect involves modifying the general standard of review, where necessary, to take into account the specific responsibilities or 'competencies' retained for members under the various WTO Agreements. This would potentially lead to different standards of review being applied in some types of WTO disputes. However, at the same time, this type of approach is likely to lead to similar standards of review being applied in respect of Agreements dealing with similar subject matters and processes. For example, this book contends that a similar standard may be applied in relation to the trade remedy agreements, comprising the Anti-Dumping, Safeguards and SCM Agreements.[6] The Anti-Dumping Agreement presently sets out a unique standard of review, which on its face, is quite different from the standard of review that is applied in respect of other WTO Agreements.[7] The development of a new standard of review will arguably eliminate any major divergence between

[3] Matthias Oesch, *Standards of Review in WTO Dispute Resolution* (Oxford University Press, 2003) 35.

[4] See for example, Andrew Stoler, 'The WTO Dispute Settlement Process: Did the Negotiators get what they wanted?' (2004) 3(1) *World Trade Review* 99, 113.

[5] See Chapter 2, Section 2.4.3.

[6] Trade remedy mechanisms are also contained within other WTO Agreements such as the Agreement on Agriculture and the Agreement on Textiles and Clothing.

[7] This specific standard is set out in Article 17.6 of the Anti-Dumping Agreement. There is no standard of review explicitly prescribed in other WTO Agreements, including in the DSU.

the anti-dumping standard of review and the standard of review applied in relation to other trade remedy measures.

There has been a modest amount of literature on what might be an appropriate standard of review for panels to apply in WTO dispute settlement.[8] The most comprehensive work to date on the subject is Oesch's *Standards of Review in WTO Dispute Resolution.*[9] However, this work as with other works is largely descriptive in nature and does not overtly prescribe a new WTO standard of review. In 1996 Croley and Jackson published an influential and thought-provoking article on the subject in which the authors conclude that some deference may be preferable in developing the WTO standard of review, but that there should be caution in applying domestic administrative law concepts to WTO dispute settlement.[10] Since then there have been various publications on the subject which put forward alternative formulations of the WTO standard of review.[11] Arguably, debate was somewhat provoked by the Appellate Body's decision in *EC-Hormones*. The reforms argued for range from a highly intensive standard of review, such as advocated by Spamann,[12] to a more deferential test suggested by Zleptnig,[13] based on the idea of deliberative democracy.[14] Button puts forward a 'reasonable regulator' test,[15] which is somewhere between a highly intensive standard of review and an extremely deferential standard of review.[16] Finally, Ehlermann and Lockhart[17] have identified that the WTO standard of review is already to some degree being applied in a flexible manner, based on the type of WTO obligations being reviewed.[18]

---

8 See Chapter 3, Section 3.2.

9 Oesch, *Standards of Review in WTO Dispute Resolution*, above n 3.

10 Stephen Croley and John H. Jackson, 'WTO Dispute Procedures, Standard of Review and Deference to National Governments' (1996) 90(2) *American Journal of International Law* 193, 208–12.

11 These works vary enormously in the level of detail in the treatment of this subject.

12 Holger Spamann, 'Standard of Review for World Trade Organization Panels in Trade Remedy Cases: A Critical Analysis' (2004) 38(3) *Journal of World Trade* 509.

13 Stefan Zlepnig, 'The Standard of Review in WTO Law: An Analysis of Law, Legitimacy and the Distribution of Legal and Political Authority' (2002) 6(17) *European Integration Online Papers* 1 (available at http://eiop.or.at/eiop/texte/2002017.htm, last accessed 31 March 2012).

14 See Chapter 3, Sections 3.2.2 and 3.2.4.

15 Catherine Button, *The Power to Protect: Trade Health and Uncertainty in the WTO* (Hart Publishing, 2004) 217.

16 See Chapter 3, Section 3.2.3.

17 Claus-Dieter Ehlermann and Nicolas Lockhart, 'Standard of Review in WTO Law' (2004) 7(3) *Journal of International Economic Law* 491.

18 See Chapter 3, Section 3.2.5.

This book concerns the search for a new WTO standard of review. My conclusion is that a standard of review that is highly intensive should be the default position. This is essential in order for the WTO to adequately enforce the WTO Agreements. However, it is appropriate to modify this default standard of review to make it more deferential in cases when the WTO Agreements provide WTO members with specific responsibilities to ensure that trade measures comply with WTO obligations. The standard of review proposed in this book would therefore not involve WTO panels applying a singular level of intensity in reviewing domestic measures, but rather the nature of the review would vary depending upon the WTO obligations being examined. Accordingly, what I am putting forward in this book is what might be described as a hybrid test.

The approach I take in this book is to critique the current standard of review and then to identify and test the merits of a new standard of review. The book is divided into two parts. In the first part, comprising Chapters 1 to 3, I identify the major conceptual issues, provide a critique of the current standard and discuss alternative approaches. The second part, as set out in Chapters 4 to 8, involves essentially a detailed description of the two limbs of the proposed standard, and a defence of its application across the most commonly litigated provisions of the major WTO Agreements.

The remainder of this chapter consists, firstly, of an introduction to the concept of a standard of review (including how standards of review are currently formulated in several other legal systems). Secondly, I will deal with the issue of how and to what extent standards of review may apply to WTO dispute settlement. Finally, I will conclude with a short summary of the major arguments, methodology and chapter outlines.

1.2 CONCEPTUAL FOUNDATIONS OF STANDARDS OF REVIEW

1.2.1 The Definition of Standards of Review

The expression 'standard of review' refers to the manner in which an adjudicative body reviews a party's compliance with a form of regulation or the correctness of prior decisions made in the same matter. It therefore conceptualizes in legal form the scope or extent of the review task performed. A number of different words and phrases are used to describe the same process. These include the expressions 'intensity of review' and 'intrusiveness of review', all of which frequently appear in literature. The key concept to bear in mind is the relative comprehensiveness of the review exercise. Therefore, if a reviewer limits the process of review, it may be said that the reviewer applies a degree of deference or restraint in relation to the conduct or decision being reviewed. In everyday language, it may be said that the reviewer exercises some 'leeway' or grants some 'room to move' to the original decision-maker.[19] It is also sometimes referred to as the 'margin of appreciation' that a reviewer exercises towards the decision or conduct being reviewed.[20] In short, it may be envisaged as a spectrum depicting the relative intrusiveness or deference exercised by the reviewer in relation to the subject under review.

Standards of review may be formulated in a wide variety of ways. Firstly, they may be directly prescribed through judicial doctrine or legislation and both in positive and negative terms. In other words, a standard may be determined through the presence or absence of any restriction on the ability of the reviewer to conduct its review, or conversely, it may refer to any positive direction as to how the review should be conducted. The absence of any restriction of itself does not equate to an intrusive standard of review. This is because the absence of any restriction, whilst permitting the reviewer to exercise an unfettered discretion in the review process, may nonetheless result in the reviewer exercising a less intrusive standard. Secondly, standards of review are shaped by (and yet must be distinguished from) a number of other adjudicative principles and techniques. The most influential example of this is the process of fact-finding prescribed, which if extensive, may lead to a more intrusive standard being applied.[21] The review process may also be affected by matters such as the burden of proof, the method of interpretation of regulation, and the degree to which the reviewer relies upon 'issue avoidance' techniques such as the use of judicial restraint, the requirement for standing or exhaustion of alternative remedies.[22] This book does not deal with these types of principles and techniques, other than to refer to them when they directly affect the standards of review being advocated.

Generally standards of review are regarded as instruments of legal procedure given that they directly concern or are a part of the process by which a proceeding or a review is conducted. However, it has been argued that standards of review are, in reality, a product of both procedural rules and the substantive regulation being examined.[23] In my view, the standard of review should still be regarded as an aspect of procedure, albeit one which has a

---

19 Button, *The Power to Protect: Trade Health and Uncertainty in the WTO*, above n 15, 164.

20 Oesch, *Standards of Review in WTO Dispute Resolution*, above n 3, 14 and 51. Specific reference is made to the development of the margin of appreciation doctrine by the European Court of Human Rights.

21 See Michelle T. Grando, *Evidence, Proof and Fact-Finding in WTO Dispute Settlement* (Oxford University Press, 2010).

22 Oesch, *Standards of Review in WTO Dispute Resolution*, above n 3, 24–5.

23 Zlepnig, above n 13, 6.

number of wider influences and effects. Certainly, substantive provisions may affect the review task because such provisions may directly dictate the type or scope of review that may be undertaken. This type of interplay between procedural and substantive rules will be discussed in the second part of the book in relation to the question of how obligations in the WTO Agreements may alter the standard of review being applied by panels.

1.2.2 Types of Standards

Standards of review are frequently identified by reference to their relative scope of review. If this scope is seen as a spectrum, then two types of standards, namely *de novo* and total deference, occupy each end of the spectrum. *De novo* review generally refers to a situation where the reviewer conducts a full merits review of a matter and is not required to defer to or accept any of the findings of the original decision-maker.[24] The expression is usually associated with a formal hearing conducted by a court or tribunal. A hearing *de novo* has been described in a domestic administrative law context as 'the administrative law equivalent of a retrial where the matter is reconsidered with evidence produced and witnesses called.'[25] Therefore, such a hearing requires a litigant to make out its case again and the court or tribunal exercise their powers based upon the evidence before them, whether or not such evidence had been before the primary decision-maker or even existed at the time of the original decision. The key point is that there is no restriction on the later decision-maker from reviewing the merits of the case to arrive at the 'correct' decision.

When a *de novo* review is conducted, usually the degree of intensity of review is not prescribed, but rather the adjudicating body has the role of examining the case as if no prior decision had been made in order to arrive at an independent decision. A major argument in favour of conducting a *de novo* review of administrative decisions in domestic law is that it provides a new and independent avenue of review of government agency decisions.[26]

---

[24] *De novo* has a literal English translation of 'Anew'. See Mick Woodley, *Osborn's Concise Law Dictionary* (Sweet & Maxwell, 11th ed, 2009) 135.

[25] William B. Lane and Simon Young, *Administrative Law in Australia* (Law Book Company, 2007) 268.

[26] A broad scope of review of this kind is primarily directed at keeping administrative behavior of governments fair, reasonable and accountable. See Kenneth F. Warren, *Administrative Law in the Political System* (Prentice Hall, 3rd ed, 1997) 330. It is also more common where there is a serious risk of harm or disadvantage such as in deportation and family law cases: see William Wade and Christopher Forsyth, *Administrative Law* (Oxford University Press, 10th ed, 2009) 309–10.

In contrast, a standard that espouses almost total deference would result in the reviewer being required to accept the findings of the original decision-maker, unless there is a major flaw in the procedures carried out by the original decision-maker.[27] This might include, for example, a failure to accord natural justice or due process to one of the parties. Total deference therefore refers to an avoidance of the responsibility of reviewing the substantive question at issue.[28]

Between *de novo* and total deference there are various intermediate standards, which usually involve a limited scope of review that is set down in procedural rules or via the application of general principles. In a sense intermediate standards may be regarded as a 'build up' or a 'build down' from the extreme standards, depending upon the approach taken. Standards that are determined by procedural rules or legislation are sometimes referred to as statutory standards, whereas the standards that are applied by courts and tribunals based on doctrine or general principles are often known as adjudicative standards.[29] One of the most pervasive adjudicative standards is that of reasonableness. In the well-known decision of *Associated Provincial Picture Houses v Wednesbury Corporation*, the English Court of Appeal established that it is the role of the Court to examine whether an administrative decision-maker has applied a level of reasonableness. In that decision, Lord Greene MR held that:

> The court is entitled to investigate the action of the local authority with a view to seeing whether they have taken into account matters which they ought not to have taken into account, or conversely, have refused to take into account or neglected to take into account matters which they ought to take into account. Once that question is answered in favour of the local authority, it may still be possible to say that, although the local authority have kept within the four corners of the matters which they ought to consider, they have nonetheless come to a conclusion so unreasonable that no reasonable authority could have ever come to it.[30]

The above extract shows the imprecise nature of utilizing concepts such as reasonableness in that the question of what conduct is reasonable may vary depending upon the circumstances or the subjective judgment of the decision-maker.[31] The same criticism may be made of similar tests such as

---

27 Spamann, above n 12, 510.

28 See Macquarie Dictionary (Macquarie, 5th ed, 2009) 444 which defines deference as '1. submission or yielding to the judgment, opinion, will etc., of another. 2. respectful or courteous regard: in deference to his wishes.'

29 Jeffrey Waincymer, *WTO Litigation: Procedural Aspects of Formal Dispute Settlement* (Cameron May, 2002) 349.

30 [1948] 1 KB 233, 228.

31 There are also different types of reasonableness tests that many domestic courts have applied. See Dean R. Knight, 'A Murky Methodology: Standards of Review in Administrative Law' (2008) 6(1) *New Zealand Journal of Public and International Law* 117.

proportionality.[32] A higher degree of subjectivity may enable a more intrusive standard of review to be exercised, as the reviewer is not going to be restricted as would be the case with a more rigorous or checklist form of standard. By the same token, the use of an adjudicative standard of this kind does give the reviewer more flexibility in carrying out the review task. It is common for courts and tribunals to have to apply a mixture of statutory and adjudicative standards of review. The various models employed to set the scope or intensity of review in some major legal systems will be discussed in the next section of this chapter.

1.2.3 Review of Facts versus Law

An important distinction needs to be drawn between the standard of review applied to the review of facts as compared with the review of questions of law. Standards of review are normally associated with a second tier of review, where the extent of the second tier of review needs to be defined.[33] In that case, the review is normally of a decision of some kind. However, the decision made will consist of interpretations of factual matters and interpretations of law. Therefore, a separate standard of review may apply to these different interpretations. The distinction between the review of facts and law is often lost because standards are most commonly associated with a review of facts. This is largely because decision-makers may reach very different factual conclusions depending upon the way the facts of a case are scrutinized. Standards of review of law are nonetheless also important as they deal with the question of whether the reviewer must accept the original decision-maker's interpretation of laws or regulation.

The review of facts can be broken down into various sub-categories dealing with matters such as the type and extent of evidence considered, the relative weight given to different evidence, the reasoning processes, and the form of conclusions that are drawn. Broadly, a review of facts can be divided into two basic parts, being a review of the 'raw' evidence that was or ought to be have been examined by the original decision-maker, and a review of the

---

[32] A lack of proportionality may be referred to as the absence of reasonable correspondence between the object or purpose of a regulation and the regulator's decision or chosen means for achieving that object or purpose. See Christopher Enright, *Federal Administrative Law* (Federation Press, 2001) 404; Roger Douglas, *Douglas and Jones's Administrative Law* (Federation Press, 6th ed, 2009) 476.

[33] The concept of a standard of review is traditionally associated with the degree of scrutiny that a reviewer applies when examining a prior decision, and therefore, arguably a standard of review does not apply to a first time review where the reviewer is simply reviewing a set of facts to determine compliance with some form of regulation.

factual conclusions subsequently drawn from the 'raw' evidence.[34] The examination of 'raw' evidence is to some extent governed by fairly practical considerations, such as the fact-finding powers of the reviewer, the extent of reasons given at first instance, and availability of expertise and resources.[35]

The distinction between facts and law is not always conceptually clear.[36] In the context of standards of review, the line is frequently blurred between factual and legal conclusions. This is because many facts, such as in the trade remedies fields, are derived from other groups of facts. These 'inferred' facts, then may become mixed questions of fact and law. A good example in WTO law is under the Safeguards Agreement, where it is necessary to prove the 'causation' of 'serious injury'.[37] Causation of injury requires a qualitative assessment of more basic facts and also involves inferences that may constitute questions of law.

In domestic legal systems, standards of review of facts are historically more likely to be deferential than standards of review of law.[38] This is due to a number of policy reasons associated with the role of the first-instance decision-maker. Such reasons include the need for finality in decision-making and the usually high level of expertise of the decision-maker in relation to the subject matter and their proximity to witnesses. For these types of reasons the decision-maker is afforded certain privileges concerning the establishment of facts and conclusions drawn. By contrast, standards of review of law are often stricter and closer to being *de novo* in nature. This is because there is normally a policy imperative of ensuring a consistency in the interpretation of laws. Therefore, the reviewer will need to ensure that original decision-makers interpret laws in a uniform manner and the reviewer will wish to retain the competency to ensure that this occurs.

The focus of this book is on the review of facts rather than law, principally because the review of facts is more open to controversy. By this I mean that under WTO law, the role of a panel is to review measures of members. A measure may be any act or omission attributable to a WTO member.[39] It is

---

34 Oesch, *Standards of Review in WTO Dispute Resolution*, above n 3, 18.

35 *Ibid.*

36 See Tania S. Voon and Alan Yanovich, 'The Facts Aside: The Limitation of WTO Appeals to Issues of Law' (2006) 40(2) *Journal of World Trade* 239, 245.

37 Agreement on Safeguards Agreement, art 4. 'Serious Injury' is defined in Article 4.1(a) and 'causation' in Article 4.2(a).

38 Waincymer, above n 29, 348.

39 Appellate Body Report, *US-Corrosion-Resistant Steel Sunset Review* [81] cited in Panel Report, *US-Oil Country Tubular Goods Sunset Reviews* [7.136] and referred to in Alan Yanovich and Tania Voon, 'What is the Measure at issue?' in Andrew D. Mitchell (ed), *Challenges and Prospects for the WTO* (Cameron May, 2005) 115, 119.

reasonably uncontroversial that the role of panels is to determine the conformity of a domestic measure with the WTO Agreements.[40] This compliance task carried out by panels is also reinforced by the role of the WTO Appellate Body to hear appeals from panel decisions on questions of law.[41] Therefore, strictly, the role of panels should be to accord no deference to the interpretations of WTO provisions relied upon by members. The more controversial consideration is whether, or to what extent, members should be accorded deference in relation to factual determinations made by members themselves. This will be explored further in the next section of this chapter.

1.2.4 Rationales for Standards of Review

A key question is why standards of review are necessary in any administrative law review process. The reviewer could simply seek to answer the question of whether the original decision-maker arrived at the correct decision, and then use whatever means are available to answer that question. Other procedural rules concerning the nature of fact-finding and legal interpretations could potentially set the boundaries of that review without the need to add a layer of complexity to the process. The difficulty with this approach is that it does not deal with the need in any sophisticated dispute settlement system for there to be general principles or rules concerning the nature of the review task so as to improve the quality of decision-making. Put simply, the general rationale for standards of review is that they enhance the quality of decision-making in dispute settlement systems.

In many domestic legal systems, standards of review may regulate the degree to which governments can be held accountable for their decisions through judicial review.[42] For many common law-based domestic legal systems they are also one of the mechanisms used to guarantee a separation of powers. This is because they predominantly concern a court's scrutiny of legislation or administrative decisions. They therefore define the parameters within which judges work and may establish 'no go' areas beyond which the

---

[40] There are also non-violation complaints where no breach of WTO obligations is alleged but instead that the measure nullifies or impairs its benefits or impedes a WTO objective. See Alan Yanovich and Tania Voon, 'What is the Measure at issue?', above n 39, 118.

[41] DSU Article 17.6 provides that 'An appeal shall be limited to issues of law covered in the panel report and legal interpretations developed by the panel.'

[42] Standards of review are heavily influenced by the design and history of the institution in which they function. See Chapter 1, Section 1.2.5. For a broader discussion of administrative law systems see Carol Harlow, *Global Administrative Law: The Quest for Principles and Values* (2006) 17(1) *European Journal of International Law* 187.

courts must accept the decisions of legislators and public officials.[43] Accordingly, they may be seen as part of the checks and balances between the judiciary and the executive and legislative arms of government. Standards of review should therefore also be viewed as an important element in the constitutional arrangements of any legal system. To link this back to the quality of decision-making point, arguably standards of review, if appropriately formulated, may enhance the quality and legitimacy of government decision-making as a whole.

From the previous discussion in this section, it can be seen that the institutional effects of standards of review are both vertical and horizontal in nature. The vertical effects exist because standards may have the capacity to alter the relationship between different levels of decision-making within the same legal system. Typically this will relate to the allocation of decision-making responsibilities between public officials or legislators and the various tiers within review courts. Standards may have horizontal effects in that they can affect the allocation of responsibilities between the different organs within an institution or constitutional system. All of these considerations may be seen as a means of allocating the responsibility for decision-making within an institutional framework. Therefore, a stricter standard imposed upon a decision-maker may lead to the transfer of more decision-making power to that decision-maker, with a consequential loss of decision-making power to other parts of the institution or system. For this reason, standards of review are usually prescribed or constructed to give an appropriate 'weighting' to these different institutional structures. This idea has been succinctly described in the following terms: 'It is nothing other than the embodiment of a carefully drawn balance between the jurisdictional and institutional competences of the actors.'[44]

In addition to constitutional considerations, standards are often based on quite practical considerations, mainly around the question of identifying appropriate review procedures. The most obvious example of this imperative is the need to prescribe the degree of a decision-maker's fact-finding powers and responsibilities in relation to the review of established facts. A common scenario, which I will cover in the next section, is the restriction on courts of review in many jurisdictions to review only questions of law. Such courts have no independent fact-finding responsibilities. These types of systems are based upon the need to avoid a duplication of judicial effort and to best use limited court resources. However, they are also frequently designed with the constitutional setting in mind, as is the case with judicial review of government decision-making within many political systems. Other than the issue of

---

[43] Douglas, *Douglas and Jones' Administrative Law*, above n 32, 56–7.

[44] Oesch, *Standards of Review in WTO Dispute Resolution*, above n 3, 23.

fact-finding powers, there are a number of other overlapping procedural considerations such as the level of expertise or experience that a decision-maker may have to deal with factual or legal matters, and whether the decision-maker has the benefit of an adversarial or inquisitorial process.[45] Standards of review may also be informed by the need for the decision-maker to exercise natural justice and due process in the treatment of the legal complaint or action.[46]

1.2.5 Standards Applied in other Relevant Jurisdictions

Prior to discussing standards of review in the WTO, it is useful to briefly outline some examples of standards of review applied in a relevant selection of other legal systems. This will allow analysis of standards in the WTO to be viewed against their application in other legal systems, particularly in relation to the question of the degree of deference exercised by courts and tribunals on factual and legal questions. This section is divided into five parts with parts one to three covering the Australian, United States and French legal systems.[47] Part four will deal with the ECJ as an example of a regional legal system and part five will deal with other selected international dispute settlement bodies. The United States and France provide good examples of how major economies with common law and civil law traditions respectively deal with the standard of review question. Australia is an example of a common law country with which I am familiar. The ECJ is somewhat unique in being a supranational court having well developed jurisprudence.[48] Finally, the selected international dispute settlement bodies comprise the ICJ, ICSID arbitral tribunals, and NAFTA panels. The ICJ is of course a central dispute settlement body in public international law and the other two are more specialized bodies dealing with international trade matters, which may be partly analogous to WTO dispute settlement.

---

45 An inquisitorial process arguably may increase the intensity of review and thus change the standard of review in practice.

46 For discussion on these principles, see Andrew Mitchell, 'Fair Crack of the Whip: Examining Procedural Fairness in WTO Disputes Using an Australian Administrative Law Framework', in *Ten Years of WTO Dispute Settlement: Australian Perspectives* (Commonwealth of Australia, 2006) 45.

47 These legal systems are examples of modern legal systems with common or civil law origins. Further these countries are significant trading nations. Whilst developing countries are not specifically represented in these examples, there is a reasonable prospect that many developing countries would apply similar standards of review due to being common or civil law based systems.

48 The ECHR, which is briefly referred to in Section 1.2.5D, could be described in similar terms.

A. Australia

Australia possesses a federal system of government in which the Commonwealth Government and the States have independent legal systems.[49] Within both systems, the judicial review powers of the courts in respect of administrative decisions are generally quite restricted in that courts are frequently cautious about encroaching on the merits of administrative decision-making, and the scope of review is predominantly limited to examining whether there has been an error of law. As a common law nation, Australia inherited *Wednesbury* reasonableness from the United Kingdom as the basic standard of review in administrative law cases.[50] Whilst this test requires some degree of intrusion into the merits of a decision, in recent times, Australian courts have often applied the test in a restrictive manner.[51] There will usually have to be something exceptional in the considerations or actions of the decision-maker for the decision to be overturned.[52] In addition, the Australian courts have been reluctant to adopt an independent test of proportionality, instead conceptualizing it as part of whether a decision is unreasonable.[53]

The standard of review applied by Australian courts in respect of legal issues may best be described as a correctness test in that courts have the responsibility for interpreting and applying the law which constrains administrative decision-makers. In other words, there is no deference to the original decision-maker in respect of legal questions. Errors of law in administrative cases commonly relate to the legality or procedural regularity of a decision. This might involve, for example, the doctrine of *ultra vires* which requires that administrative action not exceed the limit of a grant of power given to a decision-maker.[54]

The common law grounds for challenging administrative decisions as described above have been codified in relation to decisions of Federal government departments and agencies. The *Administrative Decisions (Judicial Review) Act 1977* (Cth) sets out approximately 20 separate grounds for contesting the validity of administrative decisions.[55] Unreasonableness is one of these grounds, but most of the grounds concern legal errors such as taking irrelevant considerations into account and the denial of procedural

---

[49] Douglas, *Douglas and Jones' Administrative Law*, above n 32, 56.

[50] *Associated Provincial Picture Houses Ltd v Wednesbury Corpn* [1948] 1 KB 223, discussed in D.C.M. Yardley, *Principles of Administrative Law* (Butterworths, 2nd ed, 1986) 48.

[51] Peter Cane and Leighton McDonald, *Principles of Administrative Law: Legal Regulation of Governance* (Oxford University Press, 2008) 180.

[52] *Ibid.*

[53] *Ibid.*

[54] Douglas, *Douglas and Jones' Administrative Law*, above n 32, 57.

[55] *Administrative Decisions (Judicial Review) Act 1977* (Cth) ss5–7.

fairness.[56] The role of the Federal Court is therefore quite restricted in its oversight of Federal administrative decisions.

By contrast, a different approach to the standard of review of administrative decisions is found in the jurisdiction of a federal body known as the Administrative Appeals Tribunal. The AAT was constituted through legislation in 1975 and its basic mandate is to provide a fast and effective type of review for aggrieved parties.[57] The AAT's jurisdiction does not cover all administrative decisions.[58] In a hierarchical sense the AAT sits within the Federal System between the primary decision-maker and Federal Court review process. The important difference between AAT and judicial review is that the AAT conducts a merits review.[59] This means that the AAT stands in the shoes of the primary decision-maker and will remake the decision. A merits review usually involves a full *de novo* hearing before AAT members with documentary and oral evidence being presented.[60] The AAT may examine any evidence relevant to the case, whether or not it was relied upon in arriving at the original decision.[61]

The boundary between merits review and judicial review can sometimes be difficult to draw. Where decisions are quashed by courts on the grounds of unreasonableness and are remitted back to the original decision-maker, the nature of the court decision will often leave the primary decision-maker with little choice but to make a different decision. Further, decisions on what constitute relevant and irrelevant considerations can come close to involving a merits review because the court will need to examine the facts and the original decision in some detail. This difficulty is not unique to the Australian system but is important given the very different roles of the AAT and the Federal Court in the review process. In summary, the Australian system has a mixture of deferential and non-deferential processes. The AAT affords little or

---

56 *Administrative Decisions (Judicial Review) Act 1977* (Cth) ss5–7.

57 Section 2A of the *Administrative Appeals Tribunal Act 1975* (Cth) provides: 'In carrying out its functions, the Tribunal must pursue the objective of providing a mechanism of review that is fair, just, economical, informal and quick.'

58 Section 25(1) of the *Administrative Appeals Act 1975* (Cth) provides that 'an enactment may provide that applications may be made to the Tribunal' and therefore jurisdiction is only conferred by specific reference in other legislation.

59 The expression 'merits review' does not appear in the *Administrative Appeals Act 1975* (Cth). The role has often been described as to 'make the correct and preferable decision.' (See *Drake v Minister for Immigration and Ethnic Affairs* (1979) 2 ALD 60, 78.) In addition, in order to enable the AAT to reach the correct conclusion on the review, it may exercise all the powers and discretions that are conferred on the original decision-maker, and by s43(6), the decision of the AAT is deemed to be the decision of the decision-maker.

60 *Administrative Appeals Act 1975* (Cth) s35(1).

61 *Administrative Appeals Act 1975* (Cth) s33(1).

no deference to government agencies in relation to questions of fact. By contrast, in most cases judicial review involves a very high level of deference on questions of fact and no deference on questions of law.

B. The United States

The United States does not have a specialized court or tribunal that deals with the review of federal-level administrative agency action. This task falls to the national courts possessing general jurisdiction.[62] It is suggested that the lack of a specialized administrative court or tribunal is the product of the constitutional theory of checks and balances between the different branches of government. In other words, a body that is set up by the executive branch of government as an internal review mechanism may not provide a sufficient check on the power of executive government.[63] Courts are generally regarded as an independent source of review. It is also important to note, however, that within the United States there is a large number of administrative review processes undertaken by a broad range of agencies ranging from industry regulators to government departments. Therefore, the courts are called upon to review a wide variety of actions, decisions and regulations.

In this context, it is noted that traditionally the courts in the United States have exercised considerable restraint when reviewing agency conduct. This general principle of deference is based on three major arguments.[64] Firstly, it is rooted in the separation of powers doctrine under the American constitution whereby courts are empowered to exercise judicial rather than administrative functions. Secondly, courts are mindful of the expertise possessed by agencies in their specific fields and are reluctant to second-guess decisions of agencies. Thirdly (and related to the first two arguments), courts traditionally rely on the well-established principle that they should defer to the views of administrators in relation to questions of fact. Despite these strong arguments, in recent years the United States courts have become more interventionist in administrative law matters. This has led to charges that they are overstepping their authority and interfering with public policy-making.[65] However, the courts do not have an easy role in satisfying all affected parties. This tension has been concisely described in the following terms:

---

[62] Peter L. Strauss, *An Introduction to Administrative Justice in the United States* (Carolina Academic Press, 1989) 212.

[63] *Ibid* 211.

[64] Warren, above n 26, 333.

[65] *Ibid* 329.

> Ideally, the courts should seek a scope of review broad enough to prevent dangerous administrative abuses, yet narrow enough that normal administrative operations are not disrupted by unwanted judicial interference.[66]

The scope of review of agency action is prescribed by the *Administrative Procedure Act*.[67] The APA, enacted in 1946, is largely a codification of common law principles. Under section 706 of the APA two general standards of review are provided for in relation to the review of factual findings.[68] These two standards are known as the 'substantial evidence' standard and the 'arbitrary and capricious' standard. The former applies to formal rule-making by agencies and in quasi-judicial hearings, whereas the latter applies to informal decisions or rule-making.[69]

The substantial evidence test under section 706 (2)(E) of the APA provides that:

> The reviewing court shall hold unlawful and set aside agency action, findings and conclusions found to be unsupported by substantial evidence subject to sections 556 or 557 of this title or otherwise reviewed on the record of an agency hearing provided by statute.[70]

The United States Supreme Court has determined this test to mean that courts must determine whether the agency's findings are supported by substantial evidence on the record considered as a whole.[71] Therefore, if a reviewing court finds that substantial evidence exists to support the agency determination, then its review task is complete, and it must not look any further into the matter. On its face, this standard creates a high degree of deference towards agencies due to the courts being simply asked to determine whether there is sufficient evidence to support the conclusions.

On closer inspection this standard may not necessarily afford a great deal of deference. Firstly, no clear guidance has been provided by the courts as to what constitutes 'substantial evidence'. Most of the authorities focus on the question of reasonableness, but without providing any further guidance as to how to define this expression.[72] For example, in *Consolidated Edison Co. v*

---

66 *Ibid* 330.

67 5 USC § 559 (1946).

68 The APA is a codification of judicially made administrative law principles.

69 Button, *The Power to Protect: Trade Health and Uncertainty in the WTO*, above n 15, 194.

70 Sections 556 and 557 of the APA prescribe various minimum procedural requirements for reviews by agencies.

71 *Universal Camera Corp v National Labor Relations Board*, 340 US 474 (1951).

72 See *Consolidated Edison Co. v NLRB*, 305 US 197, 299 (1938); *NLRB v*

NLRB the expression was defined to mean '…such relevant evidence as a reasonable mind might accept as adequate to support a conclusion'.[73] Secondly, in assessing the existence of substantial evidence, the courts must take into account the body of opposing evidence that may contradict the agency's position. In effect the courts are being asked to weigh up the presence of supporting and contradicting evidence, which in itself requires some qualitative review of the matter. Therefore, in the absence of more concrete direction to agencies, the courts are to a large extent assuming the responsibility for the reasonableness and fairness of agency decisions.[74]

The 'arbitrary and capricious' standard is found under section 706(2)(A) of the APA. This standard applies to informal procedures such as agency decisions that may involve written notification and reasons. Ostensibly this standard is more deferential than the substantial evidence test and is more designed to ensure that procedural fairness has taken place. In other words, that the agency has considered all relevant factors and its decision contains 'no clear error of judgment'.[75] In *Citizens to Preserve Overton Park Inc v Volpe*, Justice Marshall famously described arbitrary and capricious review as follows:

> Although this inquiry into the facts is to be searching and careful, the ultimate standard of review is a narrow one. The court is not empowered to substitute its judgment for that of the agency.[76]

Since the *Overton Park* case, a number of decisions have shown that the courts have not applied this standard in a deferential manner. This is particularly the case with questions of methodology for experiments or data collection undertaken by agencies. A well-known example is the *Industrial Union Department, AFL-CIO v American Petroleum Institute* case, which concerned the lowering of exposure limits for the chemical benzene.[77]

In the United States, a distinction is made between the standard of review applied to facts and legal questions. In *Chevron USA Inc v Natural Resources*

Columbian Enameling and Stamping Co., 306 US 292, 300 (1939); *Consolo v Federal Maritime Commission*, 383 US 607, 619 (1966), referred to in Warren, above n 26, 334.

73 *Consolidated Edison Co. v NLRB*, 305 US 197, 229 (1938).

74 *Ibid* 490. The court noted at page 489 that 'The ultimate reliance for the fair operation of any standard is a judiciary of high competence and character and the constant play of an informed professional critique upon its work.'

75 *Pacific Coast Federation of Fishermen's Associations v National Maritime Fisheries Service* 265 F 3d 1028, 1034 (9th Cir, 2001) (referring to *Arizona v Thomas* 824 F 2d 745, 748 (9th Cir, 1987), which quotes *Citizens to Preserve Overton Park Inc v Volpe* 401 US 402, 416 (1971)).

76 401 US 402, 416 (1971).

77 448 US 607, 100 (1980).

Defense Council, the Supreme Court deferred to the expertise of the Environmental Protection Authority in its interpretation of a statutory scheme.[78] The *Chevron* test will be discussed in further detail in Chapter 2 given that it was influential in the drafting of the standard of review for WTO anti-dumping disputes. However, this test stipulates that the courts must defer to an agency's interpretation of a statutory provision if the statute is ambiguous or silent and the agency's interpretation is reasonable.[79] Conversely, if Congress has 'directly spoken on the precise question at issue', then its intention must be respected.[80] Therefore, despite it being the traditional competency of the courts to review legal questions with a non-deferential standard of review, this test does provide for considerable deference. However, the apparent simplicity of this test masks a number of potential problems.[81] For example, the test leaves open the question of whether there is ambiguity over the provision, and there is always the issue of what constitutes a question of fact versus law.[82] The Courts may therefore not necessarily afford the degree of deference that is first suggested, and they may retain a moderate degree of competency in overseeing agency conduct.

C. France

France is a good example of the treatment of administrative law in a civil law country, as opposed to the countries based on the common law tradition, such as Australia and the United States.[83] Administrative law in France is very much based upon the constitutional structures that originate with the French Revolution of 1789.[84] Administrative law in France, as with many civil law countries, is categorized differently from private law, and separate administrative courts hear administrative-related disputes.[85] Such courts perform both administrative and judicial functions. The court of first instance is known as the Tribunal Administratif, from which decisions may be appealed on both

---

78 467 US 837, 104 (1984).

79 *Ibid* 842–3.

80 *Ibid.*

81 Button, *The Power to Protect: Trade Health and Uncertainty in the WTO*, above n 15, 196.

82 See David M. Wagner, 'Gonzales v Oregon: The Assisted Suicide of Chevron Deference' (2007) 2 *Michigan State Law Review* 435. This article argues that the Chevron test has been narrowed through recent cases and administrative agencies have less discretion with interpretations of regulation.

83 See Rene Chapus, *Droit du contentieux administrative* (Montchrestien, 12th ed, 2006); Pierre Laurent Frier and Jacques Petit, *Precis de Droit Administratif Mis a Jour, Precis Domat* (Montcrestien, 5th ed, 2008).

84 Rene David, *French Law: Its Structure, Sources and Methodology* (Louisiana State University Press, 1972) 127.

85 *Ibid* 128.

questions of fact and law to either the Cour Administrative d'Appel or the Conseil d'Etat.[86] The latter is considered to be at the apex of the French administrative law system.[87]

The major doctrine under French administrative law with regard to the standard of review of facts is that of 'manifest error'.[88] This is where the relevant administrative court determines that the administration, although making no mistake in the finding of facts, had nonetheless committed a manifest error in the assessment of those facts.[89] For example, in the typical case of *Rougemont*, the Conseil d'Etat categorized a decision of a local medical committee refusing to place a well-known and highly-qualified surgeon on a special list that would entitle him to charge higher fees, as being a manifest error.[90] Therefore, traditionally the standard of review of facts provided a great deal of discretion to public officials and it was only in the case of more obvious factual errors or misclassifications that a court of review would reverse the decision. In more recent years, there has been a modest trend by the courts towards a more intensive standard of review of facts. This has been through the influence of the concept of proportionality and also the use of a bilan or balance-sheet approach, whereby the courts may weigh up positive and negative factors relied upon by public officials or agencies in reaching administrative decisions.[91] This would appear to be much closer to merits review than the traditional manifest error test.

The influence of French administrative law is apparent in many other European jurisdictions including the Netherlands, Luxembourg, Italy, Spain,

---

86 An appeal before the Conseil D'Etat is known as the 'pourvoi en cassation'. Appeals may be instituted to the Conseil d'Etat either directly from the Tribunal Administratif or from the Cour Administrative d'Appel depending upon the type of dispute. The reconsideration by the Conseil d'Etat or the Cour Administrative d'Appel of a decision by the Tribunal Administratif is referred to as 'l'effet devolutif' which means that the law and facts are both subject to review.

87 David, above n 84, 128.

88 L. Neville Brown and John S. Bell, *French Administrative Law* (Clarendon Press, 5th ed, 1998) 261. There are also various categories of errors of law that are applied by the French administrative courts. These include *incompetence* (want of authority), *vice de forme* (*ultra vires*), illegality and *detournment de pouvoir* which is a more unique concept meaning 'internal illegality'.

89 The manifest error doctrine has been principally developed in France by the Conseil d'Etat.

90 *Ibid* 262. *Rougemont* Conseil d'Etat 7 July 1967. See also *La Grange*, Conseil d'Etat 15 February 1961 concerning the checking by a public official of the equivalence of diplomas. Later cases such as *Société de Lotissement de la Plage de Pampelonne*, Conseil d'Etat 29 March 1968 and *Société Anonyme Librairie François Maspero*, Conseil d'Etat 2 November 1973 have broadened out this doctrine to apply to a range of administrative functions.

91 Brown and Bell, above n 88, 263.

Portugal and Greece, all of which have separate courts to deal with administrative law disputes.[92] France has also been quite influential on the jurisprudence of the ECJ and the ECHR,[93] given that it was one of the five founding members of the European Community.[94]

D. The European Court of Justice

The European Union differs constitutionally from national legal systems in that it is a supranational organization with nation states as its members. It has evolved from a strictly trade-related body in the 1950s to become a regional polity. The present legal foundations of the European Union comprise the Treaty of the Functioning of the European Union (formerly Treaty of Rome), the Maastricht Treaty and subsequent amending treaties, the most recent of which is the Treaty of Lisbon.[95] Executive functions of the European Union are undertaken by the European Commission, with review of its actions falling to the Court of First Instance or the ECJ.[96] The Court of First Instance may review matters of fact and law, whereas the ECJ is restricted to reviewing questions of law.[97]

Article 173 of the Maastricht Treaty grants broad jurisdiction upon the ECJ to review the legality of acts of various EU institutions, including the Commission.[98] Article 189 of the treaty defines acts as 'regulations, directives, decisions, recommendations or opinions', and the ECJ has adopted a liberal interpretation of the kinds of agency conduct that may be reviewable.[99]

---

92 *Ibid* 268.

93 There is a close connection between administrative law of European Community member states and that of European law, particularly in the field of human rights. See for example, *Delcourt v Belgium* (1970) 11 Eur Court HR (ser A) where the Court found that Article 6(1) of the European Convention on Human Rights guaranteeing a fair hearing applied to the Court of Cassation in Belgium even though this Court did not deal with the merits of a case.

94 Brown and Bell, above n 88, 279.

95 L. Neville Brown and Tom Kennedy, *The Court of Justice of the European Communities* (Sweet & Maxwell, 4th ed, 1994) 124; Jurgen Schwarze, 'The Future of the European Union Legal and Political Order' in Patrick J. Birkinshaw and Mike Varney (eds), *The European Union Legal Order after Lisbon* (Kluwer Law International, 2010) 3, 22–3. See also http://europa.eu/lisbon_treaty/index_en.htm, last accessed 31 March 2012.

96 See Brown and Kennedy, above n 95, 124.

97 *Ibid.*

98 Article 173 states: 'The Court of Justice shall review the legality of acts adopted jointly by the European Parliament and the Council, of acts of the Council, of the Commission and of the European Central Bank, other than recommendations and opinions, and of acts of the European Parliament intended to produce legal effects *vis-à-vis* third parties.'

99 This is despite the apparent incongruity of s173 and s189 on the reviewability of recommendations and opinions. See Brown and Kennedy, above n 95, 124–9.

Article 173 of the Maastricht Treaty sets out four grounds for the annulment of EU acts. These are for a lack of competency (authority), infringement of an essential procedural requirement, infringement of the Maastricht Treaty or of any rule of law relating to its application, or a misuse of powers. All four grounds appear to raise only questions of law, not of fact, and at first glance do not appear to deal with the merits of the challenged act. However, the ECJ may be led inevitably into a review of the facts, (as found by the Commission), if the issue is whether there was such a manifest error in determining questions of fact, that this error would constitute an error of law.[100] Several ECJ cases have interpreted the standard of review that is to be applied. In *SA Roquette Freres v Council*, the applicant claimed that the Council had infringed the essential procedure requirement in Article 173 by adopting a regulation for the fixing of a quota on isoglucose without first receiving an opinion on the matter from the European Parliament.[101] The ECJ found in favour of the applicant but defined the standard of review in the following terms:

> When the implementation by the Council of the agricultural policy of the Community involves the need to evaluate a complex economic situation the discretion which it has does not apply exclusively to the nature and scope of the measures to be taken but also to some extent to the finding of the basic facts inasmuch as, in particular, it is open to the Council to rely if necessary on general findings. In reviewing the exercise of such a power the court must confine itself to examining whether it contains a manifest error or constitutes a misuse of power or whether the authority in question did not clearly exceed the bound of its discretion.[102]

It can be seen from the above quotation, that the ECJ defined the scope of its review in extremely limited terms. Misuse of power and lack of authority are parts of the test that mirror section 173, whereas 'manifest error' is a separate element that, although requiring the Court to examine facts, does not require a high level of scrutiny.

The 'manifest error' test was discussed by McNelis in the context of the decision of *UK v Commission*, concerning the total ban on exports of bovine animals, bovine meats and derived products from the United Kingdom to other

---

[100] *Ibid* 143.

[101] (C-179/80) [1980] ECR 3333, 3393. This case followed closely the reasoning in *Italy v Council* (C-166/78) [1979] ECR 2575 where it was also found 'To prove that the Council has made a serious mistake in the exercise of its discretion given to it would require evidence more definitive and less disputable than that adduced by the Italian government during the proceedings.' Both decisions were followed in *SAM Schiffahrt GmbH and Heinz Stapf v Bundesrupblik Deutschland* (C-248/95) [1997] ECR I-4475.

[102] *SA Roquette Freres v Council of the European Communities* (C-179/80) [1980] ECR 3333, 3393.

EU member states and to third countries in the wake of mad cow disease.[103] In that case, the Court concluded:

> Lastly, it must be recalled that, since the Commission enjoys a wide measure of discretion, particularly as to the nature and extent of the measures which it adopts, the Community judicature must, when reviewing such measures, restrict itself to examining whether the exercise of such discretion is vitiated by a manifest error or a misuse of powers or whether the Commission did not clearly exceed the bounds of its discretion.[104]

McNelis argues that a major reason for the highly deferential approach taken by the ECJ is that the ECJ is judging a member of its own institutional 'family' when it reviews Commission findings.[105] The Commission is somewhat of a protector of the advancement of the European common market, which is based on the original idea of freedom of movement of goods. It is contended that this makes the high level of deference more acceptable than the applicable standard within a national system of government that may rely upon a separation of powers doctrine to ensure proper public accountability.

The European system is complex and it would appear that not all legal disciplines are subject to the same standard of review. A case in point is in the field of merger control. In the decision of *Tetra Laval* the ECJ sanctioned a more interventionist standard by determining that the Court must examine whether the evidence is factually accurate, reliable, consistent, complete and capable of substantiating the conclusions drawn.[106] In other words, in economic assessments, the Court will conduct a detailed analysis or re-examination of the Commissions' findings as well as the economic analysis on which the decision is based. Such an approach is vastly different from a 'manifest error' approach and, in many respects, is not greatly different from *de novo* review. The Commission unsuccessfully, but perhaps correctly, argued in *Tetra Laval* that the standard of review had gone beyond a mere review of the legality of its findings.[107]

---

103 Natalie McNelis, 'The Role of the Judge in the EU and WTO: Lessons from the BSE and Hormones Cases' *Journal of International Economic Law* (2001) 189; *UK v Commission* (C-180/96) [1998] ECR I-2265.

104 *UK v Commission* (C-180/96) [1998] ECR I-2265, [60].

105 Natalie McNelis, above n 103, 202.

106 *Commission v Tetra Laval* (C-39/03) [2005] ECR I-987 as discussed in T.R. Reeves and Ninette Dodoo, 'Standards of Proof and Standards of Judicial Review in European Commission Merger Law' 29 *Fordham International Law Journal* 1034.

107 T.R. Reeves and Ninette Dodoo, 'Standards of Proof and Standards of Judicial Review in European Commission Merger Law' 29 *Fordham International Law Journal* 1034, 1035.

The uniting thread in European jurisprudence would appear to be that the ECJ will generally only have an interest in ensuring that measures are arrived at with due consideration from the Commission or other agency.[108] There is evidently some flexibility in the standard depending upon the field and level of economic analysis required. It should also be borne in mind that the standard of review, and questions of discretion are somewhat tied in with other doctrines, such as the requirement for proportionality of measures.[109] This is frequently linked to the idea that measures ought to be least trade restrictive in nature, so as to promote the free movement of goods in Europe.

Within the European system, there has also been the development of what is known as the margin of appreciation doctrine.[110] This doctrine has principally developed through the case law of the European Court of Human Rights in interpreting the European Convention on Human Rights, and was first laid down in the decision of *Handyside v United Kingdom*.[111] The margin of appreciation allows a court to apply a more deferential interpretation to measures of European Union members. This doctrine is a principle of interpretation rather than a standard of review. However, it may result in a court moving away from *de novo* review and applying a more deferential standard of review. The result is that the ECHR has moved gradually towards 'a shared baseline of human rights rules, with room for disparate national solutions at the margins'.[112] The manner in which this doctrine has been applied will also vary according to the specific right in question, the subject matter and the circumstances of each case.

It is arguable that the margin of appreciation is a unique response to the different legal, political and cultural traditions existing in European nations.[113] If this rationale is accepted, then it would make introducing such a doctrine into WTO jurisprudence difficult in light of the different context of and objectives of the WTO.[114]

---

108 Button, *The Power to Protect: Trade Health and Uncertainty in the WTO*, above n 15, 210.

109 *Ibid* 208.

110 For discussion of this doctrine see Oesch, *Standards of Review in WTO Dispute Settlement*, above n 3, 51–3.

111 (1976) 26 Eur Court HR (ser A) 47–9. The Court held that the right of freedom of expression under Article 10 of the European Convention on Human Rights was not absolute and was to be balanced against measures of members that had a legitimate aim and are necessary in a democratic society.

112 Oesch, *Standards of Review in WTO Dispute Settlement*, above n 3, 51 referencing Laurence Helfer and Anne-Marie Slaughter, 'The Effectiveness of the Council of Europe's Human Rights Regime', in Bob Reinalda and Bertjak Verbeek (eds), *Autonomous Policymaking By International Organizations* (Routledge, 1998) 141.

113 Oesch, *Standards of Review in WTO Dispute Settlement*, above n 3, 52.

114 *Ibid* 53.

E. Selected international dispute settlement bodies

In the previous sections, I have discussed the standard of review developed in several domestic legal systems and one regional system. In this section, I will briefly refer to how the concept of a standard of review is or may be treated in selected international courts and tribunals. I will deal with the ICJ, ICSID Arbitrations and NAFTA Tribunals.

The jurisdiction of the ICJ is principally governed by Article 36 of the ICJ Statute.[115] Article 36(2) provides that States may declare that they recognize as compulsory the jurisdiction of the ICJ concerning the interpretation of a treaty, any question of international law, the existence of any fact which, if established, would constitute a breach of an international obligation or the nature or extent of reparations to be made for the breach of an international obligation. The jurisdiction of the ICJ is therefore very broad and covers questions of both fact and law. However, the concept of a standard of review is not readily apparent for the ICJ as the ICJ is not necessarily undertaking an examination of domestic decisions that are administrative in character. It is therefore not likely to be carrying out a process of review that is akin to judicial review of administrative action. Given that the ICJ, in the main, deals with disputes between states on matters of public international law, it will not commonly need to address the question of whether it must defer in any way to the decision-making processes of a State. The ICJ, in most cases, would simply examine the question in issue and make a legal judgment based on the best facts available.

The above comments concerning the ICJ are also applicable concerning ICSID arbitral tribunals, which are composed in an ad hoc manner to resolve disputes concerning international investment.[116] The litigants in such matters are either states or the host state and a private investor. Disputes frequently relate to fair treatment of an investor under the provisions of a bilateral investment treaty or similar investment regulation.[117] The notion of a standard of review is not going to be important where the arbitral body is merely deciding on whether an international obligation has been observed. There is, however, the potential for it to become more relevant where the arbitral body is examining a discretionary decision of a domestic body, for example, where the dispute concerns the discretionary decision to grant an operating licence for a company.

---

[115] *Statute of the International Court of Justice* art 36.

[116] *International Convention on the Settlement of Investment Disputes between States and Nationals of Other States*, opened for signature 18 March 1965, 575 UNTS 159 (entered into force 14 October 1966) arts 36–49.

[117] See ICSID art 25.

The application of a standard of review is certainly more relevant under the NAFTA, whose members are the United States, Canada and Mexico.[118] In particular, Chapter 19 of the NAFTA provides for the establishment of ad hoc bi-national review panels to review anti-dumping and countervailing measure determinations made concerning goods imported into a NAFTA member state. This mechanism therefore specifically contemplates the review pursuant to an international agreement of domestic administrative decisions. Article 1904(3) of the NAFTA requires panels to apply the standard of review embodied in various domestic statutes of the importing country, as well as general judicial principles that would be applied in the importing country.[119] Accordingly, Chapter 19 panels will be applying a domestic law standard of review as if they were a court of review in the country that has issued the challenged measure.[120]

F. Assessment of other legal systems

The above survey of standards applied in the Australian, United States and French legal systems and by the ECJ demonstrates a high degree of deference overall towards agency conduct. The types of factors that influence the standards of review are somewhat similar, albeit the result of different institutional priorities. For instance, in all four systems there must be a prioritization of issues such as agency expertise, efficiency and authority. In all four examples, there is a significant difference between standards of review that apply to questions of law and fact. Generally, a higher degree of deference applies to questions of fact. Arguably, the rationales for deference apply more so to facts as the agency will frequently have more competence than courts to examine factual matters. Despite this, these examples show that there may be considerable ambiguity in the precise standard applied in relation to facts. This can

---

118 North American Free Trade Agreement, signed 17 December 1992 [1994] CTS 2 (entered into force 1 January 1994).

119 Article 1904(3) requires panels to apply the standard of review as defined in NAFTA Annex 1911, which provides: 'standard of review means the following standards, as may be amended from time to time by the relevant Party: (a) in the case of Canada, the grounds set out in subsection 18.1(4) of the *Federal Court Act*, as amended, with respect to all final determinations; (b) in the case of the United States, (i) the standard set out in section 516A(b)(l)(B) of the *Tariff Act* of 1930, as amended, with the exception of a determination referred to in (ii), and (ii) the standard set out in section 516A(b)(l)(A) of the *Tariff Act* of 1930, as amended, with respect to a determination by the United States International Trade Commission not to initiate a review pursuant to section 751(b) of the *Tariff Act* of 1930, as amended; and (c) in the case of Mexico, the standard set out in Article 238 of the Federal Fiscal Code ('Código Fiscal de la Federación'), or any successor statutes, based solely on the administrative record.'

120 See Michael J. Trebilcock and Robert Howse, *The Regulation of International Trade* (Routledge, 3rd ed, 2005).

give rise to a 'creeping' intrusion as in the case of the United States' substantial evidence test, or in recent developments regarding European Union merger assessments.

In the case of the international dispute settlement bodies discussed above, the application of a particular standard of review will be more apparent where the body is directly reviewing domestic agency conduct, and the converse proposition is equally valid. If, for example, the ICJ is examining the lawfulness of state conduct, then the question of whether there should be any deference towards factual and legal issues is unlikely to arise. By contrast, Chapter 19 NAFTA panels are specifically charged with the responsibility of reviewing measures that are the result of formal domestic administrative procedures. In that case, NAFTA panels must apply various domestic standards of review, but there is scope for international bodies, and particularly those reviewing technical international trade decisions, to apply an institution-specific standard of review that is based on more universal principles.

Whatever the merits or demerits of the above systems, their usefulness in the context of the WTO dispute settlement system should be considered in a cautious light. It is always a difficult proposition to transplant legal doctrines from one system to another. In this case three of the systems examined are domestic systems, and all have very different institutional designs. This does, however, lead to the important conclusion that the development of an appropriate standard of review in WTO dispute settlement is likely, to some extent, to be influenced by the function and institutional design of WTO dispute settlement system as well as its history. Further, the value in this type of comparative enquiry is also in identifying the relevant legal concepts and principles that may shape the development of a new standard of review. In this regard, the issue of the degree of deference or intrusiveness of judicial review would appear to be a universal 'tension' in dispute settlement systems, as are the underlying principles such as the allocation of judicial responsibility, expertise and efficiency. There is certainly evidence of common jurisprudential approaches evolving in international law, and the need to define what is being reviewed, and how it is to be reviewed is ever present.[121] This suggests the potential evolution of a global system of administrative law in which a common theoretical framework is adopted by courts and tribunals in different jurisdictions.[122] In the next section I will discuss how a standard of review operates as part of the WTO dispute settlement system.

[121] See for example, Daniel C. Esty, 'Good Governance at the Supranational Scale: Globalizing Administrative law' (2006) 115 *Yale Law Journal* 1490; Sabino Cassese, 'Administrative Law Without the State? The challenge of Global Regulation' 37 (2005) *New York University Journal of International Law and Politics* 663.

[122] Daniel C. Esty, above n 121, 1490.

1.3 APPLICATION OF STANDARDS OF REVIEW IN THE WTO

Having introduced standards of review on a conceptual level, in this section I will deal with the issue of how and to what extent standards of review may apply to WTO dispute settlement. This section is divided into three parts. In the first part, I will discuss how a standard of review may be relevant in the WTO panel process. In the second part, I will outline some possible limitations on developing a WTO standard of review. In the third part, I will discuss the relative usefulness of drawing upon domestic law in identifying an appropriate WTO standard of review. I conclude that the development of a standard of review is an important and inevitable aspect of WTO law, and that caution should be exercised when examining whether domestic standards of review may be transplanted into the WTO system.

1.3.1 Relevancy, Definitions and Application

WTO dispute settlement involves resolving disputes concerning the interpretation of the WTO Agreements. Panels are charged with the responsibility of providing rulings and recommendations in relation to provisions of the WTO Agreements.[123] The question therefore arises as to whether standards of review are at all relevant. Panels must simply decide whether or not a party's conduct conforms to its WTO obligations.[124] There is certainly a conceptual simplicity with this approach. However, problems arise because of the nature of the measures being reviewed. Many WTO obligations are implemented through domestic agencies. These agencies may make discretionary decisions based on a series of facts. This is particularly the case with anti-dumping, countervailing, safeguard and SPS measures. In these types of matters, panels are generally reviewing the validity of a prior decision, rather than simply laws or regulations implementing WTO obligations. In order to review a prior decision, a panel must then determine the level of intrusiveness it will apply in order to be satisfied that the measure is WTO compliant. This will involve questions of whether panels may look at any evidence, or only evidence that was before the agency, and the extent to which panels should review the reasoning undertaken by the agency. Therefore, to a significant degree, the review function of WTO panels does mirror the concept of a standard of review found in other legal systems, such as those discussed in the previous section.

---

123 DSU, art 3.2.

124 Jeffrey Waincymer, above n 29, 349.

Arguably, panels should do whatever is required in each case to determine a member's compliance with WTO obligations. However, this simply begs the question of how far panels should go in this exercise. If it is an entirely discretionary matter for panels, then there may be a significant variation both in the treatment of members and in the enforcement of the WTO Agreements. This would contradict the movement by the WTO towards having a dispute settlement system that is more 'legalized' and based upon ideas of security and predictability in the trading system.[125] In the absence of established principles, if different standards have been applied in different cases, then members may argue that they have not been afforded due process and this may encourage more WTO litigation generally. The type of WTO standard of review adopted also links in to the issue of the broader observance and enforcement of WTO obligations by the membership, that is, whether WTO rules should be totally binding, or whether the WTO Agreements should operate more in the nature of guidelines. A weaker WTO dispute settlement system may have undesirable consequences for the development of the WTO as an institution. The type of standard of review applied may also be shaped by practical issues such as the amount of resources that the WTO can afford to devote to the review of measures.[126]

The centrality of the standard of review question is brought to mind when one examines the broad range of policy issues that may be reviewable as a measure. These may include environmental, security, health, labour as well as commercial issues. It can be seen therefore how, in the WTO context, the standard of review has the potential to be a sensitive matter for members. Without too much imagination, the standard of review can lead to charges of panel intrusion into the domestic affairs of members and allegations of an erosion of national sovereignty.[127]

All legal systems face the difficulty of defining the nature of what is reviewable. In many domestic systems, this is often restricted to a decision or act mandated under legislation. Under the WTO Agreements measures being reviewed may take a wide variety of forms.[128] For example, they may be in the form of domestic legislation, or alternatively, agency decisions that are based on either formal or informal processes. This can make the formulation

[125] See DSU, art 3.2; The WTO Secretariat, *Guide to the Uruguay Round Agreements* (Kluwer Law International, 1999) 19–20.

[126] The WTO operates a very robust trade agenda with a modestly staffed secretariat.

[127] See for example, J. Greenwald, 'WTO Dispute Settlement: An exercise in Trade Law Legislation?' (2003) *Journal of International Economic Law* 6, 113.

[128] Alan Yanovich and Tania Voon, 'What is the measure at Issue?', above n 39, 115.

of a uniform standard of review very difficult, given that a uniform level of intrusion may be inappropriate. There is also the difficulty of making the traditional distinction between facts and law. Certainly the provisions of the WTO Agreements may be considered analogous to 'laws', but facts cannot so easily be treated uniformly when they may concern an analysis of domestic laws or domestic processes.[129]

WTO panels may determine disputes concerning domestic regulation as opposed to the specific application of domestic regulation.[130] This distinction is referred to as 'as such' versus 'as applied' claims. The rationale for determining 'as such' claims is that the WTO dispute settlement system is intended to protect the security and predictability of future trade and avoid a multiplicity of litigation regarding particular issues.[131] An 'as such' claim is likely to require the application by panels of a legal standard of review because these claims will generally involve an assessment of whether domestic regulation is consistent with a member's obligations under the WTO Agreements.[132] By contrast, many 'as applied' claims, especially in the trade remedy disciplines, will involve an assessment of a domestic authority's findings, and hence the standard of review of facts is likely to be more important.

Different standards of review may produce very different outcomes for the parties to a dispute. The WTO system is no exception, and the application of *de novo* review, total deference or any intermediate standard may lead to such variances. *De novo* review would give the complainant more of an opportunity to have its case heard, in that the panel would be reviewing all relevant facts, and would not be deferring in any way to the impugned domestic decision or regulation. A *de novo* standard would therefore arguably advantage complainants. The reverse would apply where the panel engages in a cursory review of the measure. The consequences may become more unpredictable if panels were to apply a standard that is value or objective-specific, such as a determination of whether the measure is reasonable, or whether it is at least trade restrictive. Arguably, these types of standards add in an unnecessary layer of complexity to the task of panels.

---

129 *Ibid* 137.

130 Appellate Body Report, *US-1916 Act* [60]–[61].

131 Appellate Body Report, *US-Corrosion Resistant Steel Sunset Review* [82].

132 This is not always the case as some factual assessment of the meaning of domestic regulation may be required. Further, there is on occasion argument about whether the regulation under review is in fact a measure at all. See for example Appellate Body Report, *US-Oil Country Tubular Goods* [186]–[187], in which the Appellate body overturned the panel's finding that a 'Sunset Policy Bulletin was not a measure'.

1.3.2 Institutional Considerations and Limitations within the WTO System

Earlier in this chapter, it was asserted that standards of review are ultimately a mechanism to enhance the quality of decision-making in dispute settlement systems, albeit within the context of particular institutional structures and objectives. Further, standards of review have both constitutional and procedural dimensions within the legal system in which they function. The WTO, like many international organizations, does not have the same historical and constitutional foundations of many domestic legal systems, but rather the legal system that has evolved is derived from international treaties and practices. In this case, the WTO administers a series of multilateral trade agreements designed principally to promote trade liberalization. It does not have a sophisticated constitution that imposes checks and balances or other constraints on the actions of its dispute settlement organs. Nor does it have the automatic benefit of judicial doctrines, such as standards of review, which may have developed over many years in conjunction with a legal system. Whilst standards of review may be prescribed legislatively or judicially, there is some scepticism as to whether the Appellate Body can formally adopt a standard of review in the absence of its direct inclusion in the text of the WTO Agreements.[133]

There is therefore a potential limitation on the degree to which a standard of review can be imposed upon the WTO membership. The WTO is an international treaty-based organization that relies on the consent of its membership. Accordingly, there is a question of whether the principle of state sovereignty could affect the type of standard of review that might be applied to domestic measures.[134] If state sovereignty is a relevant consideration then it is arguable that a more deferential standard of review should be applied by WTO panels.

The status of the WTO as a treaty-based organization also raises the question of whether it can or should be interpreted consistently with other international treaties. Articles 31 and 32 of the VCLT set out the basic rules for interpretation of international treaties. Article 31(1) provides:

> A treaty shall be interpreted in good faith in accordance with the ordinary meaning to be given to the terms of the treaty in their context and in the light of its object and purpose.

---

[133] Article 3.2 of the DSU is frequently raised in support of this proposition. The final sentence of this Article provides 'Recommendations and rulings of the DSB cannot add to or diminish the rights and obligations provided in the covered agreements.'

[134] Ian Brownlie, *Principles of Public International Law* (Oxford University Press, 7th ed, 2008) 76, 299.

The question is whether a standard of review can be developed and imported into a system that is treaty-based, and yet still be within the object and purpose of the treaty.[135] In *US-Gasoline,* the Appellate Body determined that these provisions of the VCLT apply to the interpretation of the WTO Agreements.[136] Unfortunately, the VCLT does not of itself resolve the issue of whether a 'judicial-like' standard may be introduced, and what form such a standard should take. At best, the VCLT may be a useful interpretative tool used in the examination of these issues or as part of the justification for the construction of a new standard.

In examining the place of a standard of review in WTO jurisprudence, the design of the WTO system is significant. The system grew out of the GATT 1947 and its various deficiencies experienced from the 1960s onwards.[137] It was also very much a product of vigorous negotiations that took place from 1986 to 1994, known as the Uruguay Round of negotiations. The membership was aware of the need for a permanent institution to administer the expanding range of trade agreements. Further, the membership was unsatisfied with the increasing numbers of GATT panel reports that were unadopted, and therefore unenforceable, due to a lack of member consensus in support of such decisions.[138] There was therefore considerable political will available to support basic improvements to the dispute settlement system.[139] This was particularly the case with ensuring that panel decisions were binding and enforceable on the membership. A major example of this was the introduction of the negative consensus rule whereby all members of the DSB are required to vote against panel decisions in order for them to remain unadopted.[140] Despite the development of a comprehensive dispute settlement system, the membership did not expressly include reference to a general standard of review. The DSU, which sets out the objectives of the system as well as both substantive and procedural provisions, makes no mention of any general standard of review. The Anti-Dumping Agreement does prescribe a specific standard in relation to anti-dumping matters.[141] This was a product of robust negotiations pursued by the United States that will be discussed in Chapter 2.

---

135 Asif H. Qureshi, *Interpreting WTO Agreements* (Cambridge University Press, 2006) 7–8, 224.

136 Appellate Body Report, *US-Gasoline* [30].

137 See Chapter 2, Section 2.2.1.

138 Stoler, above n 4, 99.

139 *Ibid* 100.

140 The negative consensus rule is set out in DSU Articles 6.1, 16.4, 17.14 and 22.6.

141 Anti-Dumping Agreement, art 17.6.

1.3.3 Usefulness of the Domestic Law Analogy

Given that the notion of a standard of review has predominantly developed as a domestic law concept, it is relevant to examine the extent to which the concept is transportable to the WTO context. Croley and Jackson considered whether any domestic law justifications for deference apply to WTO dispute settlement.[142] Three main arguments are raised in support of deference: expertise, democracy and efficiency. These arguments are important justifications for deference by Courts in the United States towards administrative agency conduct as discussed in section 1.2.5B above. In each case, Croley and Jackson determined that the justifications are not easily transplanted into the WTO context.[143] Firstly, it cannot be forcefully put that WTO panels have less expertise in WTO matters compared with the domestic agencies implementing the obligations.[144] Indeed, quite the reverse is true. Secondly, it does not follow that deference creates more democratic accountability, because there is no analogous constitutional structure between the WTO and a domestic political system.[145] Domestic standard of review considerations involve power sharing between different branches of government, whereas the WTO has a vertical and supranational (rather than horizontal) relationship with the member measures being reviewed. Indeed, arguably there is more democratic accountability if the WTO affords less deference to the membership, given that all members agreed to the specific obligations set down in the WTO Agreements. Thirdly, the efficiency argument fares no better for similar reasons.[146] Unlike in domestic systems, the agencies are not co-ordinators of the disciplines giving rise to the measures.[147] It is the WTO that is the 'central agency' responsible for this task. This argument, in fact, mitigates against the notion of deference because there is a risk that domestic agencies will apply their own interpretations of WTO Agreements.[148] This 'tower of Babel' argument is perhaps the strongest argument against deference. It is highly likely that multiple countries will confront interpretive questions about the same WTO provisions.[149]

---

[142] Croley and Jackson, 'WTO Dispute Procedures, Standard of Review and Deference to National Governments', above n 10, 208–12.

[143] *Ibid.*

[144] *Ibid* 208.

[145] *Ibid* 209.

[146] *Ibid* 210.

[147] *Ibid.*

[148] *Ibid.*

[149] This is correct if we consider the large number of disputes that concern a small number of provisions within the major WTO Agreements. Examples would include Article III of the GATT 1994 (national treatment), Article 5.1 of the SPS Agreement (risk assessments), the dumping and material injury provisions of the Anti-Dumping Agreement and the threat of injury provision in the Agreement on Safeguards.

Given the limitations on direct relevance of domestic law rationales, it is important to be cautious about transplanting standards of review from domestic law to the WTO forum. These conceptual models are, however, most definitely our starting point as the standard of review question does still apply to WTO dispute settlement. The key consideration when identifying appropriate standards is to carefully consider the underlying principles giving rise to those standards, and to also consider the likely effects of implementing such standards. This book will progressively deal with such issues in determining the optimal standard or standards available to the WTO. Given the domestic justifications for deference do not for the most part apply in the WTO context, there needs to be careful scrutiny of any departure from a non-deferential or intensive standard of review for panel review of domestic measures. I will be contending that a highly intensive general standard of review be adopted as a default position. However, I will also be arguing that a more deferential standard should be applied in some cases based on the wording and subject matter of the WTO Agreements.

1.4 ARGUMENT, METHODOLOGY AND CHAPTER OUTLINES

1.4.1 Summary of Argument

It is contended in this book that the present standard of review adopted by the WTO Appellate Body is inadequate, and that a new standard of review should be developed. The current standard is confusing, and is particularly unclear about the degree of deference (if any) that WTO panels should apply, and the principles that inform its construction. The new standard proposed in this book consists of two limbs. The first is to provide a general standard of review that is unrestricted in nature and that is similar to a *de novo* style of review found in many domestic legal systems. The second limb stipulates a variation to the first limb in specific instances when the WTO Agreements restrict or vary the competencies existing between WTO panels and members. In other words, the second limb will operate where the review function, that might otherwise have been carried out by panels, has been modified based upon the wording or structure of particular WTO Agreements. This model provides a new conceptual framework through which panels may apply a standard of review. In some cases the standard of review will not be any different from that which is currently prescribed or applied. Therefore, in referring to a 'new' standard of review, I am emphasizing the novelty of the approach rather than advocating any radical change in practice. The coherency and consistency of approach is, in many ways, as important as applying a more optimal standard of review.

In arguing for such a model, this book also examines the underlying principles that inform the construction of an appropriate standard of review. Three such principles are identified and comprise the need for standards of review to promote the major objectives of the WTO, the need for standards to maintain adjudicative legitimacy, and the requirement for standards to be procedurally appropriate. In this book I contend that the new proposed model satisfies such criteria, and that it will result in an improvement in the workings of the WTO dispute settlement system. This book does not make extensive claims about the suitability of the proposed standard of review for other international institutions. However, the principles, themes and arguments raised in this work do have the potential to be applied for the improvement of governance in international institutions.

1.4.2 Methodology

This book utilizes a predominantly doctrinal methodology in its approach to the subject matter. This will involve in the first instance the exposition, analysis and critical evaluation of the current WTO standard of review. From this critique, I seek to identify the principles from which a new standard of review may be developed. The work is essentially divided into two parts, the first being a critique of the current standard, and the second being the extrapolation of a new standard of review model. In this type of work, it is important to appreciate that it is quite difficult to separate argumentation from methodology. In the first part of this work, the methodology will consist of a general review of the subject matter, and a discussion of both positive and negative aspects of the current approach to the standard of review issue within the WTO system. Based upon this survey, key principles are derived that it is argued should form the basis of a new standard of review. In the second part, the new model is proposed and is described in considerable detail. It is then tested against the principles identified in the first part and against a number of anticipated criticisms. Finally, this new model is then analysed in the context of each of the major WTO Agreements to determine its appropriateness for introduction into the WTO dispute settlement system. The new model is not based upon any particular theoretical approach, such as rights-based or constitutional approaches.[150] The analysis is ultimately based upon a number of sequential research questions that focus on whether the current standard of review is adequate, and whether the new proposed model would represent an overall

---

150 See for example, Deborah Cass, 'The 'Constitutionalization' of International Trade Law: Judicial Norm Generation as the Engine of Constitutional Development in International Trade' (2001) 12(1) *European Journal of International Law* 39. There may be several other approaches to the standard of review, such as democratic or developing country approaches.

improvement to the WTO dispute settlement system. In this work I seek to identify and articulate the best normative approach to the standard of review issue in WTO dispute settlement.

1.4.3 Chapter Outlines

The purpose of this chapter has been to explain the concept of a standard of review and its importance in relation to WTO law. Chapter 2 will provide a detailed history of how the standard of review has developed within the GATT and WTO systems, and identify any major problems experienced to date. Chapter 3 will first examine a number of different theoretical approaches to the standard of review and discuss their attractiveness for adoption in the WTO. It will then identify relevant principles that may form the basis of a new standard. These principles are on the whole deduced from the common factors within (or axiomatic to) different theoretical approaches discussed by scholars. In Chapters 4 and 5 a new standard of review test is outlined and its overall strengths and weaknesses are discussed. The new test is also examined by reference to the underlying principles in order to evaluate its appropriateness within the WTO system. In Chapters 6 and 7, I will move away from a theoretical description of the new test and discuss how the standard may be practically applied. Chapters 6 and 7 will, in this regard, involve a brief assessment of how the new standard of review may be applied in relation to the major trade remedy and non-trade remedy agreements respectively. Of the non-trade remedy agreements, the following agreements will be scrutinized: the GATT 1994, the SPS Agreement and the TBT Agreement.[151] Finally, Chapter 8 is a summary of findings and a discussion of the implications for the WTO of adopting the new standard or failing to do so.

[151] These Agreements account for the vast majority of non-trade remedy based disputes. See Chapter 7 Section 7.1.

2. The development of the WTO standard of review

2.1 INTRODUCTION

This chapter concerns the historical development of the standard of review in GATT and WTO law. I will seek to put the WTO standard of review in its historical and institutional context before identifying and discussing the current standard of review test in WTO law. This chapter is divided into three major sections: its treatment under the GATT (1947–1994), during the Uruguay Round of negotiations (1986–1994), and under the WTO (1995 to the present). There is discussion of both the structure of the GATT and WTO agreements and case law as they relate to the standard of review. The bulk of the chapter concerns the 'objective assessment' test formulated in the decision of *EC-Hormones*, and its development in subsequent decisions. The final section deals with the unique standard of review prescribed for anti-dumping disputes.

This historical chapter is intended to identify trends in the current WTO standard of review and draw out any difficulties in its operation within the WTO system. The difficulties that I will seek to highlight include the lack of any clear theoretical foundation for the standard, the inconsistency in the way the standard is described and applied, and the fact that a separate standard exists solely for anti-dumping disputes. Two of the major trends in the development of the standard are adaptation of the standard depending upon the type of obligations under review, and the movement of the standard closer to *de novo* review.[1] This chapter will seek to show that whilst the current standard of review is a positive development and is part of the evolution towards a more legally-based international trading system, there are strong grounds for it to be reformed. Absent such reforms WTO members may become increasingly concerned about whether the dispute settlement system is operating effectively to protect and maintain the balance of rights and obligations enshrined in the WTO Agreements.

---

1 See Chapter 2, Section 2.4.3.

2.2 THE GENERAL AGREEMENT ON TARIFFS AND TRADE 1947

This section deals with the development of the standard of review under the GATT 1947. Its development during this period is crucial to understanding its later treatment in WTO cases because a large part of the architecture of the WTO, including the dispute settlement system, is based upon the unique nature of the GATT and its practices that have evolved since 1947.

This section will show that the development of a standard of review during the GATT years was slow and erratic. Whilst the reasons are complex, this section will focus on two major factors. Firstly, the GATT did not have a detailed dispute settlement procedure that would help develop a standard of review doctrine. Secondly, quite often decisions made by GATT panels were excessively deferential to members whose measures were being investigated. This cautiousness on the part of panels did not assist the development of a more rigorous standard of review. Both of the above factors are linked by the gradual movement of the GATT away from its diplomatic origins towards the creation of a more sophisticated legal system capable of dealing with more complex international trade disputes. This historical and institutional context is an important influence on how the WTO standard of review has developed in recent years and it without question shapes what kind of standard of review would be most suitable for WTO dispute settlement.

2.2.1 GATT 1947

The GATT is a multilateral trade agreement concluded between 23 governments in October 1947.[2] The GATT system is often described as being more of a 'power'-orientated system rather than a rule-orientated system.[3] The GATT resulted from negotiations for a broader international agreement for economic affairs, the Charter for an International Trade Organization.[4] The original signatories to the GATT were members of a 'Preparatory Committee' for the ITO Charter.[5] On 30 October 1947, the members signed a Final Act

---

2 *General Agreement on Tariffs and Trade*, opened for signature 30 October 1947, 55 UNTS 187 (entered into force 29 July 1948).

3 Ernst-Ulrich Petersmann, *The GATT/WTO Dispute Settlement System: International Law, International Organizations and Dispute Settlement* (Kluwer Law International, 1997) 66.

4 *Charter for an International Trade Organization*, UN Doc. E/Conf. 2/78 (24 March 1948). See John H. Jackson, *The World Trading System – Law and Policy of International Economic Relations* (MIT Press, 2nd ed, 1997) 37.

5 *Ibid.*

adopting the text of the GATT and a Protocol of Provisional Application. It was expected that the GATT would become part of the ITO structure once the ITO Charter was ratified. The ITO Charter was however never ratified, and therefore, the ITO did not come into existence.[6] Accordingly, the GATT was an international agreement that was provisional in nature. It did not incorporate administrative and institutional features to enable the carrying out of its objectives. The GATT was instead administered principally through the collective decision-making of its membership, known as the 'Contracting Parties'.[7] This, to a large extent, explains many of the subsequent practices which evolved in the administration of the GATT, including dispute settlement procedures.

The text of the GATT did not contain any detailed dispute settlement provisions. In analysing the structure of the GATT, Jackson notes that: 'there is no single, sharply defined dispute settlement procedure in the GATT that can be readily distinguished from the remainder of GATT activity'.[8] Two articles do however focus on dispute settlement procedures, albeit in a generalized way. Firstly, Article XXII dealt with consultations. It provided for consultations between any of the GATT contracting parties 'with respect to any matter affecting the operation of this Agreement'.[9] If these consultations were unsuccessful, consultations could, at the request of a contracting party, occur between the Contracting Parties as a whole, and other contracting parties, whose measures were claimed to be inconsistent with the GATT. The Contracting Parties initially dealt with disputes at its semi-annual meeting and during the early 1950s through an 'intersessional committee'.[10]

The second article of the GATT that concerned dispute settlement was Article XXIII, which dealt with enforcement. It provided for the suspension of concessions or other obligations afforded to parties that have 'nullified or impaired' benefits of another party, or where the attainment of any objective of the Agreement is impeded due to the failure of a contracting party to fulfil its obligations. The circumstances under which this suspension of benefits might take place were not restricted to a failure to comply with provisions of the GATT, but also extended to a case where any other measure, or the existence of any other situation, may undermine the operation of the GATT.[11]

---

6 *Ibid* 39.

7 *Ibid* 38.

8 John H. Jackson, *World Trade and the Law of the GATT* (Bobbs-Merrill Company, 1969) 64.

9 GATT 1994, art XXII, para 1.

10 Jackson, *The World Trading System – Law and Policy of International Economic Relations*, above n 4, 115.

11 GATT 1994, art XXIII, para 1.

Accordingly, this article did not exhaustively set out the exact grounds for members to be entitled to initiate a complaint. Nor did it elaborate on the procedures by which complaints were to be initiated and prosecuted.

Hudec summarizes the position as follows:

> The enforcement of these rules was left to a rather vaguely defined procedure. No formal organizational structure was created. The signatory countries, known collectively as the Contracting Parties, simply gave themselves the power to make whatever decisions were necessary to implement the agreement. It was, after all, only a provisional agreement between a small group of countries; the ITO would soon take over everything.[12]

In the 1950s the GATT Council began referring claims to bodies known as working parties that comprised a small number of the GATT membership. Hudec describes these working groups as 'ad hoc negotiating bodies'.[13] A high degree of policy cohesion existed between the founding members of the GATT and this served to ensure that disputes could be resolved mainly through informal processes. However, in 1952 a panel system was introduced with panels being assembled on an ad hoc basis with diplomats from neutral countries. Only 53 complaints were filed up until 1959, and GATT panels had a high rate of success, both in ensuring that a panel decision could be reached, and that the membership complied with recommendations and rulings made.[14]

In the 1960s there was a diversification of the GATT membership, particularly with the admission of a number of developing countries.[15] As a result, the dispute settlement system became more politicized and a number of difficult claims were filed in the early 1960s.[16] This led to a policy stalemate where the dispute settlement system was essentially inactive or dysfunctional between 1963 and 1970.[17] This set the tone for the need to reform many aspects of GATT's operation, including the need to create a more legalistic dispute resolution system. Major reform of the GATT took place during the 'Tokyo Round' of negotiations.

---

12 Robert E. Hudec, *Enforcing International Trade Law – The Evolution of the Modern GATT Legal System* (Butterworths, 1993) 30.

13 *Ibid.*

14 *Ibid* 31.

15 *Ibid* 12.

16 *Ibid* 13.

17 Terence P. Stewart and Christopher Callahan, 'Dispute Settlement Mechanisms' in Terence P. Stewart (ed), *The GATT Uruguay Round: A Negotiating History (1986–1992)* (Kluwer, 1993) Volume II, 2680.

2.2.2 Tokyo Round Codes

Tariff reductions and related issues were progressively negotiated in a series of negotiating rounds. There have been eight such rounds in the history of the GATT and WTO. The seventh round, known as the Tokyo Round took place from 1973 to 1979. The major accomplishment of this round was the introduction of a number of side-agreements or codes that set out rules concerning mainly non-tariff barrier issues. The United States was the main proponent of the Tokyo Round negotiations. Unlike in the previous Kennedy Round, it had acquired a 'fast track' procedure under its Trade Act 1974 to negotiate on many non-tariff issues, which ordinarily would require congressional approval to implement changes to United States domestic legislation.[18]

In order to reduce or remove non-trade barriers, it was recognized that detailed legal rules were required. These barriers by their nature are not as transparent as tariffs, and the terms of their reduction or removal as well as enforcement rights needed to be documented. The resulting seven codes were in total much longer than the GATT text. Significantly, many of the codes contained their own dispute settlement provisions, and the GATT's general dispute settlement procedure was also reformed. Hudec notes that 'the new codes required a strong dispute settlement procedure to make them credible' and 'unlike tariffs, NTBs could not simply be bargained away, one against the other'.[19]

The 1979 Understanding on Dispute Settlement set out the new dispute settlement procedures.[20] It was an important step in the development of a standard of review because it provided firmer foundations for formal dispute settlement techniques. Article 16 of the Understanding on Dispute Settlement dealt in general with the appropriate role of panels in reviewing domestic authorities' measures. This Article provided as follows:

> The function of a panel is to assist the Contracting Parties in discharging their responsibilities under Article XXIII:2. *Accordingly, a panel should make an objective assessment of the matter before it, including an objective assessment of the facts of the case and the applicability of and conformity with the General Agreement and, if so requested by the Contracting Parties, make such other findings as will assist the Contracting Parties in making the recommendations or in giving the rulings provided for in Article XXIII:2.* In this connection, panels should consult regularly

---

18 *Ibid* 2685.

19 Hudec, *Enforcing International Trade Law – The Evolution of the Modern GATT Legal System*, above n 12, 25.

20 Understanding Regarding Notification, Consultation, Dispute Settlement and Surveillance, L/4907, adopted 28 November 1979, BISD 26S/210. See also Stewart and Callahan, 'Dispute Settlement Mechanisms', above n 17, 2696.

> with the parties to the dispute and give them adequate opportunity to develop a mutually satisfactory solution.[21] (Emphasis added)

The second sentence of this Article gives some guidance to panels as to the applicable standard of review of facts and law. Panels are directed to conduct an objective assessment of a matter, and this would appear to be the standard for both factual and legal review. Despite the term 'objective assessment' later becoming central to the standard of review doctrine under WTO dispute settlement, no GATT dispute panels identified this Article as describing the appropriate standard of review even though it contained virtually the same wording as Article 11 of the DSU.[22]

A number of the Tokyo Round Codes also contained dispute settlement procedures that dealt with the way in which panels were to approach their review task for individual disciplines. For example, Article 18.1 of the *Subsidies Code* provided:

> The Committee shall establish a panel upon request pursuant to paragraph 3 of Article 17. A panel so established shall review the facts of the matter and, in light of such facts, shall present to the Committee its findings concerning the rights and obligations of the signatory party to the dispute under the relevant provisions of the General Agreement as interpreted and applied by this Agreement.[23]

This article does not stipulate the intensity or general method by which panels should review matters, but rather simply states that panels are obliged to review the facts and present their findings.

Neither Article 16 of the 1979 Understanding on Dispute Settlement, nor Article 17 of the Subsidies Code, therefore articulates the standard of review with any precision. In attempting to draw out some guiding principles, Oesch notes that 'At least, they indicated that panels were under no explicit obligation to defer to factual findings as established and evaluated by the domestic authorities, neither in general matters, nor in subsidy cases. Thus, neither provision openly promoted judicial restraint.'[24] However, by contrast Article 15.5(b) of the 1979 Anti-Dumping Code did cast some limitations on the fact reviewing task of panels. This provision restricted panels to an examination of 'the facts made available in conformity with appropriate domestic procedures

---

[21] Understanding Regarding Notification, Consultation, Dispute Settlement and Surveillance, L/4907, adopted 28 November 1979, BISD 26S/210.

[22] Matthias Oesch, *Standards of Review in WTO Dispute Resolution* (Oxford University Press, 2003) 61.

[23] Agreement on Interpretation and Application of Articles VI, XVI and XXIII of the General Agreement on Tariffs and Trade BISD 26S/56.

[24] Oesch, *Standards of Review in WTO Dispute Resolution*, above n 22, 62.

to the authorities of the importing country'.[25] Accordingly, panels in the anti-dumping field were generally restricted to reviewing facts placed on the record that constituted the basis for decisions made by domestic authorities.

The above provisions demonstrate that the standard of review was not significantly developed in the text of the GATT or in the subsequent Tokyo Codes. The next section deals with the treatment of the standard of review by GATT panels.

2.2.3 GATT Panel Decisions

The question as to what standard of review of facts should be applied did arise in a number of GATT panel decisions. It arose mostly in anti-dumping cases, where findings of dumping and material injury are based upon the establishment of particular facts by domestic authorities. The cases show that the treatment of the standard of review was erratic, but that on the whole, panels demonstrated a high degree of deference towards GATT members.

The first decision on point was *US-Fur Felt Hats*, which demonstrated a highly deferential approach in the early years of the GATT. In examining the right of the United States to withdraw a tariff concession, the working party decided that the United States was entitled to the benefit of any reasonable doubt in relation to the claim that increased imports of hats from Czechoslovakia had caused serious injury to its domestic industry.[26] In determining how much deference a party may be given, the working party was far from intrusive and acknowledged that members had to make difficult subjective economic judgements. The implication was that it was the prerogative of members to manage economic policies, and that only when there was obvious discrimination against imports would the working party intervene to overturn a measure. With this in mind, the working party noted: 'It would not be proper to regard the consequent withdrawal of a tariff concession as ipso facto contrary to Article XIX unless the weight attached by the government concerning such factors was clearly unreasonably great.'[27] Therefore the working party appeared to be allowing members a high level of subjective decision-making and would only intervene where the measure was obviously unreasonable.

By the 1970s, the administration of the GATT had changed considerably and disputes were becoming more complex. Some panels were taking a more robust approach in reviewing measures, with the 'high watermark' being *New*

---

[25] Agreement on Implementation of Article VI of the General Agreement on Tariffs and Trade BISD 26S/171.

[26] GATT Panel Report, *US-Fur Felt Hats* [30].

[27] *Ibid* [48].

Zealand-Finnish Transformers. In that case, which concerned the right to impose anti-dumping duties, the panel rejected the proposition that domestic authority findings on material injury were to be accepted as being correct. The panel noted: 'To conclude otherwise would give governments complete freedom and unrestricted discretion in deciding anti-dumping cases without any possibility to review the action taken in the GATT.'[28] The panel in this decision appeared to sanction a more intrusive standard of review. The panel performed a detailed analysis of whether the findings of dumping and material injury were sustainable. However, the panel did not take the opportunity to positively define what its review task was. It has been suggested that the panel's approach in *New Zealand-Finnish Transformers* equated to a *de novo* review of facts, although this point is unclear.[29] Hudec comments in relation to this decision that:

> While the case clearly served as another solid building block in GATT's legal reputation, in retrospect it might have been wiser to spend more time defining the degree of review GATT panels were to conduct in antidumping and countervailing cases.[30]

In the 1990s panels were dealing with a higher number of anti-dumping disputes. Such disputes were becoming more factually complex, and the approach by panels in reviewing measures was increasingly seen by members as being a key determinant of outcomes. However, despite parties making submissions in a number of cases as to the appropriate standard of review, panels were not willing to prescribe a specific standard for the benefit of parties. For example, in *US-Swedish Steel*, the United States and Sweden put forward opposing views on the role of the panel in reviewing facts. The United States argued that the role of a panel was to perform a 'systemic analysis', which would act as a check against blatantly poor decision making, but that anything short of bias or serious neglect should not be liable to be overturned by panels.[31] Sweden, by contrast, argued that it was impossible for a panel to decide whether a party has acted consistently with the anti-dumping agreement without undertaking a detailed analysis of the facts.[32] In this case, the panel declined to articulate a general standard of review believing it was more appropriate for these matters to be decided on a case-by-case basis.[33]

---

28 GATT Panel Report, *New Zealand-Finnish Transformers* [4.4].

29 Oesch, *Standards of Review in WTO Dispute Resolution*, above n 22, 65.

30 Hudec, *Enforcing International Trade Law – The Evolution of the Modern GATT Legal System*, above n 12, 174.

31 GATT Panel Report, *US-Swedish Steel* [3.11].

32 *Ibid* [3.12].

33 *Ibid* [5.3].

During this period panels continued to take a cautious and highly deferential approach to the review of facts. However, this stopped short of fully accepting factual determinations of domestic authorities. In *Korea-Resins* and *US-Norwegian Salmon AD*, the panels made it clear that their role was not to make an independent evaluation of facts.[34] Instead, their role was to determine whether the facts reasonably supported the conclusions of the authorities. In other words, as long as there was positive evidence that addressed the criteria for making findings, panels would not disturb the decisions of national authorities.

In analysing the treatment of the standard of review during the GATT years, Croley and Jackson summarised the position as follows:

> Thus it can be seen that the standard-of-review question is recurring and delicate, and one that to some extent goes to the core of an international procedure that (in a rule-based system) must assess a national government's actions against treaty or other international norms. Indeed, a more detailed review of these and other cases would show that quite a few concepts invoked by panels over the years relate to the broader question of the appropriate relationship of international dispute settlement proceedings to national government actions.[35]

This fundamental question of the allocation of power between international dispute settlement bodies and national governments was one of the key issues debated during the Uruguay Round of negotiations.

2.3 THE URUGUAY ROUND NEGOTIATIONS

The Uruguay Round of negotiations took place between November 1986 and December 1993, and the outcome was the conclusion of the agreement establishing the WTO and a number of other agreements dealing with trade liberalization and related issues.[36] The United States was the chief architect of the Round.[37] In addition to reforms of substantive disciplines, the reform of GATT dispute settlement was a high priority. Major reforms of the dispute settlement

---

34 GATT Panel Report, *Korea-Resins* [227]; GATT Panel Report, *US-Norwegian Salmon AD* [494].

35 Stephen Croley and John H. Jackson, 'WTO Dispute Procedures, Standard of Review and Deference to National Governments' (1996) 90(2) *American Journal of International Law* 197.

36 *Agreement Establishing the World Trade Organization*, opened for signature 15 April 1994, 1867 UNTS 3 (entered into force 1 January 1995) ('Marrakesh Agreement').

37 Hudec, *Enforcing International Trade Law – The Evolution of the Modern GATT Legal System*, above n 12, 182.

system, including the introduction of appellate review and the negative consensus, were the most prominent achievements.[38] However, towards the end of the Round, the United States was forcefully advocating a more deferential standard of review for panels to apply, particularly in trade remedy disputes.[39] At that time, the United States was imposing anti-dumping duties on a relatively large number of imported products.[40] Accordingly the United States was concerned that WTO panels would overturn many of these anti-dumping measures, even where there was a reasonable basis for their imposition.[41]

The first United States standard of review proposal, put forward in November 1992, was extremely deferential. On the question of review of facts, it stipulated that WTO panels must accept factual findings of domestic authorities, unless there was no interpretation of the factual information before the authority that could support its findings.[42] This proposal was rejected by other members that participated in the negotiations. The United States, however, put forward a number of other proposals. For example, in October 1993, it proposed that a restrictive standard apply to all Uruguay Round agreements, and not just in relation to anti-dumping and countervailing measures.[43] This was to take the form of notes to Article 11.1 of the DSU that would prevent an overturning of factual findings where a member's evaluation was consistent with a reasonable interpretation of those facts. This proposal was withdrawn because United States intellectual property groups sought broad grounds (an intrusive standard of review) to overturn intellectual property decisions of other members.[44] The final proposal put forward in November 1993 was significantly less restrictive and formed the basis of what became Article 17.6 of the Anti-Dumping Agreement. This proposal stipulated the requirement for panels to undertake an objective assessment of facts in order to determine whether the domestic authority's evaluation of those facts was reasonable.[45]

---

38 See DSU, arts 16.4 and 17.

39 Gary N. Horlick and Peggy A. Clarke, 'Standards for Panels Reviewing Anti-Dumping Determinations under the GATT' in Ernst-Ulrich Petersmann (ed), *International Trade Law and the GATT and WTO Dispute Settlement System* (Kluwer Law International, 1997) 295, 297. The United States' proposals were strenuously opposed by most other GATT Contracting Parties.

40 Oesch, *Standards of Review in WTO Dispute Resolution*, above n 22, 73.

41 *Ibid.*

42 Horlick and Clarke, 'Standards for Panels Reviewing Anti-Dumping Determinations under the GATT', above n 39, 298.

43 *Ibid* 299.

44 *Ibid.*

45 *Ibid* 300.

In the final stages of the Uruguay Round negotiations, discussions concerning the proposed standard of review became central to the timely conclusion of the round as a whole. It has been suggested that the standard of review issue became a 'deal breaker' for the Uruguay Round.[46] Debate centred around whether it was appropriate to allow authorities the scope of 'reasonableness' in making factual and legal findings. Some members believed that this would lead to too much inconsistency in the application of the WTO Agreements, and also that there was the potential for abuse by members.[47] As a compromise, references to reasonableness were removed from the proposal and instead other language was adopted, with panels not being able to overturn 'permissible' legal interpretations by domestic authorities. Further, this restrictive standard of review was limited in application to the Anti-Dumping Agreement, with a Ministerial Declaration being drawn up calling for consideration within three years, as to whether the new standard was capable of general application across all WTO Agreements.[48] There was hence recognition that further work was required in the quest to formulate an appropriate standard of review.

The results of the Uruguay Round of negotiations posed a number of challenges for the development of a general standard of review. These challenges are a product of the consensus-driven nature of the WTO. The United States wanted, at a minimum, to achieve a deferential standard in the anti-dumping field. However, this left open the question of what standard would apply in respect of all other disciplines. This problem was not addressed and there were no express provisions in the DSU which guided panels on this issue.[49] Would panels apply two different standards of review and would there be justification for this? There may be some justification for adopting a more restrictive standard in anti-dumping matters as they involve a review of decisions arrived at through judicial or administrative processes. However, how is this different from disputes concerning countervailing measures or any other trade remedies? Further, how would panels apply Article 17.6 anyway? Would it in fact result in a more deferential standard of review as intended by the United States?

The above questions and issues were not resolved in the drafting of the WTO Agreements. There was no express standard of review prescribed in the

---

[46] Oesch, *Standards of Review in WTO Dispute Resolution*, above n 22, 76.

[47] Croley and Jackson, 'WTO Dispute Procedures, Standard of Review and Deference to National Governments', above n 35, 197–9.

[48] Decision on Review of Article 17.6 of the Agreement on Implementation of Article VI of the General Agreement on Tariffs and Trade 1994, Final Act Embodying the Results of the Uruguay Round of Multilateral Trade Negotiations 15 April 1994 33 ILM 1140 (1994).

[49] Oesch, *Standards of Review in WTO Dispute Resolution*, above n 22, 77.

DSU or in agreements covering substantive disciplines, other than in the Anti-Dumping Agreement. As a result of these unresolved drafting problems, the task of formulating a general standard of review has been left to the DSB, and more particularly to the Appellate Body.[50] Without express guidance, the Appellate Body has had to tread carefully in balancing the need to create certainty for litigants, and at the same time, not exceeding its mandate and the scope of the WTO Agreements.

2.4 THE WORLD TRADE ORGANIZATION

2.4.1 Decisions prior to *EC-Hormones*

Given that the DSU does not prescribe a particular standard of review, there was considerable academic analysis in the immediate post-Uruguay period as to the type of approach panels might take. The WTO Agreements, being more legalistic in nature than the GATT 1947, provided scope for a more interventionist approach by panels. Despite this, certain provisions in the DSU could be interpreted as requiring a more cautious approach by panels.[51] For example, Article 3.2 provided that 'Recommendations and rulings of the DSB cannot add to or diminish the rights and obligations provided in the covered agreements.'[52] This and similar provisions supported the idea that the WTO Agreements were an exhaustive source of the rights and obligations of members and that panels should not interpret the Agreements in ways that may change the nature of rights and obligations that have been carefully negotiated.[53] This approach was also reinforced by comments made by the Appellate Body in its first decision, *US-Gasoline*.[54] In this decision, the Appellate Body upheld the panel's ruling that the United States measure (restricting imported petroleum not meeting particular environmental standards) was not justified under GATT Article XX.[55] However, the Appellate Body heavily emphasized

---

50 *Ibid.*

51 Croley and Jackson, 'WTO Dispute Procedures, Standard of Review and Deference to National Governments', above n 35, 199–200.

52 DSU, art 3.2, first sentence.

53 John H. Jackson, 'The Great 1994 Sovereignty Debate: United States Acceptance and Implementation of the Uruguay Round Results' (1997) 36 *Columbia General of Transnational Law* 157, 174.

54 Appellate Body Report, *US-Gasoline* 30.

55 The Appellate Body did however modify some panel findings. For example, the Appellate Body reversed the panel's finding that the measure was not justified under GATT Article XX(g) and instead found that it was not justified under the chapeau to GATT Article XX.

that this decision was not signalling the wider impingement of the autonomy of members to make decisions in key policy areas.[56] This cautious approach was consistent with the conclusions of Croley and Jackson in 1996 on how the WTO standard of review may be best formulated.[57]

Before discussing the line of cases concerning the WTO standard of review, it is appropriate to make reference to the issue of legal precedent. Not long after the inception of the WTO, the Appellate Body clearly stated that there was no formal doctrine of *stare decisis* in the WTO dispute settlement system.[58] This was in the context of the Appellate Body disagreeing with a panel's finding that panel reports adopted by the DSB constituted 'subsequent practice' within the meaning of Article 31 of the VCLT.[59] In support of this conclusion, the Appellate Body referred to the exclusive authority of the Ministerial Conference and General Council to adopt interpretations of the WTO Agreements under Article IX:2 of the Marrakesh Agreement.[60] However, panel decisions do nonetheless create reasonable expectations that a similar dispute would be decided in a similar manner.[61] This proposition has been reinforced by the comments made by the Appellate Body in relation to the large number of WTO cases concerning the practice of zeroing.[62] WTO law therefore does have the opportunity to develop through the DSB's adoption of panel decisions, which may be subject to scrutiny and clarification by the Appellate Body.[63] This 'de facto' concept of precedent is, in my view, critical to the effective functioning of the WTO dispute settlement system.

---

56 Appellate Body Report, *US-Gasoline* 30.

57 Croley and Jackson, 'WTO Dispute Procedures, Standard of Review and Deference to National Governments', above n 35, 193.

58 See Appellate Body Report, *Japan-Alcoholic Beverages II*, 13–14.

59 *Ibid.*

60 *Ibid.*

61 See Michelle Sanson, 'The Effectiveness of the WTO Dispute Settlement System' in Australian Department of Foreign Affairs and Trade (ed), *Ten Years of WTO Dispute Settlement: Australian Perspectives* (Commonwealth of Australia, 2006) 100.

62 See Appellate Body Report, *US-Stainless Steel (Mexico)*, [145]–[162] where at paragraph 161 the Appellate Body states: 'The Panel's failure to follow previously adopted Appellate Body reports addressing the same issues undermines the development of a coherent and predictable body of jurisprudence clarifying Members' rights and obligations under the covered agreements as contemplated under the DSU.'

63 Further, the Appellate Body does not have a strong degree of 'legislative' oversight given that it is very difficult to correct interpretations of the Appellate Body though an amendment to the WTO Agreements. This would require agreement of all WTO members, usually at the Ministerial Conference. See Mitsuo Matsushita, Thomas J. Schoenbaum and Petros C. Mavroidis, *The World Trade Organization: Law, Practice and Policy* (Oxford University Press, 2nd ed, 2006) 131–2.

Between 1995 and 1998, there were two panel decisions in which panels expressly made findings concerning the appropriate standard of review to be applied. *US-Underwear* and *US-Wool Shirts and Blouses* both concerned the safeguard provisions of the Agreement on Textiles and Clothing and in both cases the panels relied upon Article 11 of the DSU.[64] In *US-Underwear*, the panel was forced to choose between the United States proposal that the *US-Fur Felt Hats* reasonableness standard should be adopted, versus the Costa Rica proposal for a review based on identified criteria, which included ensuring that the establishment of facts by the domestic authority was proper, and that there was an objective evaluation of facts by the panel. In agreeing with much of Costa Rica's submission, the panel determined that its review task was primarily based on Article 11 of the DSU, which requires panels to undertake an objective assessment of the matter.[65] The panel then found that an objective assessment would involve an examination of whether the domestic authority had examined all relevant factors before it, whether an adequate explanation had been provided about how the facts as a whole supported the determination made and whether the determination was consistent with a party's international obligations.[66]

The first two criteria identified by the panel in *US-Underwear* relate to the process of factual review, whereas the third criterion concerns the standard of review of law. This early decision is remarkably detailed in its prescription of the standard of review and these findings were significantly developed by the Appellate Body in *EC-Hormones*.

2.4.2 *EC-Hormones*

EC-Hormones marks the first occasion when the Appellate Body directly considered the standard of review question.[67] The Appellate Body was reviewing a panel decision concerning whether European Union[68] measures prohibiting the importation of hormone treated meat was consistent with the SPS Agreement.[69] Central to the dispute was the panel's finding that the European Union measures were not 'based upon' a risk assessment as required by Article 5.1 of the SPS Agreement. Of critical importance to the outcome of the appeal

64 Panel Report, *US-Underwear*, Panel Report, *US-Wool Shirts and Blouses*.

65 Panel Report, *US-Underwear* [7.9]–[7.10].

66 Panel Report, *US-Underwear* [7.13].

67 Appellate Body Report, *EC-Hormones*.

68 The European Union was formally known as the European Communities within the WTO until 30 November 2009. The EU is a WTO member in its own right as are each of its 27 member states, making 28 WTO members altogether.

69 Appellate Body Report, *EC-Hormones* [2]–[5].

was therefore the identification of the panel's review task. The European Union argued that the panel had improperly applied a *de novo* standard of review, particularly by imposing its own assessment of scientific evidence.[70] The United States, by contrast, argued that the panel had correctly carried out its role in determining whether the scientific evidence was sufficient to show that the measure was based on a risk assessment.[71]

In rejecting the arguments of both parties, the Appellate Body articulated the standard of review in the following terms:

> In our view, Article 11 of the DSU bears directly on this matter and, in effect, articulates with great succinctness but with sufficient clarity the appropriate standard of review for panels in respect of both the ascertainment of facts and the legal characterization of such facts under the relevant agreements.[72]

The Appellate Body then set out Article 11 with the following emphasis:

> The function of panels is to assist the DSB in discharging its responsibilities under this Understanding and the covered agreements. Accordingly, a panel should make an <u>objective assessment of the matter</u> before it, including <u>an objective assessment of the facts</u> of the case and the <u>applicability of and conformity with the relevant covered agreements</u>, and make other such findings as will assist the DSB in making the recommendations or in giving the rulings provided in the covered agreements. Panels should consult regularly with parties to the dispute and give them adequate opportunity to develop a mutually satisfactory solution. [Underlining added][73]

In applying Article 11, the Appellate Body noted that: 'The duty to make an objective assessment of the facts is, among other things, an obligation to consider the evidence presented to a panel and to make factual findings on the basis of that evidence.'[74] Conversely, the Appellate Body stated that the failure by a panel to consider evidence or the wilful distortion or misrepresentation of evidence is incompatible with an objective assessment of the facts and '... impl[ies] not simply an error of judgment in the appreciation of the evidence but rather an egregious error that calls into question the good faith of the panel.'[75]

The Appellate Body made it clear that a *de novo* review of facts is not required, and by implication an objective assessment involves a degree of scrutiny that is more restricted than in the case of *de novo* review. To put it

70 *Ibid* [14]–[15].
71 *Ibid* [41].
72 *Ibid* [116].
73 *Ibid.*
74 *Ibid* [133].
75 *Ibid.*

another way, objective assessment is somewhere between *de novo* review and total deference. The Appellate Body stated that:

> So far as fact-finding by panels is concerned, their activities are always constrained by the mandate of Article 11 of the DSU: the applicable standard is neither *de novo* review as such, nor "total deference", but rather the "objective assessment of the facts".[76]

This decision also made it clear that objective assessment was the applicable standard for the review of both facts and law.[77] Whilst the Appellate Body provides examples in *EC-Hormones* of what does not constitute objective assessment, no positive definition of this term is provided. The use of the concept of objective assessment without the addition of further criteria therefore poses a number of difficulties.

The major difficulty with this type of definition is that an objective assessment does not really signify any particular degree of deference or intrusion for panels to adopt in examining measures. There is therefore an absence of conceptual sophistication that would provide guidance to panels in their review of measures. For instance, in an early critique of this issue, one commentator noted:

> Clearly the 'objective assessment' principle is not all that helpful in ascertaining towards which extreme (*de novo* or total deference) the Appellate Body would lean. The notion of objectivity rather assumes an alternative to the EC's proposals for the development of an appropriate standard of review. The question is if the Appellate Body will further develop the confines of this review through the principle of objectivity rather than vacillating between total deference and *de novo* review.[78]

It has also been suggested that not only is the notion of objective assessment inadequate to support the intended jurisprudence, but that it suggests a highly intensive form of review that is akin to *de novo* review.[79] Other commentators have been equally concerned, with a common response being that the use of Article 11 as a standard of review 'is unclear, misses the mark conceptually and generates confusion'.[80] The conclusion to be drawn from these reactions is that the Appellate Body would appear to have simply identified a general

---

[76] *Ibid* [117].

[77] *Ibid* [118].

[78] G. Axel Desmedt, 'Hormones: Objective Assessment and (or as) Standard of Review' (1998) 1 *Journal of International Economic Law* 695, 697.

[79] Holger Spamann, 'Standard of Review for World Trade Organization Panels in Trade Remedy Cases: A Critical Analysis' (2004) 38(3) *Journal of World Trade* 540.

[80] Catherine Button, *The Power to Protect: Trade Health and Uncertainty in the WTO* (Hart Publishing, 2004) 168.

provision in the DSU (which was already in the Tokyo Round DSU) as a convenient source of the standard of review.

Part of the conceptual confusion regarding the objective assessment test is that the Appellate Body, in *EC-Hormones* (and in some subsequent decisions), has equated the failure of a panel to apply the correct standard of review to a failure by a panel to review the evidence in good faith.[81] In *EC-Hormones*, the Appellate Body in turn referred to a failure to exercise good faith as including instances of wilful distortion or misrepresentation of evidence and other conduct that amounted to a denial of natural justice or due process.[82] It is arguable that the methodology of assessing facts and questions of good faith are conceptually distinct. In other words, it may be possible to apply the incorrect standard of review without failing to exercise good faith or vice versa.

The net effect of this decision is that the standard of review was not narrowly defined. This lack of clarity has not been substantially remedied in subsequent cases because of the ongoing adherence to the concept of objective assessment. In the next section I will discuss the major developments regarding the standard following *EC-Hormones*. Panels were initially given a wide discretion in their approach to the assessment of facts, which did make it difficult to succeed with a claim that a panel had failed to apply DSU Article 11.

2.4.3 Post *EC-Hormones*

In a number of decisions following *EC-Hormones* the Appellate Body and panels have seen fit to make statements to clarify the standard of review and, in doing so, the standard has been varied, both in the way it is formally expressed and in the way it is applied. This has provided panels and parties with some degree of guidance on how cases should be reviewed where they deal with different obligations under the various WTO Agreements. However, the development of the standard of review test has been slow, sometimes inconsistent and difficult for parties to interpret clearly. The cases also evidence at least two critical developments: the movement towards a *de novo* standard, and the adaptation of the standard to the specific provisions of different WTO agreements, thus potentially creating more than one standard.

The movement towards *de novo* review has been gradual, with the Appellate Body through a number of decisions expanding the requirements of panel review. In *Argentina-Footwear (EC)*, the Appellate Body determined that the panel had correctly identified Article 11 as the source of the standard of review (save for in anti-dumping matters) but that this review task involved

---

81 Appellate Body Report, *EC-Hormones* [133]; Appellate Body Report, *EC-Poultry* [134].

82 Appellate Body Report, *EC-Hormones* [133].

examining, in the context of a safeguard injury determination, whether the relevant domestic agency had considered all the relevant facts and adequately explained how the facts supported the determinations that were made.[83] Such an approach was subsequently developed in a number of other safeguard decisions, such as in *US-Lamb* and *US-Cotton Yarn*.[84] In *US-Lamb*, the Appellate Body emphasized that a panel can only assess whether an agency explanation for a safeguard determination is reasoned and adequate if the panel critically examines that explanation in depth and in light of the facts before the panel.[85] In other words, panels have a duty to review a domestic agency's reasoning and conclusions thoroughly, and this will not be considered to be engaging in a *de novo* review.[86] In *US-Cotton Yarn*, the Appellate Body drew upon the earlier safeguard decisions of *Argentina-Footwear (EC)*, *US-Lamb* and *US-Wheat Gluten* and described the standard of review of facts as follows:

> The standard may be summarized as follows: panels must examine whether the competent authority has evaluated all relevant factors; they must assess whether the competent authority has examined all pertinent facts and assessed whether an adequate explanation has been provided as to how those facts support the determination; and they must also consider whether the competent authority's explanation addresses fully the nature and complexities of the data and responds to other plausible interpretations of the data. However, panels must not conduct a *de novo* review of the evidence nor substitute their judgment for that of the competent authority.[87]

This intensive approach arguably had its high-water mark in *US-Softwood Lumber VI (Article 21.5-Canada)* which dealt with compliance in respect of threatened injury determinations under the SCM and Anti-Dumping Agreements. The Appellate Body found that the panel had not applied the correct standard of review in reviewing the USITC's determinations in that it 'failed to engage in the type of critical and searching analysis called for by Article 11 of the DSU'.[88] The Appellate Body was quite critical of the panel's acceptance that the USITC's explanation of the measures provided reasoned support for its conclusion.[89] The Appellate Body suggested that a panel must

---

83 Appellate Body Report, *Argentina-Footwear (EC)* [121].

84 Appellate Body Report, *US-Lamb* [106]; Appellate Body Report, *US-Cotton Yarn* [74].

85 Appellate Body Report, *US-Lamb* [106].

86 *Ibid* [107].

87 Appellate Body Report, *US-Cotton Yarn* [74]; Appellate Body Report, *US-Wheat Gluten* [110]–[117].

88 Appellate Body Report, *US-Softwood Lumber VI (Article 21.5-Canada)* [113].

89 Appellate Body Report, *US-Softwood Lumber VI (Article 21.5-Canada)* [124].

determine whether the domestic authority's conclusions are reasoned and adequate and that this should involve the following kinds of steps:

> The panel should test whether the reasoning of the authority is coherent and internally consistent.
>
> The panel must undertake an in-depth examination of whether the explanations given disclose how the investigating authority treated the facts and evidence in the record and whether there was positive evidence before it to support the inferences made and conclusions reached by it.
>
> The panel must examine whether the explanations provided demonstrate that the investigating authority took proper account of the complexities of the data before it, and that it explained why it rejected or discounted alternative explanations and interpretations of the record evidence.
>
> A panel must be open to the possibility that the explanations given by the authority are not reasoned or adequate in the light of other plausible alternative explanations.
>
> ...and must take care not to assume itself the role of initial trier of facts, nor to be passive by "simply *accept[ing]* the conclusions of the competent authorities."[90]

The above extracts demonstrate the present requirement for panels to conduct an extensive review of the issues, but without somehow engaging in *de novo* review.[91]

A similar outcome occurred in *US-Countervailing Duty Investigation on DRAMS*[92] and *US-Continued Zeroing*.[93] In both of these decisions, the Appellate Body overturned certain panel findings on the basis that panels had failed to evaluate evidence in its totality in order to draw conclusions about whether the measures were justified. In *US-Continued Zeroing* the Appellate Body noted that compliance with Article 11 means that a panel must:

---

90 Appellate Body Report, *US-Softwood Lumber VI (Article 21.5-Canada)* [93]. This final extract, including the quotation with original emphasis, is a citation from Appellate Body Report, *US-Lamb* [106].

91 In *US-Softwood Lumber VI (Article 21.5-Canada)*, the result was that the Appellate Body overturned some of the panel's findings concerning injury to the local producers, but it could not complete the analysis, which left parts of the dispute unresolved. Based on the subsequent decision of *US-Continued Suspension* (discussed below), arguably this decision represents the high watermark in the Appellate Body prescribing a highly intensive standard of review.

92 Appellate Body Report, *US-Countervailing Duty Investigation on DRAMS* [144]–[158], [188].

93 Appellate Body Report, *US-Continued Zeroing*.

> ...evaluate evidence in its totality, by which we mean the duty to weigh collectively all of the evidence and in relation to one another, even if no piece of evidence is by itself determinative of an asserted fact or claim.[94]

In that case, the European Union successfully argued that the panel did not engage in any cumulative appreciation of the evidence in failing to consider the dumping margin calculations to corroborate the fact that the zeroing methodology was used.[95] Once again, a highly intensive form of review was required to be exercised by the panel.

Subsequently, in *US-Continued Suspension*, the Appellate Body overturned a key panel finding on the basis that the panel had applied a standard of review that was not sufficiently deferential. The Appellate Body noted:

> [Instead] the Panel seems to have conducted a survey of the advice presented by the scientific experts and based its decisions on whether the majority of the experts, or the opinion that was most thoroughly reasoned or specific to the question at issue, agreed with the conclusion drawn in the European Communities' risk assessment. This approach is not consistent with the applicable standard of review under the *SPS Agreement*.[96]

The Appellate Body found that the panel had not applied the correct standard of review because the panel sought to determine whether the risk assessment relied upon by the European Union was based on the correct scientific evidence, instead of determining whether the risk assessment is supported by coherent reasoning and reputable scientific evidence.[97] This strongly suggested that a more deferential or lower standard of review needed to be applied by the panel.

The approach taken in *US-Continued Suspension* was more recently applied in *Australia-Apples*, where the panel unequivocally stated: 'The Panel finds no reason to articulate a standard of review that departs from such guidance.'[98] In *Australia-Apples*, Australia argued strongly in support of a more deferential and agreement-specific standard of review.[99] Australia contended that the standard of review should be informed by the particular WTO Agreement and obligation in issue.[100] Further, Australia argued that the standard of review must maintain the balance between trade liberalization goals

94 Appellate Body Report, *US-Continued Zeroing* [336].
95 Appellate Body Report, *US-Continued Zeroing* [337].
96 Appellate Body Report, *United States-Continued Suspension* [598].
97 Appellate Body Report, *United States-Continued Suspension* [590].
98 Panel Report, *Australia-Apples* [7.226].
99 *Australia-Apples, First Written Submissions of Australia* [175]–[189].
100 *Australia-Apples, First Written Submissions of Australia* [175]–[179].

and domestic regulatory rights.[101] These arguments were not accepted by the panel and there was no formal recognition of a more deferential standard of review, but such arguments may nonetheless have influenced the intensity of the panel's analysis of the issues.[102] Australia unsuccessfully appealed these findings, with the Appellate Body reaffirming the approach taken in *US-Continued Suspension*.[103]

It would appear from the findings in *US-Continued Suspension* and *Australia-Apples* that the Appellate Body has signalled the development of a more deferential standard of review, at least in the case of disputes concerning Article 5.1 of the SPS Agreement. Through these decisions, the Appellate Body has strongly emphasized that panels should not second guess national governments in respect of health and safety measures that have a reputable scientific basis. It nonetheless remains unclear whether these cases represent a more permanent shift in the approach of the Appellate Body. In particular, it is not absolutely clear whether the Appellate Body would apply a similar approach in disputes concerning other WTO Agreements, but the inference from subsequent trade remedy cases is that this more deferential approach may be confined to disputes under the SPS Agreement.[104]

Despite the Appellate Body repeatedly emphasizing that a panel's role was not *de novo* in nature, the line of authorities described above demonstrates that generally a greater onus has been placed on panels to thoroughly review member measures. Various commentators have suggested that the approach required of panels is close to a *de novo* standard of review in relation to the assessment of facts.[105] Despite this ostensibly high onus placed on panels,

---

101 *Australia-Apples, First Written Submissions of Australia* [180]–[183].

102 Panel Report, *Australia-Apples* [7.216]–[7.229].

103 Appellate Body Report, *Australia-Apples* [222]. For the grounds of appeal relied upon by Australia see: *Australia-Apples, Notification of an Appeal by Australia*, WT/DS367/13. Australia claimed *inter alia* that the panel erred in its interpretation and application of what constitutes a proper risk assessment under Articles 5.1 and 5.2 of the SPS Agreement. New Zealand also appealed certain findings. See *Australia-Apples, Notification of an Appeal by New Zealand*, WT/DS367/14.

104 See for example, Appellate Body Report, *US-Anti-Dumping and Countervailing Duties (China)* [491]–[527]; Panel Report, *United States-Measures Affecting Imports of Certain Passenger Vehicle and Light Truck Tyres from China* [7.15]–[7.21]; Appellate Body Report, *United States-Measures Affecting Imports of Certain Passenger Vehicle and Light Truck Tyres from China* [122]–[125] and [257].

105 Matthias Oesch, 'Standards of Review in WTO Dispute Resolution' (2003) 6(3) *Journal of International Economic Law* 635, 650; Spamann, 'Standard of Review for World Trade Organization Panels in Trade Remedy Cases, above n 79, 540.

there have only been a relatively small number of cases to date where the Appellate Body has overturned panel findings based on a failure to comply with Article 11.[106] It is difficult to definitively account for this outcome but likely contributing factors are the already rigorous approach to review shown by panels and the reasonably wide discretion still afforded to panels in their factual findings. This last factor may lead to a disconnection between the standard proclaimed by the Appellate Body and the standard that is actually applied in some cases. The conceptual confusion about what is meant by objective assessment has not made the position clear for panels or WTO members.

The second major trend in the development of the standard of review has been the movement towards a more agreement-specific standard. The effect of this approach is that the objective assessment test is increasingly not applied in a uniform manner but rather it is treated as a general legal principle that may be applied in a different manner depending upon the WTO obligations being reviewed. Arguably this approach is an attempt to give practical effect to the wide variety of measures in sometimes quite divergent fields that come before WTO panels.[107] This trend was first signalled by the Appellate Body in *US-Lamb* where it stated that the precise nature of an examination conducted by a panel, in reviewing a claim under Article 4.2 of the Safeguards Agreement, stems in part from the panel's obligation to make an objective assessment of the matter under Article 11 of the DSU, and, in part, from the obligations imposed by Article 4.2 of the Safeguards Agreement.[108] This provision requires domestic authorities to investigate whether imports have caused or are threatening to cause serious injury to a domestic industry using certain criteria, and to publish a detailed analysis of the case. This type of provision prescribes various requirements for

---

106 The decisions are: Appellate Body Report, *US-Wheat Gluten*; Appellate Body Report, *US-Lamb*; Appellate Body Report, *US-Cotton Yarn*; Appellate Body Report, *US-Countervailing Duty Investigation on DRAMS*; Appellate Body Report, *US-Softwood Lumber VI (Article 21.5-Canada)*; Appellate Body Report, *Japan-DRAMs (Korea)*; Appellate Body Report, *US-Upland Cotton (Article 21.5-Brazil)*; Appellate Body Report, *US-Continued Suspension*; Appellate Body Report, *Canada-Continued Suspension*; Appellate Body Report, *US-Continued Zeroing*, Appellate Body Report, *US-Anti-Dumping and Countervailing Duties (China)* [491]–[527]. In Appellate Body Report, *US-Wheat Gluten* and Appellate Body Report, *US-Cotton Yarn* the panel errors are more in the nature of reasoning errors rather than the panel applying a less intensive standard.

107 Claus-Dieter Ehlermann and Nicolas Lockhart, 'Standard of Review in WTO Law' (2004) 7(3) *Journal of International Economic Law* 491.

108 Appellate Body Report, *US-Lamb* [105]. See also discussion of WTO member obligations under the Safeguards Agreement in Chapter 6, Section 6.5.

members to satisfy, but it also provides a degree of flexibility for domestic authorities to reach their own conclusions.[109]

Subsequently, in *US-Countervailing Duty Investigation on DRAMS*, the Appellate Body has reinforced and possibly extended this approach when describing the standard of review in the following terms:

> Nevertheless, we recall that an 'objective assessment' under Article 11 of the DSU must be considered in the light of the obligations of the particular covered agreement at issue in order to derive the more specific contours of the appropriate standard of review.[110]

In that case the Appellate Body was reviewing whether a subsidy determination complied with the terms of the SCM Agreement and in applying this approach stated that an objective assessment is informed by the panel's examination of whether a domestic authority has provided a reasoned and adequate explanation of how the evidence supported its findings and how the findings supported an overall subsidy determination.[111] The Appellate Body also determined that a similar standard of review would apply to like obligations normally carried out by domestic authorities under the various trade remedy agreements.[112] This is logical in that all trade remedy disputes involve a 'second tier' review of national-level investigations that, of themselves, incorporate similar processes. Where panels are performing a 'second tier' review, generally their scope of review is limited to reviewing the approach by the domestic authority in establishing facts, and the reasoning and explanation associated with the decision made.[113] It is not clear from these statements whether it was intended that this approach would vary the relative intensity or deference of the standard of review in the trade remedies context. However, if the standard of review continues to be applied in this manner, the overall level of scrutiny must change as the review task becomes regulated by the obligations at issue.

---

109 See *US-Steel Safeguards* [276]–[278], [298]–[299]. The requirement to publish reasons is an important part of a panel applying a standard of review that is different from *de novo* review. Where there are no published reasons it is likely to be difficult for a panel to avoid applying a standard of review that is akin to *de novo* review. More broadly, panels must be careful to restrict their analysis to evidence that was available at the time of the original investigation by the competent authority: see *US-Wool Shirts and Blouses* [7.21] discussed in Chapter 4, Section 4.2.1.

110 Appellate Body Report, *US-Countervailing Duty Investigation on DRAMS* [184].

111 *Ibid* [186].

112 *Ibid* [184].

113 Spamann, 'Standard of Review for World Trade Organization Panels in Trade Remedy Cases, above n 79, 514.

Subsequently, in *US-Continued Suspension*, the Appellate Body confirmed that the objective assessment test may vary depending upon the specific obligations being reviewed.[114] In particular, the Appellate Body framed the standard around the obligation for the member to conduct a risk assessment under Article 5.1 of the SPS Agreement prior to introducing an SPS measure.[115] The panel's attempt to draw its own conclusions from expert evidence rather than simply examining the quality of the risk assessment was determined not to be in keeping with the 'contours' of Article 5.1.

With the standard of review becoming more agreement-specific there is potential for the standard to be more deferential towards the decisions of domestic authorities. However, at present this agreement-specific trend does not appear to be resulting in more deference in most cases. Accordingly, panels are required to tread a 'fine line' of having to thoroughly review a domestic authority decision, but without substituting the reasoning and factual conclusions of agencies and thereby engaging in *de novo* review. This is particularly relevant in trade remedy cases where members may allege that panels have reviewed factual issues to a point where it is akin to *de novo* review.[116] Panels must exercise caution to ensure that they are acting as the '*reviewer* of agency action, rather than as *initial trier of fact*'.[117] The question of whether a more specialized standard of review ought to be framed is taken up in Chapter 5.

2.4.4 The Anti-dumping Standard of Review

As outlined in Section 2.3, the Uruguay Round of negotiations produced a separate standard of review for panels to apply in anti-dumping disputes. In this section, I outline how Article 17.6 of the Anti-Dumping Agreement has been interpreted to date, discuss any present difficulties and provide some comment on how this provision should be interpreted. The negotiating history

---

114 Appellate Body Report, *US-Continued Suspension* [590]–[593]. The Appellate Body has also signalled the further advancement of this approach in *Australia-Apples* when it distinguished the degree of deference to be applied by a panel in reviewing a claim under Article 5.1 of the SPS Agreement versus a claim under Article 5.6 of that Agreement: See Appellate Body Report, *Australia-Apples* [356]–[359].

115 Appellate Body Report, *US-Continued Suspension* [590]–[593]. See also Chapter 7, Section 7.3.2.

116 There are various restrictions on panel review of trade remedies. For example, panels are restricted in their review to the reasoning of the domestic agency arising out of the published determination and panels must limit their examination to evidence that was before the agency during the course of the original investigation.

117 Appellate Body Report, *US-Countervailing Duty Investigation on DRAMS* [188].

evidences that this standard was intended to be somewhat deferential in nature and thus afford domestic authorities a reasonable margin of appreciation in their factual investigations and findings.[118] The United States Statement of Administrative Action for the Uruguay Round Agreements is insightful as to the intention of Article 17.6, in which the following remarks are made:

> Article 17.6 ensures that WTO panels will not second-guess the factual conclusions of the agencies, even in situations where the panel might have reached a conclusion different from that of the agency. In addition, Article 17.6 ensures that panels will not be able to rewrite, under any guise of legal interpretation, the provisions of the Agreement, many of which were deliberately drafted to accommodate a variety of methodologies.[119]

The focus of scholarly attention with Article 17.6 has centred on the question of what kind of a standard of review Article 17.6 actually produces. Related to this question, scholars have also considered whether the anti-dumping standard is in fact any different from the standard that is applicable to other agreements, and if it is different, whether this is justified from a policy perspective. It is necessary to frame any analysis by recalling that the wording of Article 17.6 was agreed to with some haste in the final days of the Uruguay Round negotiations, and perhaps even more so than other provisions of trade agreements, it was a political compromise.[120]

Article 17.6 contains two limbs, the first of which prescribes a standard for the review of facts, and the second sets out the applicable standard for matters of law. The article reads as follows:

> 17.6 In examining the matter referred to in paragraph 5:
>
> (i) in its assessment of the facts of the matter, the panel shall determine whether the authorities' establishment of the facts was proper and whether their evaluation of those facts was unbiased and objective. If the establishment of the facts was proper and the evaluation was unbiased and objective, even though the panel might have reached a different conclusion, the evaluation shall not be overturned;
>
> (ii) the panel shall interpret the relevant provisions of the Agreement in accordance with customary rules of interpretation of public international law. Where the panel finds that a relevant provision of the Agreement admits of more than one permissible interpretation, the panel shall find the authorities' measure to be in conformity with the Agreement if it rests upon one of those permissible interpretations.

---

[118] Horlick and Clarke, 'Standards for Panels Reviewing Anti-Dumping Determinations under the GATT', above n 39, 300.

[119] Statement of Administrative Action for the Uruguay Round Agreements Act, Pub.L. 103–465 Stat. 4809 (1994), 19 USC 3501 [12].

[120] Andrew Stoler, 'The WTO Dispute Settlement Process: Did the Negotiators get what they wanted?' (2004) 3(1) *World Trade Review* 105.

It is clear from Article 17.6(i) that the article is designed to exclude panels from applying a *de novo* standard of review of facts.[121] This is borne out by limiting the role of a panel to examining whether the establishment of facts was proper and whether the evaluation of those facts was unbiased and objective, even if the panel may have reached a different conclusion. In other words, it would appear that panel review is really concerned with ensuring that adequate due process has been carried out by domestic authorities, rather than necessarily arriving at the correct conclusion. However, it is doubtful that Article 17.6 has resulted in a more deferential standard of review. For instance, there is a level of ambiguity about what is meant by a 'proper' establishment of facts, and an 'unbiased and objective' evaluation. Central to defining these terms is the amount of analysis or degree of intrusion that panels can undertake, and no guidance is given to aid panels in this task.[122] Another way of putting it is that there is some ambiguity about where in the spectrum between *de novo* and total deference the role of a panel lies.[123] Arguably there is sufficient ambiguity to allow for different degrees of intensity by panels, but on balance more deference should be shown given the intention of this provision.

Article 17.6(ii) is no less problematic. The first sentence of this Article directs panels to interpret provisions of the Anti-Dumping Agreement in accordance with customary rules of interpretation of public international law. This is generally accepted as referring to Articles 31 and 32 of the VCLT, which requires that treaty provisions shall be read in good faith according to their ordinary meaning and context, and in light of their object and purpose.[124] However, the second sentence of Article 17.6(ii) contemplates that a provision may have more than one permissible interpretation, and in which case the panel should not overturn a domestic measure if it accords with one or more such interpretations. On its face, the inclusion of the notion of 'permissible interpretations', gives the appearance of a degree of deference being afforded to legal interpretations. The problem with this, as explained below, is that the VCLT arguably only contemplates a single interpretation of any one provision of an international treaty.[125]

A number of panel and Appellate Body decisions have given further guidance on the interpretation of Article 17.6(i). In *Thailand-H-Beams*, the Appellate Body interpreted the words 'establishment' and 'proper' in relation to review of facts to make it clear that panels must ensure that a full and accu-

121 Oesch, *Standards of Review in WTO Dispute Resolution*, above n 22, 61.
122 *Ibid.*
123 *Ibid.*
124 See VCLT, art 31(1).
125 VCLT, arts 31, 32. See below n 284.

rate factual record was the basis for findings of domestic authorities.[126] On the question of unbiased and objective evaluation as required by Article 17.6(i), a number of decisions support a practical approach whereby the panel must determine whether the investigating authority could properly have reached the conclusions based on the factual record. For example, in *US-DRAMS*, the panel determined its role to be 'given the record before the DOC, an unbiased and objective investigating authority could properly have found that the Flamm study did not "reasonably reflect the costs associated with the production and sale" of DRAMS.'[127] In *Guatemala-Cement I* the panel described this standard as 'objective sufficiency'.[128] Irrespective of whether this standard is in fact based on reasonableness or objective grounds, the requirement for deference to domestic agencies distinguishes it from the standard of review under Article 11 of the DSU. This distinction has been succinctly described in the following terms: 'in general this provision results in fairly deferential review; panels do not overturn simply because they think it would have been preferable for the authorities to come to a different conclusion'.[129]

However, some decisions support the proposition that an unbiased and objective evaluation requires a more intrusive approach by panels. In *US-Hot-Rolled Steel* the Appellate Body stated as follows:

> Under Article 17.6(i) the task of Panels is simply to review the investigating authorities' 'establishment' and 'evaluation' of the facts. To that end, Article 17.6(i) requires panels to make an '*assessment of the facts*'. The language of this phrase reflects closely the obligation imposed on panels under Article 11 of the DSU to make an '*objective assessment* of the *facts*'. Thus the text of both provisions requires panels to 'assess' the facts and this, in our view, clearly necessitates an active review or examination of pertinent facts. Article 17.6(i) of the *Anti-Dumping Agreement* does not expressly state that panels are obliged to make an assessment of the facts which is '*objective*'. However, it is inconceivable that Article 17.6(i) should require anything other than panels make an *objective* 'assessment of the facts of the matter'. In this respect we see no 'conflict' between Article 17.6(i) of the *Anti-Dumping Agreement* and Article 11 of the DSU.[130]

---

126 Appellate Body Report, *Thailand-H-Beams* [116] where the Appellate Body stated that the ordinary meaning of establishment suggests 'place beyond dispute; ascertain, demonstrate, prove' and the ordinary meaning of 'proper' suggests 'accurate' or 'correct'.

127 Panel Report, *US-DRAMS* [6.67].

128 Panel Report, *Guatemala-Cement I* [7.57]. The appeal of Guatemala before the Appellate Body was successful on the basis that Mexico had failed to identify the specific anti-dumping measure in issue in its panel request.

129 Button, *The Power to Protect: Trade Health and Uncertainty in the WTO*, above n 80, 184.

130 Appellate Body Report, *US-Hot Rolled Steel* [55].

These comments by the Appellate Body clearly define the role of panels as more than merely confirming the due establishment of facts and rational basis of findings. They also raise the possibility that the standard of review of facts under Article 17.6 may not in fact be very different from the general standard relied upon in Article 11 of the DSU.

There is considerable disagreement amongst scholars as to the interpretation of Article 17.6(i). Ehlermann and Lockhart believe that this provision is designed to afford a considerable amount of discretion and panels are not to undertake their own independent assessment of facts. The role of panels is to determine whether the authority 'was balanced, impartial and open-minded in its evaluation of the facts'.[131] By contrast a number of other scholars suggest that Article 17.6(i) does not result in much deference towards decisions of domestic authorities. This is because panels will not just consider evidence supporting an authority's determination but will also weigh up evidence that contradicts such findings.[132] In other words, the wording of Article 17.6(i) does not resolve the debate about the degree of intensity of review, which is also a fundamental problem for the standard of review under DSU Article 11. This problem will be addressed in Chapter 5, but irrespective of the exact test adopted, undoubtedly there should be more deference given the extensive role of domestic authorities in the anti-dumping review process.

Article 17.6(ii) concerns the standard of review of law. It is instructive to examine its treatment in cases in order to understand the Appellate Body's attitude to the standard of review question more generally. This article has its origins in the *Chevron doctrine*, which is discussed in Chapter 1.[133] This United States administrative law principle stipulates that courts' agencies must defer to interpretations of statute by administrative agencies if the statute is ambiguous and the agency's interpretation is reasonable.[134]

Article 17.6(ii) is different from the *Chevron doctrine* in that it refers to 'permissible' rather than 'reasonable' interpretations and all interpretations must primarily conform to customary rules of interpretation of public international law.[135] In some cases, panels have skirted around the question of

131 Ehlermann and Lockhart, 'Standard of Review in WTO Law', above n 107, 504.

132 Horlick and Clarke, 'Standards for Panels Reviewing Anti-Dumping Determinations under the GATT', above n 39, 302.

133 See Chapter 1, Section 1.2.5B.

134 *Chevron USA Inc v National Resources Defense Council Inc*, 467 US 837 (1984). See also Chapter 1, Section 1.2.5B. The question of ambiguity is often couched in terms of whether congress has 'directly spoken to the precise issue in question'. See Croley and Jackson, 'WTO Dispute Procedures, Standard of Review and Deference to National Governments', above n 35, 202.

135 Anti-Dumping Agreement, art 17.6(ii), Second Sentence.

whether the relevant provisions of the VCLT, which contemplates only one interpretation, conflict with the admittance of more than one 'permissible interpretation'.[136] Article 31(1) of the VCLT provides that 'a treaty shall be interpreted in good faith in accordance with the ordinary meaning to be given to the terms of the treaty in their context and in light of its object and purpose.' In *US-DRAMS*, the panel analysed the Anti-Dumping Agreement having regard to Article 31(1), and rejected the argument of the United States that the relevant measures constituted a 'permissible interpretation' of Article 11.2 of the Anti-Dumping Agreement.[137] Therefore, the panel focussed upon the VCLT as being the basis of interpretation of Article 17.6(ii).

The cases on this point bear out that the Appellate Body and panels will not entertain multiple interpretations of WTO agreement provisions.[138] For example, in *EC-Bed Linen*, the Appellate Body upheld a panel decision on the EC's zeroing of dumping margins and noted that the practice of zeroing was inconsistent with the agreement, and therefore the panel 'was not faced with a choice among multiple 'permissible' interpretations which would have required it, under Article 17.6(ii), to give deference to the interpretation relied upon by the European Communities.'[139] However, the Appellate Body noted in *US-Hot-Rolled Steel* that it has not totally discounted the possibility that the WTO agreements may admit more than one permissible interpretation.[140] In the later decision of *US-Continued Zeroing*, the Appellate Body has confirmed such an approach by stating that the application of the VCLT may give rise to an interpretive range, but yet the application of the VCLT in that case did not allow for conflicting interpretations.[141]

---

[136] See Appellate Body Report, *US-Stainless Steel (Mexico)* [76], [136]; Panel Report, *US-Stainless Steel (Mexico*, [7.64]–[149]; Appellate Body Report, *US-Zeroing (Japan)* [188]–[189]; Panel Report, *US-Zeroing (Japan)* [7.142]; Appellate Body Report, *US-Softwood Lumber VI (Article 21.5-Canada)* [123]; Appellate Body Report, *US-Hot Rolled Steel* [57]–[62]. The problem of the interpretation of Anti-Dumping provisions has been particularly highlighted in the various zeroing cases.

[137] Panel Report, *US-DRAMS* [6.54] n 499.

[138] The position adopted by the Appellate Body on this issue has not escaped criticism, with it arguably reading Article 17.6(ii) out of the Anti-Dumping Agreement, contrary to the principle of effectiveness in treaty interpretation. See Stoler, 'The WTO Dispute Settlement Process', above n 120, 109–12.

[139] Appellate Body Report, *EC-Bed Linen* [65].

[140] Appellate Body Report, *US-Hot-Rolled Steel* [61].

[141] Appellate Body Report, *US-Continued Zeroing* [259]–[317].

2.5 CONCLUSION

It is evident from this chapter that the standard of review has quickly become a prominent issue in WTO dispute settlement. Its relative importance has grown commensurate with the development of formal dispute settlement processes and the WTO treaty system as a whole. This process has accelerated with the conclusion of the Uruguay Round Agreements and the operation of the WTO's new dispute settlement processes. However, with the exception of the Anti-Dumping Agreement, the WTO Agreements do not expressly set out a standard of review for panels to apply. Further, the DSU has only had approximately 16 years for the development of a standard of review doctrine. The Appellate Body's decision in *EC-Hormones* does not provide an adequate theoretical basis for a standard of review. Further, the question as to how the standard may be adapted to take into account different agreements requires clarification. Despite the wording of Article 17.6 of the Anti-Dumping Agreement, one must query whether the effective standard created by this article is any different from the standard applied in respect of other WTO Agreements, and in particular, other trade remedy agreements.

A fundamental issue is whether the evolution of the objective assessment test or the misapplication of Article 17.6 of the Anti-Dumping Agreement has shifted the balance of substantive WTO rights and obligations and what, if any, effect this might have on the operation of and confidence in the WTO system. To date, there have been no proposals put forward as part of the DSU reform negotiations for the adoption of a new standard of review.[142] It is in this context that in Chapter 3, I will be examining some alterative standard of review proposals before setting out the basis of a new standard of review in Chapters 4 and 5.

---

[142] A new Chairman's text of the DSU was circulated in 2003 that did not address the standard of review issue. This text is discussed in Thomas A. Zimmermann, 'The DSU Review (1998–2004) Negotiations, Problems and Perspectives', in Dencho Georgiev and Kim Van der Borght (eds), *Reform and Development to the Dispute Settlement System* (Cameron May, 2006) 451. Further, new texts of the Anti-Dumping Agreement and SCM Agreement were circulated by the Chairman of the negotiating group on rules on 19 December 2008 (WTO doc TN/RL/W/236). There was no change to Article 17.6 of the draft Anti-Dumping text and no specific reference to a standard of review in the draft SCM text.

3. Alternative models and principles for the development of a WTO standard of review

3.1 INTRODUCTION

In this chapter I will examine the major proposals that have been put forward for a WTO standard of review and then I will seek to draw from these proposals some of the main principles upon which a new standard of review should be based. This chapter may be seen as dealing with possible solutions for the creation of a new standard of review, in contrast with Chapter 2, which dealt with the difficulties of the current standard as well as historical and institutional factors relevant to the current standard.

WTO dispute settlement is considerably more legalistic in nature than GATT dispute settlement. Further, the measures reviewed by WTO panels are often very factually complex and may have involved prior assessment under domestic law. It is therefore not surprising that the standard of review has become a contentious subject. As pointed out in Chapter 2, the current objective assessment test does not provide any guidance to panels as to what level of scrutiny they should apply when reviewing measures. The fact that the current standard is drawn from DSU Article 11 rather than from more general administrative law principles signifies the reluctance by the Appellate Body to formulate an independent standard of review doctrine.[1] The inadequacy of the objective assessment test is evidenced by certain trends in case law, such as the increasing intensity of the standard and the movement towards a more agreement-specific standard, both of which bear no relationship to the concept of objective assessment.[2] The interpretation of the anti-dumping standard and its relationship to the objective assessment test has also been demonstrated to be problematic.[3]

---

[1] Catherine Button, *The Power to Protect: Trade Health and Uncertainty in the WTO* (Hart Publishing, 2004) 171.

[2] See Chapter 2, Section 2.4.3.

[3] See Chapter 2, Section 2.4.4.

In response to these kinds of problems, it is appropriate to examine the literature in which the current standard of review is criticized and a different approach to this issue is advocated. On the whole, most scholars have been cautious in proposing a strict doctrine that may be adopted within the WTO system. The drafting of a new test is not straightforward and it may result in unintended consequences, such as favouring or disadvantaging particular members depending upon whether they are likely to be a complainant or a respondent.[4] Some of the literature also focuses on how different standards of review may affect the broader relationship between the WTO and the membership both generally and in key policy areas. For example, there has been concern that a more intensive standard of review may unduly affect the right of members to maintain their own SPS measures where there may be a legitimate basis for such measures.[5]

Although in this chapter I discuss the different treatment of this subject by various scholars, I do not refer to Oesch's work in detail here because he does not advocate any particular standard of review test.[6] Oesch appears to favour a more deferential standard of review.[7] He notes that 'Sensitive subject-matters in particular may require panels to apply a deferential standard of review and to not interfere lightly with national policy determinations.'[8] However, Oesch suggests that a more deferential approach is unlikely to be adopted unless the WTO first moves away from a strict approach to treaty interpretation to a more flexible approach whereby panels would have more of a role in balancing and weighing up policy goals in order to promote welfare in a broader sense.[9]

In this chapter I will endeavour to identify, critique and then group the various approaches for the development of the WTO standard of review. It is worth prefacing the analysis by stating that the type of standard of review proposed depends very much on the way in which the function of the standard

---

4 A standard of review that is less deferential should, all things being equal, result in more domestic measures being found to be WTO-inconsistent.

5 Gavin Goh, 'Tipping the Apple Cart: The Limits of Science and Law in the SPS Agreement after *Japan-Apples*' (2006) 40 *Journal of World Trade* 655, 676–87; Michael M. Du, 'Standard of Review under the SPS Agreement after *EC-Hormones II*' (2010) 59(2) *International & Comparatively Law Quarterly* 441, 449.

6 Matthias Oesch, *Standards of Review in WTO Dispute Resolution* (Oxford University Press, 2003). This work and others are introduced in Chapter 1, Section 1.1.

7 *Ibid* 32.

8 *Ibid.*

9 *Ibid* 242–3. Oesch describes this shift as being from functionalism to constitutionalism. Functionalism is described as mechanically assessing compliance of state conduct whereas constitutionalism would allow consideration of and deference to sensitivities and political preferences and would permit a more nuanced and flexible standard of review.

is viewed. In taking a broader approach, the standard may be viewed as a mechanism to regulate the allocation of power between the WTO and its members, or as part of the overall means of interpreting the WTO Agreements.[10] Alternatively, it may be viewed in a more limited way as a procedural mechanism to give certainty to parties about the review process and to provide for efficient dispute settlement outcomes. I contend in this book that the standard of review should be viewed in a more limited way as an element of procedure, but that it does nonetheless play an important role in the overall approach to interpretation of the WTO Agreements.

By the end of this chapter I will be seeking to identify relevant principles or issues for the development of a new standard of review. The principles that I will identify are firstly, the requirement for the standard of review to support the key objectives of WTO dispute settlement; secondly, the need to maintain legitimacy of the WTO through dispute settlement; and thirdly, the need to design appropriate and workable dispute settlement procedures. The key question that an examination of the prior literature raises is what, if any, model of review best ensures that the WTO membership acts in accordance with the WTO Agreements. The standard of review should meaningfully contribute to the overall interpretation and application of the WTO Agreements. The conclusions drawn through the analysis in this chapter will form the basis of the new standard of review I will be advocating in Chapters 4 to 7.

3.2 ALTERNATIVE STANDARD OF REVIEW MODELS

3.2.1 The Sovereignty Perspective and Chevron Analogy

Croley and Jackson, in the first detailed analysis of the WTO standard of review, do not advocate any particular model or test for the standard of review.[11] Nor do they argue in favour of any particular degree of deference to be exercised by panels. They instead are quite cautious as to how panels should treat this issue. In this regard, they note:

> Of course, we do not here prescribe any particular standard of review for panels considering national governments' interpretation of treaty obligations. Time and experience with particular cases will likely clarify the appropriate standard, or standards (since these may vary with different subject matters). Indeed, perhaps all that

---

[10] See discussion in Chapter 1, Section 1.3.2.

[11] Croley and Jackson, 'WTO Dispute Procedures, Standard of Review and Deference to National Governments' (1996) 90 *The American Journal of International Law* 193.

> is required is that panels (including appellate panels) perceive and show sensitivity toward the issues involved when an international body reviews the legal appropriateness of national government authorities' actions. In this connection, panels should keep the relevant purposes, strengths and limitations of their institution in mind.[12]

With the above approach the emphasis is on panels maintaining a level of institutional sensitivity that is appropriate depending upon the nature of the issues being adjudicated. The last sentence of the above extract suggests that the discretion of panels in such matters should be circumscribed by reference to the aims and structure of the WTO as an institution. Whilst the importance of the institutional context seems self-evident, it is noteworthy that this work was published in 1996, only a year after the formation of the WTO and almost two years prior to the decision of the Appellate Body in *EC-Hormones*.

Certainly part of Croley's and Jackson's caution is due to them identifying the standard of review 'problem' through the lens of sovereignty.[13] They describe this problem as an identification of the mediating principles between international policy values and the preservation of the national sovereignty of members.[14] Whilst they concede that definitions of sovereignty are complex and even outdated, they frame the standard of review question in the following terms:

> The GATT dispute settlement procedures have increasingly confronted these questions, including the degree to which, in a GATT (and now WTO) dispute settlement procedure, an international body should "second guess" a decision of a national government agency concerning economic regulations that are allegedly inconsistent with an international rule.[15]

Arguably, there is always going to be some degree of sovereignty erosion in the WTO setting and members may contend that a panel has interpreted an agreement differently from that member's perceived meaning of the agreement. This could result in the allegation that the WTO has violated state sovereignty.[16] Certainly, sovereignty is an important consideration, but it is not the

---

12 *Ibid* 212.

13 *Ibid* 194. For further discussion on the effects of the WTO on member sovereignty see John H. Jackson, 'The Great 1994 Sovereignty Debate: United States Acceptance and Implementation of the Uruguay Round Results' (1997) 36 *Columbia Journal of Transnational Law* 204.

14 Stephen Croley and John H. Jackson, 'WTO Dispute Procedures, Standard of Review and Deference to National Governments' (1996) 90(2) *American Journal of International Law* 193, 212.

15 *Ibid.*

16 In the context of dispute settlement an adverse interpretation may also provide the other party with a benefit which might be seen as an enhancement of sovereignty.

only consideration in formulating a standard of review. Croley and Jackson define the expression sovereignty as 'policies and concepts that focus on an appropriate allocation of power between international and national governments'.[17] However, the difficulty with formulating a standard of review around the notion of allocation of power, or the retaining of sovereignty, is that it does not provide any positive basis or criteria for defining a standard of review. It will be determined by the degree to which the advocate of this position believes that sovereignty ought to be sacrificed in favour of effective international co-operation between member states. It is certainly feasible to argue for more or less deference in the construction of a standard of review based on the perceived national interest that is being adjudicated.

In examining whether there are other principles that may inform the construction of a standard of review in the WTO context, Croley and Jackson note that certain national-level doctrines may be useful. In particular, they refer to the United States administrative law rule known as the Chevron doctrine, which was influential in the drafting of Article 17.6 of the Anti-Dumping Agreement.[18] As discussed in Chapter 1, the Chevron doctrine arises from the 1984 United States Supreme Court decision of *Chevron USA Inc v Natural Resources Defense Council Inc*, in which the court formulated a new standard of review for judicial review of administrative decisions.[19] The doctrine instructs courts to defer to the statutory interpretations of government administrative authorities if, and only if, the statute in question is ambiguous and the authority's interpretation is reasonable.[20] Arguably, this doctrine has resulted in a significant shift in power from courts to authorities, and is justified by reference to three underlying principles of United States administrative law, being expertise of the authority, (democratic) accountability and efficiency (or consistency) of interpretation by an authority.[21]

Croley and Jackson then go on to review how effectively the Chevron doctrine might be if transplanted into WTO dispute settlement.[22] They conclude that the major rationales identified above that support the argument for Chevron-style deference carry very little weight when transplanted into the context of WTO dispute settlement.[23] For instance, domestic authorities

---

17 Croley and Jackson, 'WTO Dispute Procedures, Standard of Review and Deference to National Governments', above n 14, 211.

18 *Ibid* 202.

19 467 US 837 (1984).

20 For a more detailed description of the Chevron doctrine see Chapter 1, Section 1.2.5 B.

21 Croley and Jackson, 'WTO Dispute Procedures, Standard of Review and Deference to National Governments', above n 14, 206–8.

22 *Ibid* 209–11.

23 *Ibid* 211.

certainly do not have more expertise than WTO panels in the task of interpreting and applying the WTO Agreements.[24] In the case of democratic accountability, WTO panel decisions do not reduce accountability by potentially restricting the scope of decision-making of authorities.[25] This is because WTO panels are not accountable directly to the citizens of each member but to the membership at large. Accordingly, introducing Chevron-style deference would, on this basis, reduce democratic accountability by weakening the relationship between the WTO and the membership. Finally, Chevron-style deference would not promote efficiency in WTO dispute settlement because it is likely to lead to multiple interpretations of WTO Agreements and there is the potential for reciprocity by members in the form of protectionist trade measures.[26] Multiple interpretations of statutes are much less likely in a domestic context. In short, the constitutional relationship between actors in an international and domestic setting are quite different and this makes the reasons behind introducing the Chevron test less relevant.

Croley and Jackson, to some degree, leave open the question of what principles or criteria might assist in defining an appropriate standard of review.[27] They conclude that whilst Chevron-style deference may not be justified on the basis of criteria such as expertise, accountability and efficiency, this does not suggest that this type of approach is unjustifiable.[28] However, they argue that the justification would have to come from outside the Chevron paradigm.[29] What Croley and Jackson conclude is that there should be some level of deference as a trade-off between international policy coordination and national sovereignty.[30] Nevertheless, they do not put forward a specific test. There is also equivocation in that, on the one hand, they caution against panels becoming too activist-like in nature, which could, in their view, alienate the members and threaten the stability of the dispute settlement procedure.[31] However, they also emphasize the central role that dispute-settlement plays in supporting the implementation, effectiveness and credibility of the WTO rules.[32] It is perhaps understandable, given that this work was published at the beginning of the development of WTO jurisprudence, that the standard of review was not analysed by reference to practical considerations, such as the role of procedure, and in particular the limits of fact-finding and review. In my view, the

---

24 *Ibid* 208.
25 *Ibid* 209.
26 *Ibid* 212.
27 *Ibid.*
28 *Ibid* 211.
29 *Ibid* 212.
30 *Ibid.*
31 *Ibid.*
32 *Ibid* 213.

analysis of Croley and Jackson is broadly correct, and it suggests that the WTO standard of review ought not to be directly based on domestic administrative law systems, and that the unique institutional setting of the WTO must be taken into account.

3.2.2 The 'Deliberation Test'

Zleptnig suggests that the standard of review in WTO cases be formulated by reference to what he terms a deliberation test.[33] The essence of this test is that panels should look into the evidence provided by WTO members in order to determine whether a proper deliberative process had taken place prior to the enactment of the national measure.[34] In cases where such a deliberative process was absent, then panels should be less inclined to defer to domestic authorities and they ought to instead strictly scrutinize decisions of domestic authorities.[35] Zleptnig argues that this test will 'lead to more deferential treatment of well-founded, rational policy choices and less deference in the absence of suitable public deliberation.'[36]

This proposal is based upon a number of underlying principles identified by Zleptnig. The basic premise of this test is that whilst the standard of review is, *prima facie*, a procedural provision, it is and should be seen as an aspect of dispute settlement that has a wider impact upon WTO law and policy.[37]

Zleptnig therefore contends that the standard of review should be concerned with promoting issues such as due process rights, transparency and public deliberation.[38] Whilst these terms are not defined, it is clear that it is based around the central theme of adequate public deliberation being linked to the legitimacy of the WTO.[39] The test and its ramifications are described in the following terms:

> Too much deference to measures enacted without sufficient deliberation might namely lead to a situation where narrowly defined, protectionist and non-transparent interests prevail over broader stakeholder concerns. Alternatively, each time that a national public discourse takes place in a transparent and deliberative environment, stakeholders are able to raise their voice and authorities must engage in a

---

33 Stefan Zlepnig, 'The Standard of Review in WTO Law: An Analysis of Law, Legitimacy and the Distribution of Legal and Political Authority' (2002) 6(17) *European Integration Online Papers* 1 (available at http://eiop.or.at/eiop/texte/2002-017.htm, last accessed 31 March 2012).

34 *Ibid* 16.

35 *Ibid.*

36 *Ibid* 1.

37 *Ibid* 6.

38 *Ibid.*

39 See Chapter 3, Section 3.3.3 for further discussion of the notion of legitimacy.

> careful interest-balancing between different values. The dispute settlement system is subsequently better equipped to assess national regulatory determinations and to make, on a supranational level, important trade-offs deeply affecting national constituencies. *Bearing the theory of deliberative democracy in mind, it is arguable that in situations where stakeholders can present their views through a rational discourse, international adjudication is less likely to be regarded as impinging upon democratic and sovereign policy choices and deliberatively to disregard important societal values.*[40] (Emphasis added)

It is evident that Zleptnig is concerned with the question of the legitimacy of WTO dispute settlement. In his work, he discusses the background to his proposal as being based around what he terms a legitimacy crisis and he asks the question as to how greater democratic legitimacy can be achieved.[41] He argues that WTO dispute settlement has been particularly affected by the 'trade and' evolution, in which new policy areas such as environment, health and safety have progressively become part of the international trade agenda.[42] On this basis, it is contended that WTO dispute settlement may intrude into non-economic policy areas and constrain the ability of members to regulate these areas. With a broader trade agenda panels must therefore increasingly balance economic and non-economic values in resolving disputes, and giving priority to economic values may curtail the attainment of social goals at a domestic level.[43]

At its core, Zleptnig's proposal is based on the notion that the standard of review is an important mechanism in the constitutionalization of the WTO. The term, constitutionalization can have many different meanings. However, Zleptnig identifies it as essentially a particular framework governing the conduct of nation states and the division of power between different layers of governance within states.[44] He then asserts that 'the standard of review can be re-thought as an important constitutional feature of WTO law'.[45] This link is made by viewing judicial review as an important element in the constitutional framework of the WTO and, ultimately, as a doctrine that affects the allocation of power between the WTO and its members.[46]

---

40 Zlepnig, above n 33, 16.

41 *Ibid* 14. Cf Robert Howse, 'Democracy, Science and Free Trade: Risk Regulation on Trial at the World Trade Organization' (2000) 98 *Michigan Law Review* 2329 in which it is argued that SPS provisions do not usurp legitimate democratic choices but instead they enhance the quality of rational democratic deliberation about risk and its control.

42 Zlepnig, above n 33, 10.

43 *Ibid.*

44 *Ibid.*

45 *Ibid* 9.

46 *Ibid.*

Zleptnig's proposal is also based heavily around his concern about panels being required to adjudicate complex disputes arising under the SPS Agreement. Further, he argues that panelists, usually with a background in law or economics, are ill-equipped to assess the correctness or truth of competing scientific material.[47] He argues that a well-defined standard of review can play a decisive role in mitigating concerns about encroaching judicial intervention in science-related regulation.[48]

This proposal's main positive feature is that it directly addresses the issue of how the WTO dispute settlement process might deal with criticism that it is eroding the autonomy of decision-making by members in key policy areas. The deliberative test is based on the premise that it would increase legitimacy of WTO dispute settlement amongst the membership. However, this test suffers from a number of difficulties. First of all, there are a number of presumptions that need to be accepted. For example, the presumption that the WTO is suffering problems with maintaining legitimacy and, that the dispute settlement function is somehow eroding the national sovereignty of members. Then there is the presumption that the standard of review is indeed an important constitutional mechanism for allocating power between the WTO and the membership.

Even if these matters are accepted, the major difficulty is that the deliberation test is not qualitative. No amount of deliberation will absolve a panel from needing to determine whether the domestic measures conform with WTO obligations. A panel will still be required to examine whether a quarantine measure is sufficiently based upon a risk assessment as required by Article 5.1 of the SPS Agreement. A similar review process would have to be undertaken in the case of anti-dumping and countervailing measures. Further, the deliberation test cannot be easily applied in the case of a review of measures that are based on national-level legislation, rather than a review process conducted by a domestic authority.[49]

The deliberation test speaks of balancing competing trade and non-trade values. However, it is perhaps not the function of the dispute settlement system to balance these competing values.[50] Such a process should arguably be part of the negotiating mandate of the WTO and, so far as possible, the dispute settlement process should not be concerned with this. The risk is that

---

47 *Ibid* 12.

48 *Ibid.*

49 This is because the parliamentary system of a state (if any) would have to be examined, as opposed to simply examining the transparency and accountability of an administrative review process.

50 See Carol Harlow, *Global Administrative Law: The Quest for Principles and Values* (2006) 17(1) *European Journal of International Law* 187.

by rewarding states that have an extensive deliberation process, too much deference could be given to some members, and there could be also less consistency in the way the WTO Agreements are interpreted by members. Whilst there is an emphasis on legitimacy, there is no emphasis on the standard of review supporting the enforcement of the WTO rules. In other words, the standard of review is not being viewed as a procedural rule that assists panels to efficiently interpret measures and to ensure compliance with the WTO Agreements.

3.2.3 The 'Reasonable Regulator' Test

Catherine Button argues that a standard of review that would provide panels with clear guidance is what she terms the 'reasonable regulator' test.[51] Under this test, panels would undertake their review by considering what the decision-maker responsible for the measures might reasonably conclude, based upon the evidence before such decision-maker.[52] This test would be moderately deferential in nature because it would place a qualitative limit on the amount of panel scrutiny. Button bases this test largely upon the approach taken by the panel in the *EC-Asbestos* case, which provides a strong example concerning competing scientific evidence. In that case, on the question of whether crysotile cement products posed a risk to human health, the panel determined that a decision-maker responsible for taking public health measures might reasonably conclude that the products posed such a risk.[53] Whilst the reasonable regulator test was put forward in relation to disputes under the SPS Agreement, and particularly those involving scientific controversy, it is nonetheless worthy of consideration for general application.

This test does provide a stronger conceptual basis for the standard of review than the objective assessment test.[54] Unlike the objective assessment test, a reasonable regulator test would give panels much more guidance as to how intrusive their review of measures should be. This is because a panel would be directed to consider whether a regulator has exercised reasonable judgment in determining the validity of a measure. This would not involve 'standing in the shoes' of a regulator and remaking a decision, but instead judging the actions of a regulator from the perspective of what a reasonable regulator in the same situation would have decided.[55] Further, anticipating the Appellate Body's

---

[51] Button, *The Power to Protect: Trade Health and Uncertainty in the WTO*, above n 1, 217.

[52] *Ibid* 218.

[53] Panel Report, *EC-Asbestos* [8.193].

[54] See discussion of the objective assessment test in Chapter 2, Section 2.4.2.

[55] The reasonable regulator test therefore has both objective and subjective elements.

ongoing reluctance to move away from the objective assessment test, Button suggests that this test may be applied in addition to, rather than instead of the objective assessment test.[56] In other words, reasonableness could answer the question as to what level of deference should apply in health and similar cases.

A test based upon reasonableness may also better mediate complex scientific issues in that panels would make a pragmatic assessment of any competing scientific opinions because the panel's starting point for the review is whether the member's own evaluations were reasonable. Button argues that scientific evidence is rarely unambiguous, and by allowing regulators to look at evidence though the lens of reasonableness avoids an 'all or nothing' approach where measures may be deemed inconsistent with WTO obligations because of a lack of evidence as to harm.[57] In this arena involving competing issues of scientific uncertainty and scientific justification, Button describes the benefit of the reasonable regulator test in the following terms:

> By explicitly developing the interpretation of contentious disciplines, the Appellate Body would be able to craft constraints that strike the best balance between the individual member's desire for regulatory autonomy and the Member's collective need for a disciplined, science-based approach to health regulation.[58]

Button also argues that panels would not have great difficulty in applying the concept of reasonableness as part of a standard of review given that the expression 'reasonableness' is written into a number of WTO provisions, including various provisions in the SPS and TBT Agreements and GATT 1994.[59] Further, many panels and the Appellate Body have utilized this concept in resolving many disputes, such as in defining the necessity of health measures under GATT 1994 Article XX(b) in terms of the least restrictive trade measure reasonably available.[60]

The lynchpin of Button's proposition is that a reasonableness standard sets a moderate form of review.[61] This occurs both in terms of procedure and a wider policy perspective. Reasonableness sets out more of a middle path between the extremes of *de novo* review and total deference. It would require

56 Button, *The Power to Protect: Trade Health and Uncertainty in the WTO*, above n 1, 225.

57 *Ibid* 221.

58 *Ibid* 222.

59 *Ibid* 220.

60 See for example, Appellate Body Report, *EC-Asbestos* [167]–[168]; Panel Report, *US-Gasoline* [6.26] and [6.28]. In relation to GATT 1947 see Panel Report, *US-Section 337 Tariff Act* [5.26].

61 Button, *The Power to Protect: Trade Health and Uncertainty in the WTO*, above n 1, 220.

panels to consider the issues from the perspective of the regulator to determine the WTO-consistency of the measures. There would be more deference afforded to regulators because they would need to show reasonably supported scientific conclusions as opposed to full scientific justification.[62] However, Button argues that this test would not result in too much deference because the assessment as to reasonableness would have to be made within a specific regulatory environment.[63] By contrast, a *de novo* approach would involve a panel assessing evidence outside a regulatory context and position panels as the expert final arbiter of disputes.[64] From a policy point of view, it is argued that this standard is consistent with the Uruguay Round outcomes, with members balancing trade liberalization with the right to take trade-limiting action to protect health and other similar objectives.[65] In other words, it provides a certain amount of 'policy space' for domestic regulation of scientific, social or cultural matters.

The reasonable regulator test does, on an initial appraisal, seem to be an attractive approach. It has a strong conceptual foundation that is likely to be acceptable to the membership, and at the same time it would provide sufficient flexibility in the interpretation of the WTO Agreements.[66] It would also assist in easing tensions between the WTO and national regulators in key policy areas, particularly those falling under the ambit of the SPS Agreement. However, this approach does suffer from a number of weaknesses and difficulties. Firstly, a standard of review based on the notion of reasonableness is not new and has been already rejected by the Appellate Body.[67] In *EC-Hormones*, the European Union advocated that panels should adopt a 'deferential reasonableness standard' in all complex factual

---

62 The concept of reasonableness in this context is also consistent with the precautionary principle, which in general terms, provides that conclusive scientific evidence should not be required before measures are introduced by governments for the protection of the environment or human health.

63 Button, *The Power to Protect: Trade Health and Uncertainty in the WTO*, above n 1, 221–2.

64 *Ibid* 222. Button expresses this as the proposition that *de novo* review would give panels a monopoly on truth in contentious matters dealing with science and culture.

65 *Ibid* 220. This notion is referred to or embodied in the following WTO Agreements: SPS Agreement Preamble, art 2.1 thereof; the TBT Agreement Preamble and GATT 1994, art XX(b).

66 It would appear to be quite similar to *Wednesbury* reasonableness: see Chapter 1, Section 1.2.2.

67 Appellate Body Report, *EC-Hormones* [112]–[113], [119]. The idea of reasonableness as a standard of review was also discussed in various GATT panel decisions but there is no consistent line of authority adopting such an approach. See Chapter 2, Section 2.2.3.

situations.[68] In advancing this argument, the European Union was attempting to extend the standard of review in Article 17.6 of the Anti-Dumping Agreement to other kinds of disputes. The Appellate Body expressly rejected this approach when it proclaimed the objective assessment test pursuant to Article 11 of the DSU.[69] It is certainly possible for the Appellate Body to embrace a new doctrine founded on reasonableness, but thus far the Appellate Body has shown caution about deviating from a largely textual approach in interpreting the WTO Agreements.[70]

A second and related criticism of the Button test is that reasonableness is a malleable concept that could create too much variance in the implementation of WTO obligations, and potentially erode the trade liberalization outcomes of Uruguay Round.[71] This was a concern of many WTO members at the conclusion of the Uruguay Round negotiations when the membership rejected a United States proposal to sanction reasonable interpretations of anti-dumping measures by domestic authorities.[72] Reasonableness may simply be too flexible to be used as a central principle, and therefore it may provide too much deference to the membership, with a potential consequence that the WTO Agreements could become more like regulatory guidelines rather than international obligations. In my view, this is the most compelling reason why reasonableness is not a particularly attractive basis for a standard of review in WTO disputes.

Finally, there is the question of how this test might apply as a general standard of review across all WTO Agreements. Button has only advocated this test in the context of health regulation. It may also be possible for it to be applied to measures where a regulator has to undertake a quasi-judicial process or formal administrative review, such as in trade remedy matters. However, the reasonable regulator test, as the name suggests, cannot be read-

---

[68] Appellate Body Report, *EC-Hormones* [112]–[113]. This is further discussed in Button, *The Power to Protect: Trade Health and Uncertainty in the WTO*, above n 1, 169.

[69] Appellate Body Report, *EC-Hormones* [112]–[113].

[70] See Federico Ortino, 'Treaty Interpretation and the WTO Appellate Body Report in US-Gambling: A Critique' (2006) 9(1) *Journal of International Economic Law* 117 where Ortino argues in discussing *US-Gambling* that the Appellate Body has not moved significantly from a rigorous textual approach despite signs that it is attempting to do so.

[71] See Dean R. Knight, 'A Murky Methodology: Standards of Review in Administrative Law' (2008) 6(1) *New Zealand Journal of Public and International Law*, in which the different types of reasonableness are discussed.

[72] Gary N. Horlick and Peggy A. Clarke, 'Standards for Panels Reviewing Anti-Dumping Determinations under the GATT' in Ernst-Ulrich Petersmann (ed), *International Trade Law and the GATT and WTO Dispute Settlement System* (Kluwer Law International,1997) 298.

ily applied absent some kind of domestic regulatory process. For instance, a case brought under Article III:2 of GATT 1994 concerning like products will generally not involve a prior regulatory decision but some kind of standard of review of facts will still be required. Even if a general standard of review of reasonableness could be applied to all WTO Agreements, its application would be quite difficult due to its imprecise meaning and the fact that, in some cases, it would be applied to WTO obligations that are already complex without the addition of a qualitative adjudicatory standard.

3.2.4 *De Novo* Review

Spamann suggests that a *de novo* review of facts is the most beneficial standard to apply, at least in the case of trade remedy disputes.[73] It is not clear why Spamann restricts his analysis to the trade remedy agreements, but the fact that arguments about the standard of review have commonly featured in disputes brought under these Agreements is no doubt an important factor. Panel review of facts in trade remedy disputes will usually involve the review of a prior adjudication of facts by administrative agencies. The existence of these prior domestic review processes would perhaps, depending upon the comprehensiveness of such processes, weaken the argument for *de novo* review. However, Spamann addresses this in a number of ways.

The first important element in his approach is the way in which *de novo* review is defined. What is emphasized is the adversarial rather than inquisitorial nature of panel proceedings, and the fact that panels are not required to gather evidence in the same detailed way as domestic authorities. He notes:

> Fact-finding therefore means no more for a Panel than assessing the evidence presented by the parties on these specific points, and *de novo* review does not mean more than assessing this evidence independently of what the national authorities saw in that evidence regarding these issues.[74]

Spamann also argues that the independent establishment and evaluation of facts by panels will not involve 'starting from scratch' by, for example, visiting factories and compiling data. Rather, it would mostly involve a reasoning exercise where more 'complex' facts are inferred from the domestic authority's record and conclusions are drawn.[75] In many trade remedy cases, facts usually concern pivotal issues, such as the establishment of injury to local

[73] Holger Spamann, 'Standard of Review for World Trade Organization Panels in Trade Remedy Cases: A Critical Analysis' (2004) 38(3) *Journal of World Trade* 509.

[74] *Ibid* 551.

[75] *Ibid* 552.

industry and whether such injury is caused by imports or other factors. In these areas, Spamann argues that panels should not face any major difficulties in fulfilling their review task.[76] Facts should be readily available and able to be interpreted, and there should be no resourcing problems for panels.

The second aspect of Spamann's approach is to argue that *de novo* review may be simpler than an intermediate standard of review, and enable parties to focus on substantive rights and obligations, rather than aspects of procedure.[77] For example, the 'all relevant factors' and 'reasoned and adequate explanation' test that has developed for trade remedies disputes has the capacity to shift the focus of panels from the measure itself to the reasoning of domestic authorities.[78] This could lead panels towards a check list type of approach where the failure to consider one or more factors, or to include such consideration in written reasons, could lead to the overturning of the measure. A greater emphasis on procedure could therefore create distortions in dispute settlement outcomes, with some domestic authorities being protected from adverse panel findings and others being found to be in violation of WTO rules despite substantive compliance.

A third and related argument raised by Spamann is that an intermediate standard of review, such as the 'all relevant factors' and 'reasoned and adequate explanation' test, does not in reality afford members a large degree of deference as compared with a *de novo* approach.[79] The expressions 'relevant', 'reasoned' and 'adequate' are very broad, and lend themselves to a comprehensive review approach. Despite the Appellate Body stressing in decisions such as *US-Lamb* that panels must not substitute their views for those of the domestic authorities, it is very difficult to see how this distinction is to be maintained if there is to be any substantive review of panel decisions at all.[80] Spamann argues that these expressions suggest an expansive role for panels in ensuring that the measures satisfy the substantive issue, namely compliance with the WTO rules.

Finally, Spamann concludes his analysis by touching upon the question of sovereignty.[81] He agrees that the standard of review does affect the sovereignty of members because it is a mechanism affecting the vertical relationship between the WTO and its members. However, he argues that sovereignty is not helpful in formulating an appropriate standard of review because what-

---

76 *Ibid.*

77 *Ibid* 540.

78 See for example, Appellate Body Report, *United States-Lamb*, [74]; Appellate Body Report, *US-Wheat Gluten* [110]–[117].

79 Spamann, 'Standard of Review for World Trade Organization Panels in Trade Remedy Cases', above n 73, 540.

80 *Ibid* 541.

81 *Ibid* 553. On this analysis the standard of review is an expression of sovereignty, rather than a limitation on the exercise of sovereignty by a state.

ever impact the standard of review may have on member sovereignty, it is voluntarily assumed by the members through their agreement to the WTO texts, including the interpretation of the WTO Agreements by panels and the Appellate Body.[82]

The major advantage of a *de novo* standard is its simplicity. There is less emphasis on procedural issues and more emphasis on ensuring compliance with substantive obligations. In my view, it appears that *de novo* review or a standard similar to *de novo* review would be appropriate for at least some kinds of WTO disputes, and particularly where there is less controversy or uncertainty concerning the facts or relevant scientific or technical evidence.

The major difficulty of *de novo* review is that it may not be politically palatable and, therefore, its application has the potential to undermine the legitimacy of the dispute settlement function as a whole. Those member constituencies that view the WTO rules as having resulted in a ceding of national sovereignty are likely to argue that *de novo* review, without any other procedural or institutional constraints, will result in greater intrusion by the WTO into the domestic affairs of members. It would, at a minimum, be important for the Appellate Body to more accurately define the scope of fact finding were a *de novo* standard to be introduced. For instance, there may be scope for more guidance on when panels should seek expert evidence as opposed to merely relying on the factual record.

There is also the issue of whether *de novo* review is equally useful in reviewing different types of national measures, such as safeguard versus SPS measures. The argument for *de novo* review of trade remedies is perhaps weaker due to the formality of domestic regulatory processes. By contrast, *de novo* review of SPS measures may be more justifiable but at the same time the review process may be more politically sensitive. Given that it is extremely difficult to depoliticize WTO dispute settlement, the issue of political implications should not be an overriding consideration in the design of a standard of review. Nonetheless, it may be more appropriate to formulate a standard that does not contribute to the perception that the WTO is over-reaching its institutional mandate through the dispute settlement process.

3.2.5 A Flexible Standard of Review

Ehlermann and Lockhart identify that the approach of WTO tribunals to date in relation to the standard of review has varied depending upon the nature of the measures and WTO obligations that are in issue.[83] In other words, they

82 *Ibid.*

83 Claus-Dieter Ehlermann and Nicolas Lockhart, 'Standard of Review in WTO Law' (2004) 7(3) *Journal of International Economic Law* 491.

suggest that the current objective assessment test, with its 'one size fits all' approach, must function with another, more detailed, underlying standard of review.[84] These authors argue that this development is due to major differences in the nature of various WTO obligations and in the structure of the WTO Agreements.[85] It is contended that these differences have resulted in a variation in the scope and intensity of panel review depending upon the type of dispute.[86] One of the major variables in determining the standard is the primacy given to a national level investigation in the text of the relevant agreement. Thus, in trade remedy cases, the panel is restricted to reviewing the domestic authority findings arrived at through a formal process, and by implication, the standard of review of facts is going to be more deferential.[87] By contrast, measures that do not result from a formal national level investigatory process do not impose constraints on the standard of review. Disputes under Articles III and XX of GATT 1994 fall into this category.[88] SPS and TBT disputes are arguably between these two extremes in that there is no treaty-mandated investigation of the kind required by the trade remedy agreements, but there is the need for some scientific or technological evaluation at the national level prior to the adoption of the measure.[89]

As with many other commentators, this approach is founded on the premise that the current objective assessment test does not provide substantive guidance on the nature and intensity of panel review.[90] It is for this reason that the objective assessment test must therefore operate with another more detailed underlying standard of review.[91] Ehlermann and Lockhart argue that the objective assessment test is in fact dividing into several discrete standards as the Appellate Body develops jurisprudence under the various WTO Agreements.[92] They cite the 'reasoned and adequate explanation' test for the line of safeguard cases as evidencing greater deference towards domestic authority decisions.[93] By contrast, in *Chile-Alcoholic Beverages*, a like product dispute under Article III:2 of GATT 1994 required a *de novo* analysis of the competitive relationship between beverages.[94]

84 *Ibid* 495.
85 *Ibid* 503.
86 *Ibid* 496.
87 *Ibid* 508.
88 *Ibid* 520.
89 *Ibid.*
90 *Ibid* 495.
91 *Ibid.*
92 *Ibid* 503.
93 *Ibid* 512.
94 Appellate Body Report, *Chile-Alcoholic Beverages* [303].

This flexible standard approach is based not just upon the structure and context of each agreement, but also upon the central idea that a standard of review is designed to enhance the quality and legitimacy of decision-making.[95] In this regard, Ehlermann and Lockhart focus on Article 3.2 of the DSU and, in particular, the statements that the dispute settlement system 'is a central element in providing security and predictability to the multilateral trading system' and that the dispute settlement system serves to preserve the balance of WTO member rights and obligations.[96] These statements exemplify the inherent tension between ensuring a predictable and relatively uniform dispute settlement system, with the need to allow sufficient discretion to members in key policy areas. This test allows sufficient flexibility for panels to find this balance across a broad list of subject matters.

The main potential weakness of this test is whether it may engender too much variability in the interpretation of different WTO Agreements. Part of this variability may be the difficulty for panels conducting a robust review in matters that involve significant national sensitivity. Further, if this test was adopted, then the objective assessment test would operate as a mere general label, with no ability to apply a definitive general standard across the agreements to provide consistency of approach. In my view, this criticism cannot be dismissed lightly. It may, however, be feasible to prescribe a general 'gateway' standard that can be applied and then adapted across the various agreements. This is the approach proposed in Chapters 4 to 7.

There is also a risk that a flexible standard could become captive to a policy debate about how the agreements should be interpreted. The risk is that the standard of review could be viewed as a major tool of interpretation of the agreements and its primary role as an element of procedure may be de-emphasized. Due to this risk there is certainly logic in the Appellate Body's current 'soft' approach to developing the standard. Overall, however, this test (based as it is on dispute settlement trends) is quite far sighted and would go a long way to developing jurisprudence for the standard in commonly litigated disciplines. It may even aid the development of a common approach for anti-dumping and similar trade remedy disciplines.

3.2.6 Other Theoretical Approaches: Constitutionalization and Harmonization

Cass argues that the debate surrounding the standard of review is part of a

[95] Ehlermann and Lockhart, 'Standard of Review in WTO Law', above n 83, 493.
[96] *Ibid* 494.

larger 'constitutionalization' process that the WTO is undergoing.[97] Through this theoretical approach, it is contended that the standard of review is a key concept via which the vertical relationship between the WTO and the membership is determined. Cass frames the standard of review in the following terms:

> Once the debate moves out of the confines of a national setting, and the actors are a review tribunal established under international treaty, and the executive bodies of national states, then the question of the standard of review moves out of the domain of legal procedure and becomes imbued with constitutional meaning.[98]

The consequence of this approach is that any type of standard that lies on the spectrum between *de novo* review and total deference will influence the allocation of power between members and the WTO. Further, any particular standard (be it too intrusive or too deferential) has the capacity to alter the finely drawn jurisdictional competencies between the WTO and the membership that is reflected in the text of the WTO Agreements. Cass argues that the Appellate Body in *EC-Hormones* was acutely aware of this difficulty, and the choice of the undefined objective assessment test was made in order to deal with the constitutional effects on a gradual and case-by-case basis.[99]

The formulation of any standard based on this constitutional 'lens' is fraught with difficulty. Firstly, it is highly debatable whether the WTO as a whole is subject to any sort of constitutionalization process.[100] There are a number of theoretical approaches to the WTO's institutional status and development, with the main alternative approach being that the WTO simply operates as an ordinary treaty arrangement between parties which are almost exclusively sovereign states.[101] Secondly, there are many other architectural and doctrinal aspects of the WTO that affect the relationship between the WTO and the membership more directly, such as the way negotiation and voting is conducted or the negative consensus rule in dispute settlement.[102]

---

97 Deborah Cass, 'The "Constitutionalization" of International Trade Law: Judicial Norm-Generation as the Engine of Constitutional Development in International Trade' (2001) 12(1) *European Journal of International Law* 39; Deborah Cass, *The Constitutionalization of the World Trade Organization* (Oxford University Press, 2005).

98 Cass, 'The "Constitutionalization" of International Trade Law: Judicial Norm-Generation as the Engine of Constitutional Development in International Trade', above n 97, 39.

99 *Ibid* 59.

100 See for example John H. Jackson, *The World Trading System – Law and Policy of International Economic Relations* (MIT Press, 2nd ed, 1997) 339.

101 Cass, *The Constitutionalization of the World Trade Organization*, above n 97, 53.

102 DSU Article 16.4 prescribes the negative consensus rule.

Thirdly, and most importantly, a purely constitutional analysis does not place any weight on other important factors in the formulation of a standard, such as procedural factors or whether the standard supports key objectives of the WTO Agreements.

Heiskanen offers an alternative theoretical perspective in arguing that the WTO Agreements may be divided into negative and positive harmonization agreements.[103] Negative harmonization agreements refer to those that are predominantly concerned with ensuring uniform reductions in trade barriers and non-discrimination, through the application of principles such as most favoured nation and national treatment.[104] This is mainly embodied in GATT 1994 with various privileges, qualifications and exceptions being regulated through more specific disciplines such as subsidies and anti-dumping.[105] By contrast, positive harmonization agreements mainly deal with the harmonization of international standards or rights, such as in health, technical or intellectual property matters.[106] Heiskanen argues that if a panel is dealing with a negative harmonization or non-discrimination type of provision, then a more stringent standard of review ought to be applied than when reviewing a positive harmonization provision.[107] Heiskanen suggests that WTO Tribunals have already applied this distinction in *EC-Hormones* and *EC-Sardines* concerning the appropriate burden of proof. [108] Further, this distinction has been identified by the Appellate Body in *EC-Hormones* in relation to the standard of review, where the respondent was only required to show that its measure was a rational (but not necessary) means of achieving compliance with WTO obligations.[109] This type of deference discussed by Heiskanen relates to the standard of review of law, and not facts, given that the standard would be adjusted

---

103 Veijo Heiskanen, 'The Regulatory Philosophy of International Trade Law' (2004) 38(1) *Journal of World Trade* 1, 32.

104 See also Federico Ortino, *Basic Legal Instruments for the Liberalization of Trade: A Comparative Analysis of EC and WTO Law* (Hart Publishing, 2004) 17–27, where the similar concepts of negative and positive integration are discussed. Ortino notes that the distinction between negative and positive integration may become blurred. For example, the national treatment obligation referred to in GATT Article III:4 may be characterized as a positive obligation imposed on WTO members.

105 *Ibid* 4.

106 The TRIPS Agreement is a good example of a positive harmonization agreement. Arguably the TRIPS Agreement extends the notion of positive harmonization further than the TBT and SPS Agreements because its purpose is arguably protectionist rather than promoting regulatory harmonization. See, Heiskanen, 'The Regulatory Philosophy of International Trade Law', above n 103, 11–13.

107 *Ibid* 32.

108 *Ibid*. See also Panel Report, *EC-Sardines* [304]–[311].

109 Heiskanen, 'The Regulatory Philosophy of International Trade Law', above n 103, 33.

according to the specific WTO obligation that is in issue. However, this regulatory philosophy could equally inform the standard of review of facts.

Part of the problem with this theoretical approach is that the policy rationales for various WTO Agreements are more complex and multifaceted than suggested by Heiskanen. This approach in a broad sense may assist with the question of legitimacy because the 'new' agreements may be interpreted less strictly than the 'old' ones. However, this 'boxing' of agreements, by employing a particular standard for a group of agreements but not other agreements may not provide sufficient flexibility and may be considered arbitrary. This, in turn, may not accurately promote the objectives of particular agreements, nor promote legitimacy of the dispute settlement process as a whole. Further, this theoretical perspective focuses attention on the overriding telos of the various WTO Agreements, but does not focus on how the standard might be constructed from a procedural point of view.

3.2.7 Deference Based upon a 'Margin of Appreciation' or 'Policy Space'

The final test or approach to be considered is the case for a degree of deference to be exercised by panels based upon the need for members to implement their WTO obligations in a manner that is sensitive to domestic policy considerations. The WTO Agreements are an international set of rules that are inevitably going to be implemented by members in different ways. There are many issues that, from a practical point of view, mitigate from a strict universal interpretation of the WTO Agreements. Major factors that potentially lead to a divergence in the implementation of WTO commitments include subjective political considerations and universal issues such as the use of science in trade disputes. Disputes concerning Article 5.1 of the SPS Agreement are a case in point. Under that provision, domestic measures must be 'based upon' an assessment 'as appropriate to the circumstances' of risks to human, animal or plant life or health. The expression 'based upon' was interpreted by the Appellate Body in *EC-Hormones* as not requiring strict conformity with the scientific outcomes of the risk assessment, but rather that there needs to be a rational relationship between the risk assessment and the measure.[110] The concept of margin of appreciation is closely related to the principle of

[110] Appellate Body Report, *EC-Hormones* [193]. This approach is reinforced by findings of the Appellate Body, *United States-Continued Suspension* [590] that the role of the panel is to determine whether a risk assessment is supported by coherent reasoning and reputable scientific evidence, rather than assessing the correctness of the scientific evidence. See Chapter 2, Section 2.4.3.

subsidiarity, which would dictate that the precise parameters of implementing WTO obligations should be left to WTO members.[111]

A standard of review that grants WTO members a margin of discretion in observing their WTO obligations would potentially create a number of problems. Any material deference that panels recognize in reviewing member measures could result in a significant variance in the extent of conformity to WTO obligations and a general dilution of the WTO commitments. The main problem with any particular test that affords deference is how to delineate the nature and extent of panel scrutiny in relation to the various divergent types of WTO obligations. In other words, what criteria may be uniformly applied to justify deference towards different types of measures that are in turn rooted in subjective domestic policy considerations? The rational relationship test is not well defined and may have a different meaning in different contexts. It may be appropriate in certain SPS disputes, but not in trade remedy disputes. The same would apply for any similar test based on principles such as whether a measure is necessary or is least trade restrictive in nature. These types of tests are, in the end, quite subjective and add a layer of analysis to panel review that would not only create complications, but could change the character of the WTO obligations being reviewed.

3.3 IDENTIFICATION OF PRINCIPLES FOR THE DEVELOPMENT OF A WTO STANDARD OF REVIEW

It is very difficult to assess comparatively the major standard of review approaches discussed in the previous section. Ultimately the key variable in these approaches is the degree of deference (if any) that should be granted to members. Deference can be seen as a sliding scale ranging from complete *de novo* review to total deference. The position of a particular test within such a scale is in turn informed by the type of factors or principles that are emphasized. This includes the relative importance attributed to factors such as efficiency of decision-making, accountability of the DSB and enforcement of international trade rules. An underlying theme that frequently determines the emphasis placed on these sorts of factors is the overall perceived function of the standard of review. Those who view the standard as an important determinant

111 See Oesch, *Standards of Review*, above n 6, 31–2; Jonas Tallberg, 'Delegation to Supranational Institutions: Why, How, and with What Consequences?' (2002) 25(1) *West European Politics* 23; Matthew Windsor, 'A Fine Balance? Delegation, Standards of Review, and Subsidiarity in WTO Dispute Settlement' (2008) 14 *Auckland University Law Review* 41. See also Chapter 1, Section 1.2.5D where the margin of appreciation principle is referred to in the context of the ECHR.

of the allocation of power between the WTO and its members are more likely to argue for a standard that achieves a considerable degree of deference towards members. By contrast, those who define the standard as a general tool of interpretation or as a procedural rule, are more likely to argue in favour of a stricter standard. In this way, the standard may be seen as one of many procedural or substantive aspects of dispute settlement that may influence the way the agreements are interpreted. For example, procedural rules like the burden of proof or interpretive principles such as *in dubio mitius* may significantly influence the outcome of cases.[112]

Most of the scholars discussed in this chapter view the standard of review in power-orientated terms and do advocate a degree of deference on the basis that there should be some balance between the need for the WTO to enforce the agreements, and the need for members to be allowed some flexibility in the implementation and maintenance of their WTO commitments. Both the reasonable regulator and deliberation tests are examples of this.[113] In each case, the domestic authority is allowed some level of decision-making autonomy that may not be challenged by WTO panels. Further, both tests rely on similar factors to justify this position, including accountability, expertise, legitimacy and a balancing or mediating of trade and social issues.

Croley and Jackson also identify the standard of review as a mediating principle that can change the balance in the vertical relationship between the WTO and the membership.[114] However, from the outset their analysis discounts the relevance of factors such as expertise, efficiency and accountability because they assert that these administrative law principles, that help define the standard of review of domestic courts in respect of administrative authority decisions, do not apply equally between WTO panels and the membership. Indeed the only major consideration that Croley and Jackson cite is the need for the

---

112 Appellate Body Report, *EC-Hormones* [165] contains the following footnote: 'The interpretative principle of *in dubio mitius*, widely recognized in international law as a 'supplementary means of interpretation', has been expressed in the following terms: 'The principle of *in dubio mitius* applies in interpreting treaties, in deference to the sovereignty of states. If the meaning of a term is ambiguous, the meaning is to be preferred which is less onerous to the party assuming an obligation, or which interferes less with the territorial and personal supremacy of a party, or involves less general restrictions upon the parties' (from Robert Jennings and Arthur Watts (eds), *Oppenheim's International Law* (9th ed, 1992) vol 1, 1278). The context of this footnote at paragraph 165 was: 'We cannot lightly assume that sovereign states intended to impose upon themselves the more onerous, rather than the less burdensome, obligation by mandating *conformity or compliance* with such standards, guidelines and recommendations.'

113 See Chapter 3, Sections 3.2.2 and 3.2.3.

114 See Chapter 3, Section 3.2.1.

standard to preserve or enhance the institutional legitimacy of the WTO.[115] The problem is, however, that legitimacy alone cannot help to define a standard of review as different members may have different expectations of how intrusive panels should be, and this of course may vary from case to case. Certainly, Croley and Jackson were mindful of the shaky foundations of this principle in stating that the whole standard of review issue was 'recurring and delicate', and it is arguably a major reason why they did not put forward any particular model standard.[116]

The articulation by Spamann about why a *de novo* standard could be favourable is based on a number of flaws which he identifies with a deferential standard.[117] Like Croley and Jackson, he believes that the analogy with domestic administrative law is misplaced.[118] However, he also argues persuasively that any type of deferential standard of review is likely to move the attention of the panel from an assessment of substantive compliance to whether procedures have been adhered to, or the reasoning used in arriving at a measure.[119] For example, the 'all relevant factors' and 'adequate explanation' test utilized in recent safeguard cases could have this effect.[120] On the positive side, Spamann identifies the principle of certainty and the need for panels to be able to enforce the WTO commitments as paramount. A *de novo* standard is the most obvious way of achieving this, and the competing factor of adjudicative efficiency is not necessarily impeded, provided that the scope of fact finding is well defined.[121] Spamann also sees the standard of review as one of a number of procedures and principles that may affect the degree of scrutiny that panels exercise and therefore, arguably, members should not be overly concerned with panels adopting a *de novo* style of review.[122]

Ehlermann and Lockhart base their suggestion for a flexible standard not on any particular administrative principles, but rather on the practical need for panels to exercise a level of deference where the nature of the agreements lend themselves to such an approach.[123] In this regard, they echo Croley and Jackson in emphasizing the importance of the standard in enhancing the legitimacy of

---

115 Croley and Jackson, 'WTO Dispute Procedures, Standard of Review and Deference to National Governments', above n 14, 212.

116 *Ibid* 197. See also the quotation in Chapter 2, Section 2.2.3.

117 See Chapter 3, Section 3.2.4.

118 Spamann, 'Standard of Review for World Trade Organization Panels in Trade Remedy Cases, above n 73, 547.

119 *Ibid* 543.

120 *Ibid* 540.

121 *Ibid* 549–50.

122 *Ibid* 549.

123 See Chapter 3, Section 3.2.5.

decision-making.[124] Importantly, a flexible standard appears in some measure to be based not simply on the delineation of competencies in decision-making, but also on the need to allow members to pursue other non-trade policy goals, such as the protection of health and the environment.[125]

Ultimately, the degree of deference advocated is linked with the question of what sort of dispute settlement system the WTO membership should have. Those who support the need for a robust dispute settlement system are more likely to have no objection to a *de novo* standard being adopted. By contrast, those who view the WTO as already unaccountable to the membership are likely to be suspicious of any reforms that provide panels with greater powers. All the tests discussed above grapple with this fundamental tension between these competing visions. In the next section I will identify and discuss the principal aims of the dispute settlement system. The identification of these aims will assist to inform the major elements for the design of a new standard of review.

3.3.1 Relevant Principles

From the above discussion, it appears that there is an inherent tension between two recurring themes: legitimacy of the dispute settlement system as determined by the membership, and the ability of the system to fulfil its stated aims. There exists a complex relationship between these two principles, because, for instance, part of any institution's legitimacy includes the ability to achieve to a large degree its aims and objectives. In addition to these principles, it is evident that procedural efficiency is also an important determinant of an appropriate standard of review. This is predominantly due to practical considerations such as resource and time limitations. However, it is also inevitably linked to the other two principles identified. For example, an extremely deferential standard of review may require few judicial and secretariat resources, but it may result in lesser adherence by members with their WTO commitments, and arguably it may reduce legitimacy.

In this section, I will therefore discuss three major principles that are critical for the development of a preferred standard of review. These are, in summary, the requirement to develop a standard that supports the key aims of WTO dispute settlement, the need to maintain adjudicative legitimacy, and the importance of having appropriate procedures. I will attempt to define these principles, which can then be used as a basis for both critiquing the present

---

124 Ehlermann and Lockhart, 'Standard of Review in WTO Law', above n 83, 493.

125 *Ibid* 520.

standard and formulating a new standard. It is also noteworthy that these types of criteria are also a useful means of judging the overall success of the WTO dispute settlement system. The following extract, although dealing with the overall success of the system, could arguably apply to an analysis of the present standard of review:

> There are a number of perspectives from which one could examine the early results of the operation of this system. One obvious perspective would be that of practical success, the ability to effectively settle disputes in a timely and cost-efficient fashion. Another perspective would be that of trade liberalization as a value: to what extent has the jurisprudence generated by the new system produced rulings that unleash the liberalizing and integrating potential of WTO legal strictures? This chapter will adopt yet another perspective in its assessment of the first four years of dispute settlement – that of legitimacy. What are the characteristics of international adjudication that tend to allow for the rulings of these tribunals to be considered as legitimate by those whose values or interests are implicated or affected? To what extent has the jurisprudence of the WTO to date displayed or exemplified these characteristics?[126]

Practical success and legitimacy are identified above as potential markers of a successful WTO dispute system. Further, the above passage draws the connection between the dispute settlement system and the broader WTO objectives concerning trade liberalization. It is not my intention in this book to analyse the standard of review against the success or failure of the WTO to achieve its stated objectives. Such an analysis is unlikely to be productive given the lack of any quantifiable nexus between the standard and trade outcomes. Rather, the approach taken in this book is to focus on how the standard of review can operate as an important element of the dispute settlement architecture. A well-designed system will, in turn, enable the fulfilment of substantive objectives.

3.3.2 Developing a Standard that Supports the Key Aims of WTO Dispute Settlement

Given that the standard of review functions as an important element of the dispute settlement system, it is imperative that a standard of review supports the fundamental aims of the dispute settlement process. The key aims of the dispute settlement system are set out in the text of the DSU, and principally in Article 3.2, which provides:

---

[126] Robert Howse, 'Adjudicative Legitimacy and Treaty Interpretation in International Trade Law: The Early Years of WTO Jurisprudence' in Joseph Weiler (ed), The *EU, the WTO and the NAFTA: Toward a Common Law of International Trade* (Oxford University Press, 2000) 35.

> The dispute settlement system of the WTO is a central element in providing security and predictability to the multilateral trading system. The Members recognize that it serves to preserve the rights and obligations of Members under the covered agreements, and to clarify the existing provisions of those agreements in accordance with customary rules of interpretation of public international law. Recommendations and rulings of the DSB cannot add to or diminish the rights and obligations provided in the covered agreements.

Article 3.2 can be broken down into three discrete objectives: security and predictability, preservation of rights and obligations, and clarification of the meaning of WTO provisions. The main theme that unites these objectives (and particularly the first two) is the need to preserve the Uruguay Round outcomes.[127] Therefore, dispute settlement panels are charged with the responsibility of ensuring that members carry out their WTO obligations, and panels must not, through their decision-making, change the nature of the rights and obligations contained in the WTO Agreements. This is also emphasized in Article 19.2 of the DSU, which provides:

> In accordance with paragraph 2 of Article 3, in their findings and recommendations, the panel and the Appellate Body cannot add to or diminish the rights and obligations provided in the covered agreements.[128]

In addition, pursuant to Article IX:2 of GATT 1994, it is the exclusive competence of the Ministerial Conference and the General Council to adopt 'authoritative' interpretations of the provisions of the WTO Agreements, and Article 3.9 of the DSU stipulates that the provisions of the DSU are without prejudice to the rights of members to seek such 'authoritative' interpretations.

---

127 There was also the need to rectify perceived failings of the GATT dispute settlement system, principally by making the WTO dispute settlement system more legalistic and binding upon the membership. See Robert E. Hudec, *Enforcing International Trade Law – The Evolution of the Modern GATT Legal System* (Butterworths, 1993) 182–3; Maki, Peter, 'Interpreting GATT using the Vienna Convention on the law of treaties: a method to increase the legitimacy of the dispute settlement system' (2000) 9(1) *Minnesota Journal of Global Trade* 343, 347; WTO Secretariat, *Guide to the Uruguay Round Agreements* (Kluwer Law International, 1999) 19–20.

128 It is acknowledged that despite the wording of DSU Articles 3.2 and 19.2, there is considerable debate about the objectives of WTO dispute settlement. This is arguably part of larger debates concerning *inter alia* treaty interpretation and the application of public international law. See Jeffrey Waincymer, *WTO Litigation: Procedural Aspects of Formal Dispute Settlement* (Cameron May, 2002) 438–9; Isabella Van Damme, *Treaty Interpretation by the WTO Appellate Body* (Oxford University Press, 2009) 24–6.

Accordingly, the DSU and provisions within other WTO Agreements caution the dispute settlement system against 'judicial activism'.[129] The Appellate Body has recognized the importance of this judicial restraint in *US-Certain EC Products*, when it held:

> We observe that it is certainly not the task of either panels or the Appellate Body to amend the DSU or to adopt interpretations within the meaning of Article IX:2 of the WTO Agreement. Only WTO members have the authority to amend the DSU or to adopt such interpretations. Pursuant to article 3.2 of the DSU, the task of panels and the Appellate Body in the dispute settlement system of the WTO is to 'preserve the rights and obligations of Members under the covered agreements, and to clarify the existing provisions of those agreements in accordance with customary rules of interpretation of international law.' Determining what the rules and procedures of the DSU ought to be is not our responsibility nor the responsibility of panels, it is clearly the responsibility solely of the Members of the WTO.[130]

As with any legal system, the notion of a judicial body being faithful to what has been agreed by parties, and applying a consistent set of interpretive rules, is easier to state in the abstract and more difficult to apply in practice. For example, in areas of the WTO Agreements that have not been well articulated, panels may need to rely on a particular interpretation that is not without controversy.[131] The role of the dispute settlement body is therefore always going to involve going beyond a mere application and enforcement of the rules.[132] Despite this, the mandate of the DSB is relatively clear. Dispute settlement processes should be conducted to ensure a preservation of the agreements and certainty of the system as a whole. On this basis, a standard of review therefore should be constructed so as to ensure that these central aims can be achieved. I will be discussing the feature of particular standards that

---

[129] Peter Van den Bossche, *The Law and Policy of the World Trade Organization: Text, Cases and Materials* (Cambridge University Press, 2005) 181.

[130] Appellate Body Report, *US-Certain EC Products* [92].

[131] The issue of zeroing in the treatment of dumping margins, which fundamentally concerns Article 2.4.2 of the Anti-Dumping Agreement, is a good example of how the Appellate Body is required to interpret WTO Agreement provisions where there may be ambiguity about the meaning of such provisions has been the subject of several WTO cases. There have been several panel and Appellate Body decisions concerning this issue, with a definitive treatment contained in Appellate Body Report, *United States-Continued Zeroing*.

[132] See John H. Jackson, *The World Trade Organization Constitution and Jurisprudence*, Chatham House Papers (Royal Institute of International Affairs, 1998) 63–5 where Jackson discusses some of the controversies and tensions concerning the objectives of the WTO settlement system, including the need to resolve current disputes versus the desirability of longer-term systemic goals such as the predictability and stability of interpretation of treaty texts.

would best meet these aims in Chapters 4 and 5. However, in general terms, panels should have sufficient powers of review to ensure that members are adhering to their obligations. This supports the idea of a *de novo* review of facts and law. The difficulty, however, is that if panel review is excessively intrusive, there is a risk that panels may engage in a form of 'judicial activism' contrary to the intention of the DSU. Such activism may, of course, change the nature of the WTO commitments entered into by members. In summary, this principle therefore supports the idea of a robust standard of review, but nonetheless one which may need to be curtailed to some degree.

3.3.3 Ensuring Adjudicative Legitimacy

Adjudicative legitimacy refers broadly to the level of confidence that participants in a dispute settlement system have in the system itself. In a wide-ranging study on effective supranational adjudication, a basic definition of effective adjudication is offered in the following terms: 'the effectiveness of a particular court rests on its power to compel a party to a dispute to defend against a plaintiff's complaint and to comply with the resulting judgement.'[133] These fundamental requirements of exercising jurisdiction and ensuring compliance are closely related to the notion of any dispute settlement body possessing proper legitimacy. In the case of the WTO, compulsory jurisdiction and enforcement procedures are features of the system, but the existence of these features cannot alone create adjudicative legitimacy. It is ultimately a reasonably subjective quality that is determined by a range of legal, political, social and cultural factors.[134] However, its incidence can nonetheless be assessed by measurable indicia, such as rates of usage and levels of compliance.

Any dispute settlement body has only partial control over its legitimacy.[135]

---

133 Laurence R. Helfer and Anne-Marie Slaughter, 'Towards a Theory of Effective Supranational Adjudication' (1997) 107 *Yale Law Journal* 268, 283.

134 See for example discussion of legitimacy in the context of State sovereignty in World Trade Organization, *The Future of the WTO: Addressing institutional challenges in the new Millennium – Report by the Consultative Board to the Director-General Supachai Panitchpakdi* (World Trade Organization, 2004) [108]–[143]. At paragraph 126 the Report states: 'In all those dimensions one can ask a number of questions that would affect the allocation issue. Questions of legitimacy loom large and often; therefore, there is a focus on "democratic legitimation". This is frequently meant to challenge more traditional notions of sovereignty. Some say we are gravitating from ideas of "sovereignty for the benefit of the state" towards ideas of "sovereignty of the people."'

135 David Beetham, *The Legitimation of Power* (MacMillan, 1991) 20, where Beetham argues that legitimacy is not just a product of expressed consent or conformity to rules, but that it is also concerned with the justifiability of rules in terms of shared beliefs.

This is usually through the processes it undertakes including the form and quality of its legal reasoning, its neutrality and the degree to which its decision-making is incrementalist in nature. There are also systemic design issues that may affect legitimacy, such as rules concerning the composition of panels, the extent of resources and fact-finding powers. Despite all of these factors, procedural rules, such as the standard of review, may be significant in influencing adjudicative legitimacy if there is a perception that these rules may contribute to an erosion of a member's rights and obligations and national sovereignty.

In the context of WTO dispute settlement there are a number of other specific institutional reasons why a standard of review ought to enhance adjudicative legitimacy. Firstly, there is arguably a need for panels to be cautious in the way they review disputes due to the existence of the negative consensus rule. Negative consensus means that the entire WTO membership must reject a panel or Appellate Body decision, failing which such rulings will be adopted by the DSB at its next meeting.[136] This rule was a contentious and key reform agreed to by the membership during the Uruguay Round of negotiations. The automatic nature of this procedure means that the DSB retains a high degree of power and independence in carrying out its function. Accordingly, the membership is going to be sensitive to any claims of over-reaching on the part of the DSB.

Secondly, it is arguable that the WTO has in recent years been suffering a form of 'legitimacy crisis', because of a conflict between traditional trade liberalization objectives and several non-trade objectives concerning issues such as environment, health and labour protection.[137] It is also arguable that this situation is not helped by the fact that legitimacy is increasingly derived from an open discourse between international organizations and constituents of states, rather than being solely a product of consent exercised by states.[138]

---

136 DSU Article 16.4 stipulates: 'Within 60 days after the date of circulation of a panel report to the Members, the report shall be adopted at a DSB meeting unless a party to the dispute formally notifies the DSB of its decision to appeal or the DSB decides by consensus not to adopt the report.' Article 17.14 contains similar wording in respect of the adoption of Appellate Body Reports. There are also negative consensus or automaticy rules in DSU Articles 6.1 and 22.6 concerning the establishment of panels and the suspension of concessions respectively.

137 John H. Jackson, 'The Changing Fundamentals of International Law and Ten Years of the WTO' (2005) 8(1) *Journal of International Economic Law* 3, 7. Jackson does list several other major criticisms of the WTO system.

138 Thomas M. Franck, *The Power of Legitimacy Among Nations* (Oxford University Press, 1990) 18, 25 where Franck posits a working definition of legitimacy as follows: 'Legitimacy is a property of a rule or rule-making institution which itself exerts a pull toward compliance on those addressed normatively because those

Accordingly, panels need to be cautious in the way they review domestic regulatory measures designed to afford protection in these non-trade areas, otherwise there is a risk of further erosion of legitimacy. There have been a number of panel and Appellate Body decisions over the past decade that have led to controversy over the scope of the WTO mandate.[139]

Based upon the above reasoning, it may be advocated that the standard of review should be more deferential in nature, or at least more flexible in its application. This, however, is not necessarily the case because if the standard was designed in this manner, it may reduce adjudicative legitimacy on the basis either that there is inadequate enforcement of the WTO Agreements or that there is a lack of certainty in the way in which measures are reviewed. Adjudicative legitimacy therefore demands a consistent and reasonably intrusive standard of review, but one that is somehow sensitive to the concerns of the membership.

3.3.4 Developing Appropriate Procedures

In addition to the principles of enhancing dispute settlement objectives and adjudicative legitimacy, there is also the need for a standard of review to function in conjunction with appropriate dispute settlement procedures. In other words, standards of review must be consistent with other aspects of procedure in order for a particular standard to be capable of effective application. Further, the reverse is also important, in that the standard of review ought to promote, or at least not diminish, certain procedural objectives. The major aspects of procedure that I have identified as having such a mutual relationship with the standard of review are the scope of fact-finding, expertise, efficiency of decision-making and procedural fairness. Given that these aspects are complete subjects in their own right, it is not feasible to deal with them in any detail. These aspects will now be briefly discussed and the short exposition is intended to demonstrate that, to some extent, they are conflicting and must be traded off in order to produce a workable standard of review.[140]

---

addressed believe that the rule or institution has come into being and operates in accordance with generally accepted principles of right process.' Franck notes that another way of expressing legitimacy is to describe the phenomenon other than in terms of coercion which explains habitual compliance in any system of governance.

[139] For example: Appellate Body Report, *EC-Hormones;* Appellate Body and Panel Reports, *US-Shrimp*; Panel Report, *EC-Approval and Marketing of Biotech Products*.

[140] See for example, the checklist of elements of effective international dispute settlement bodies provided by Helfer and Slaughter in 'Toward a Theory of Effective Supranational Adjudication', above n 133, 298.

A. Scope of fact-finding and expertise

The scope of fact-finding is dealt with in Article 13.1 of the DSU, which permits panels to seek information and technical advice from any individual or body as is appropriate.[141] Since the inception of the WTO there has been a tendency for panel rulings to involve the review of extensive and complex evidence. A very wide fact-finding process does not necessarily equate to a more intrusive form of standard, because only where a panel analyses the facts and draws conclusions is a particular standard exercised. However, there is certainly a direct relationship between the fact-finding process and the standard of review, with the former being a prerequisite for developing a more intrusive standard. On the question of expertise, Article 13.2 grants panels the power to consult experts concerning scientific or other technical matters. There is certainly no basis for a panel to absolve itself from the review of evidence on the basis that a domestic authority or government has greater expertise. Even in extremely contentious matters, such as those involving scientific risk assessments, panels may review expert evidence with the aid of the parties and other experts, and this has generally been their practice.[142] Therefore, these aspects of procedure provide panels with considerable flexibility and pose no obvious limitation on the type of standard of review that might be adopted by panels.

B. Efficiency

Procedural efficiency is an important principle for ensuring that panel processes are carried out promptly, and that decisions are published in a timely fashion. It generally prioritizes the speed of outcomes over due process. Advocates of a more deferential standard of review have frequently contended that a *de novo* standard would not be workable, on the basis that panels would spend an unjustified amount of time reviewing evidence, and rulings would not then be published within the time frames stipulated in the DSU.[143] Such advocates also pair the efficiency argument with the point that the DSB only has quite limited human and financial resources to deal with a more comprehensive review process. Based upon Spamann's analysis discussed earlier in this chapter, the requirement for adjudicative efficiency is not necessarily incompatible with a *de novo* standard of review.[144] Further, other procedural

---

141 See Appellate Body Report, *Canada-Aircraft* [203] which establishes the principle that an adverse inference may be drawn by a panel for the failure to comply with a panel's request to supply information without good reason.

142 See Waincymer, *WTO Litigation: Procedural Aspects of Formal Dispute Settlement*, above n 128, 589–93.

143 See DSU Article 20 which stipulates an indicative maximum timeframe of nine months for panels to hear and determine cases.

144 Spamann, 'Standard of Review for World Trade Organization Panels in Trade Remedy Cases', above n 73, 551–2.

reforms could be undertaken, such as shortening the length of submissions or of panel reports, which can influence efficiency irrespective of the type of standard of review adopted. Accordingly, whilst it is unlikely that the need for efficiency would, of itself, exclude the possibility of adopting particular standards of review, a more highly intensive standard is more likely to put pressure on judicial resources.

C. Procedural fairness

Procedural fairness is the requirement for a dispute settlement process to ensure that neither the complainant nor respondent is subject to any serious disadvantage in putting their case as a result of procedural deficiencies.[145] It is therefore, to some extent, a mediating principle operating between the fact-finding scope and procedural efficiency, which may conflict with each other. For example, the consistent use by panels of extensive fact-finding powers may result in an overly intrusive process, whereas a high emphasis on speed and efficiency of outcomes may reduce the precision of the findings. Consideration of procedural fairness will therefore require an adjudicator to balance the rights of the parties in the dispute settlement process. Accordingly, any standard of review must retain sufficient elements of procedural fairness, failing which the parties may not respect the outcomes. Procedural fairness is therefore intimately connected with the question of legitimacy of a dispute settlement system given that parties are likely to be involved in disputes as both an aggrieved party and as a party whose measures are under review. Therefore, procedural fairness should be taken into account in the formulation of a standard of review.

The above procedural factors, scope of fact-finding, expertise, efficiency and procedural fairness, all influence the workability of any particular standard of review. Standards of review are limited by the design of the dispute settlement system. At the same time, standards of review that expressly favour particular procedural objectives will have an influence on other procedural objectives and the operation of the dispute settlement system as a whole. For instance, a standard of review that emphasizes unlimited fact-finding powers will potentially undermine the dispute settlement system as panel reports may not be published within designated timeframes and parties may lose confidence in the system. By contrast, a standard that overemphasises the requirement for efficiency may lead to allegations of 'rough justice' and potentially lead to more appeals. A standard of review that sufficiently accommodates or balances these competing procedural objectives will result in a higher level of

---

145 Procedural Fairness may be regarded as part of the broader principle of due process: see Andrew D. Mitchell, *Legal Principles in WTO Disputes* (Cambridge University Press, 2008) 122–3.

consistency between the standard of review and these objectives, and is thus in turn is more likely to improve the quality of WTO dispute settlement processes.

3.4 CONCLUSION

This chapter has examined the different approaches to the standard of review question advocated by scholars since the inception of the WTO in 1995. It has been established that there is clearly no single and readily obvious standard that can be adopted by panels. Various tests, such as that of *de novo* review or the reasonable regulator test, suffer from disadvantages such as a lack of clear definition, or the fact that they may not be appropriate for application under particular agreements. Proponents of particular tests also tend to base their arguments on their view of the relative importance of the standard of review in WTO jurisprudence. That is, whether the standard has a more direct effect on the relative power between the WTO as an institution and the membership, or whether it functions more as a procedural mechanism, albeit with an important role. The purpose of this chapter has also been to draw out the main principles that inform the construction of an appropriate standard of review. It is contended that the standard should meaningfully contribute to the interpretation of the WTO agreements utilizing the principles identified in Section 3.3 above. In the next chapter, the first limb of a new standard of review shall be advanced based upon these principles and other relevant considerations.

4. A new general standard of review

4.1 INTRODUCTION

In the first three chapters of this book, I have identified and critiqued the current WTO standard of review. Chapter 2 highlighted some of the problems associated with the current standard, and Chapter 3 dealt with alternative approaches as to how an improved standard might be formulated. This chapter marks the beginning of the second part of this work, in which a new standard of review is proposed. The new standard consists of two discrete tests, the first of which is a general standard that may be applied in relation to all WTO Agreements. The second test involves a modification of the general standard where the structure or wording of WTO Agreements provides for a change in the review process undertaken by panels. The second test therefore seeks to take into account the differing nature of WTO Agreements. This new standard of review would accordingly be applied as a singular general standard, or as a variation of the general standard depending upon which WTO obligations were the subject of a dispute. It is a singular standard, but the result may be to vary the standard that is actually applied in different types of disputes. References in subsequent chapters to 'the new standard of review' or 'new test' shall refer to the new standard of review as a whole, whereas references to a 'general standard' and 'specific standard' shall refer to the separate limbs of the new standard.[1] In this chapter I shall deal with the general standard of review and I will be dealing with the specific standard in Chapter 5.

The fact that the new standard of review consists of a two-stage test is quite different from other approaches put forward to date.[2] Most of these approaches have involved the development of a single uniform standard to be applied in relation to all WTO Agreements. The adoption of a uniform standard is a difficult proposition, in my view, because the subject matter of the WTO Agreements is extremely diverse.[3] A single standard of review rigidly

[1] A specific standard is also sometimes referred to in this book as a flexible standard of review or a modified standard of review.

[2] See Chapter 3, Section 3.2.

[3] See Sharif Bhuiyan, *National Law in WTO Law: Effectiveness and Good Governance in the World Trading System* (Cambridge University Press, 2007) 144.

applied across all WTO Agreements may also potentially have negative consequences, including the perception that panels are being too intrusive or too deferential in their approach. Given these potential problems, authors such as Ehlermann and Lockhart, have taken the opposite approach of highlighting the need for a fully flexible standard of review in which independent standards of review apply to different WTO Agreements.[4] This may involve the objective assessment test or another broadly-based test dividing more clearly into discrete standards, and there would not be a two-stage test as is contemplated in this book. The problems that may be associated with a flexible standard of review provide the basis for the argument for retaining some form of general standard of review. I put forward two major reasons for retaining a general standard of review. Firstly, a general standard will serve the function of setting out basic rules for reviewing measures, and thereby ensure that a fundamentally consistent approach is taken by panels.[5] Secondly, under many WTO Agreements, such as GATT 1994, there may be no textual or teleological basis for determining a standard of review. In such instances, a general standard is needed as a default position that will offer panels guidance in the way they review measures.

In the first section of this chapter, I will examine the major features of a new general standard of review. The general standard consists of two discrete parts: the requirement for panels to examine all available and sufficient evidence, and the requirement for panels to conduct a comprehensive review. These two parts provide the necessary conditions for panels to carry out their review function. In other words, the central rationale for the design of the general standard is that it directly supports the function and purpose of panel review, being to determine whether a member has complied with its WTO obligations. The general standard will more clearly focus the attention of all WTO stakeholders on the need for panels to have sufficient authority to determine compliance. It will provide a clear and principled framework and support the fundamental aims of the dispute settlement system, including the objective

---

4 See Claus-Dieter Ehlermann and Nicolas Lockhart, 'Standard of Review in WTO Law' (2004) 7(3) *Journal of International Economic Law* 491. See discussion in Chapter 3, Section 3.2.5.

5 See Bhuiyan, *National Law in WTO Law*, above n 3, 148, where the author notes: 'Undue deference to questionable interpretation and application of WTO law by individual WTO members would defeat uniform interpretation and application – and hence effectiveness of WTO law. In such circumstances the rights and obligations of WTO Members would differ from Member to Member, undermining the core objectives of security, predictability and effectiveness. Accordingly, the level of deference to be accorded by panels and the AB to contested national laws and measures is – indeed should be – conditioned by the objective of ensuring effectiveness of WTO rules and discipline.'

of providing security and predictability to the multilateral trading system. With this in mind, I will describe these two parts of the general standard in further detail, and I will contend that both of these parts are, to a large extent, already integrated into WTO jurisprudence. There is ample authority in the DSU and in various cases despite the ongoing citation of the objective assessment test. Accordingly, no great shift in WTO jurisprudence would be required in order to introduce the general standard of review. I will then conclude this section of the chapter by examining how the new general standard may be applied in relation to factual as opposed to legal questions. I will contend that the general standard should be applied in both instances.

In the second section of this chapter, I will seek to justify why the new general standard of review should be adopted. I will do this in four stages. Firstly, I will identify the sources of international law supporting its adoption. This is particularly important given that there is no direct textual basis for the general standard. Secondly, I will analyse the new general standard against guiding principles discussed in Chapter 3; thirdly, I will identify how the general standard would be an improvement over the objective assessment test and alternative approaches. Fourthly, I will conclude by explaining how the general standard will operate in conjunction with the standard under Article 17.6 of the Anti-Dumping Agreement.

4.2 FEATURES OF A NEW GENERAL STANDARD OF REVIEW

The general standard of review has a number of broader characteristics over and above the two parts that will be described in this section. As a whole, it could be categorized as a highly intensive standard because it will commit panels to a thorough and searching review of matters in dispute. This is necessary because a high proportion of disputes involve complex factual and legal issues that require a detailed form of review in order for panels to properly determine these issues.[6] Further, the general standard does not prescribe any particular degree of deference towards measures being reviewed. This is an important point given that the question of deference has been the subject of so much debate by scholars and the WTO membership. Consistent with no specific deference, the general standard will also allow panels a wide discretion in relation to their appreciation of evidence. However, despite this highly

[6] See discussion of the measures at issue in Appellate Body Report, *India-Patents (US)* referred to in Michael J. Trebilcock and Robert Howse, *The Regulation of International Trade* (Routledge, 3rd ed, 2005) 130.

intensive approach, the general standard is quite distinct from *de novo* review because it is a more confined process of review conducted within the framework of the DSU.

The general standard's two parts comprising the 'examine all available and sufficient evidence' and 'comprehensive review' tests are intended to be applied in a discrete and sequential manner by panels. The 'examine all available and sufficient evidence' test is concerned with the scope of review rather than the manner in which the review is undertaken. It is therefore a more formal or procedural, rather than substantive, aspect of the general standard. This part focuses on how panels establish a factual record and the extent of independent fact-finding undertaken by panels. The 'comprehensive review' test is concerned with the process of panel review and it is therefore the 'active' or 'substantive' aspect of the standard of review that more directly mediates the intensity of the review. This part concerns the requirement for panels to conduct a detailed analysis of the evidence and to draw conclusions that are consistent with such an analysis. These parts, when taken together highlight the need for panels to ensure that due process is observed. When discussing each part, I will examine the extent to which they are already being utilized through the application of procedural aspects of the DSU and in WTO case law. I will conclude that a marked change in the approach of panels is not required in order for the general standard to be implemented. A number of DSU provisions and Appellate Body rulings do in fact provide a firm foundation for the establishment of a new general standard.

4.2.1 The Requirement to Examine all Available and Sufficient Evidence

The 'all available and sufficient evidence' test would direct panels to examine all evidence that has been presented before them and to ensure that the body of evidence comprising the factual record is, at a minimum, sufficient to determine the issues in dispute. This part of the general standard is concerned with ensuring that a panel satisfies certain minimum conditions when establishing its factual record. The most critical aspect of the test is the requirement for the factual record to consist of sufficient evidence upon which a panel can make an informed decision as to member compliance. To put this central idea another way, could a panel objectively make an informed decision as to whether a member has acted consistently with its WTO obligations based on the material examined?

It is not feasible to attempt to define the expression 'sufficient' in the present context. This will vary greatly in each dispute, depending upon the nature and complexity of the facts and WTO provisions involved. Panels should, however, view this requirement as a minimum threshold that will not be contravened so long as an active and robust approach is taken to compiling the factual record. In other words, panels should seek to gather as much relevant evidence as is possible, within the confines of the dispute settlement system. For example, it would be appropriate for a panel to obtain its own expert scientific evidence where cases involve complex scientific issues or there are any important discrepancies between the expert evidence presented by the parties.[7] However, the 'all available' evidence requirement is also important because it ensures panels do not disregard evidence presented by the parties were sufficiency the only basis of this test.

As this test sets the minimum conditions for evidence to be reviewed, it does not seek to define the nature of evidence that panels should examine. For example, it does not direct panels to restrict the review to evidence that is determined as relevant to the dispute, or to evidence that is being relied upon by the parties. It is my contention that these descriptors are highly problematic and impose definitional complexity upon WTO members. Arguably, this is what has occurred with the current standard of review, where the Appellate Body has made statements in a number of decisions about what sort of review by panels will equate to an objective assessment.[8] No all-encompassing definition or exhaustive set of conditions should therefore be applied when determining the factual record. These matters do not need to be tightly regulated. If panels estimate that the parties have not presented sufficient evidence, then the factual record should be supplemented by additional evidence to ensure that the minimum obligations under this test are satisfied. Panels should retain a high degree of discretion about the circumstances in which the factual record is required to be supplemented, and by what type and quantity of evidence. Further, there should be no deference to the wishes of the parties with regards to compiling the factual record.

The 'all available and sufficient test' may be subject to allegations that it would force panels to take an overly expansive approach to evidence in order to avoid the prospect of not satisfying the test. One such allegation may be that panels may be forced to examine irrelevant evidence thereby slowing down the panel decision-making process. I do not agree that such criticisms have

---

[7] See DSU, art 13.2, SPS Agreement, art 11.2. For further discussion see also Joanne Scott, *The WTO Agreement on Sanitary and Phytosanity Measures: A Commentary* (Oxford University Press, 2007) 133–6.

[8] Various statements on the meaning of the objective assessment test have been made to date in the following Appellate Body decisions: *EC-Hormones* [115]–[117]; *Argentina-Footwear (EC)* [484]–[485]; *US-Wheat Gluten* [55]; *EC-Poultry* [135]; *Australia-Salmon* [26]; *US-Lamb* [103]–[104]; *US-Cotton Yarn* [74]; *Japan-Apples* [217]–[222]; *US-Countervailing Duty Investigation on DRAMS* [180]–[192]; *US-Softwood Lumber VI (Article 21.5-Canada)* [89]–[140]; *US-Continued Zeroing* [336]–[337]; *US-Continued Suspension* [590]–[598]; *US-Anti-Dumping and Countervailing Duties (China)* [519]–[527].

merit. The reason for this is that the dispute settlement system already has appropriate safeguards to ensure that the scope of evidence being reviewed is appropriately circumscribed and that it does not render the system inefficient. I will examine two aspects that help regulate the factual record of panels.

The first feature of the dispute settlement system that regulates the scope of the factual record of panels is the basic 'architecture' of panel proceedings. The type of adjudication utilized has a significant bearing on the nature and extent of evidence that a panel can consider. Under the present WTO system, panel proceedings are predominantly adversarial, rather than inquisitorial, in nature.[9] This means that panels adjudicate disputes primarily by reference to the issues and arguments presented by the parties. Panels do not initiate nor maintain the carriage of disputes, as may be the case under a more inquisitorial system. The effect of this is that the factual record is likely to be confined to facts and issues that are raised by the parties. A narrower factual record constructed predominantly from material presented by the parties is likely to narrow the standard of review, irrespective of the intensity of review undertaken. Accordingly, the factual record does not need to be curtailed through prescription under the general standard of review. A number of provisions in the DSU, and in particular the panel working procedures annexed to the DSU, reflect this basic approach to dispute settlement.[10] These provisions create a structure that gives the parties a relatively high degree of control over the process and this ultimately provides a suitable framework for a panel's findings.

The second feature of the dispute settlement system that circumscribes the scope of review of evidence is the limitation on certain types of evidence that a panel may consider. In trade remedy disputes, a major issue is whether a panel should consider evidence that was not before a domestic authority, either because the evidence was not tendered by a party, or it was not in existence at the time of the national level investigation. On the first of these scenarios, a number of panels have decided to limit evidence that they may consider to that

[9] For discussion of this point see Holger Spamann, 'Standard of Review for World Trade Organization Panels in Trade Remedy Cases: A Critical Analysis' (2004) 38(3) *Journal of World Trade* 551.

[10] Examples of adversarial provisions include: 1. DSU Appendix 3, Paragraph 5 (working procedures) which states: At its first substantive meeting with the parties, the panel shall ask the party which has brought the complaint to present its case. Subsequently, and still at the same meeting, the party against which the complaint has been brought shall be asked to present its point of view. 2. DSU Appendix 3, Paragraph 7 provides for formal rebuttals to be made by the parties at a second substantive meeting of the panel. 3. DSU Article 7.1 allows parties to agree to an alternative terms of reference for a panel. 4. DSU Article 12.1 allows the panel to depart from the standard working procedures at the request of the parties. The DSU also permits the parties to settle disputes at any stage during panel or Appellate Body proceedings, and complainants may withdraw complaints at any time.

which was available to the domestic authority at the time the authority made its determination.[11] There is a clear logical basis for this approach, and a failure to adhere to this approach would inevitably mean introducing elements of *de novo* review. This is because a panel would be required to assess new evidence rather than to review the evidence that led to the imposition of the measure. In *US-Wool Shirts and Blouses*, the panel analysed the position in the following terms:

> When assessing the WTO compatibility of the decision to impose national trade remedies, DSU panels do not reinvestigate the market situation but rather limit themselves to the evidence used by the importing Member in making its determination to impose the measure.[12]

Similarly, in *US-Wheat Gluten*, the panel stated that 'It is not our role to collect new data, nor to consider evidence which could have been presented to the USITC by interested parties, but was not.'[13]

On the question of evidence that was not in existence at the time of the determination, the position is generally the same as applies to non-record evidence, although there is some conflicting authority.[14] In *US-Cotton Yarn*, the Appellate Body definitively ruled that a panel must not consider evidence which did not exist at the time of a member's determination.[15] The Appellate Body also noted that if a panel did examine such evidence, it would, in effect, be conducting a *de novo* review. This is to be contrasted with an earlier decision of *Argentina-Footwear (EC)*, in which the panel ruled that evidence of invoices rendered after consultations were initiated were considered as admissible on the basis that they were relevant for the panel's understanding of how the tariff system in question functioned.[16] Whilst *Argentina-Footwear (EC)* may not be in line with the Appellate Body's position, the important consideration is that WTO jurisprudence does already place narrow limitations upon the admission of new evidence on temporal grounds.

The Appellate Body has not to date formulated an approach that is similar to the 'all available and sufficient evidence' test, and instead, it has focussed

---

[11] See Panel Report, *US-Wool Shirts and Blouses*; Panel Report, *EC-Hormones*; Panel Report, *US-Hot-Rolled Steel*; Panel Report, *US-Wheat Gluten*; Panel Report, *Korea-Dairy*.

[12] Panel Report, *US-Wool Shirts and Blouses* [7.21].

[13] Panel Report, *US-Wheat Gluten* [8.6].

[14] Expert evidence relied upon by panels is unlikely to have been prepared prior to the date of the impugned measure, but expert evidence is distinguishable from the 'raw facts' that gave rise to the measure in the first instance.

[15] The relevant information was official census data that was published after the member determination.

[16] Panel Report, *Argentina-Footwear (EC)* [8.213].

its attention on developing a standard of review that deals more with the nature, rather than the scope of review per se. However, there is ample authority within the DSU and existing WTO cases to support its adoption. In particular, there is authority for the proposition that panels must examine not only evidence presented, but also other evidence that may be relevant to the dispute. In *EC-Hormones* the Appellate Body described an objective assessment of facts in part as an obligation to consider the evidence presented.[17] In subsequent decisions developing the standard of review, such as *Argentina-Footwear (EC)*, *US-Lamb* and *US-Cotton Yarn*, the Appellate Body has extended this obligation by describing the nature of the panel review process in extremely comprehensive terms. For example, in *Argentina-Footwear (EC)* the panel was required to examine whether the domestic authority has considered all relevant facts and adequately explained how the facts supported the determination.[18] It is implicit in such a broad description of the review process that panels are required to review a body of evidence that is sufficient to determine the issues in dispute.

Further guidance on the requirement to examine sufficient evidence is found in Article 13 of the DSU. Under Article 13.1, a panel has the right to seek information and technical advice from any individual or body which it deems appropriate.[19] In interpreting Article 13.1, the Appellate Body in *Canada-Aircraft* determined that Article 13.1 imposes no conditions on the exercise of a panel's discretionary authority to obtain factual information.[20] Under Article 13.2, panels may consult experts or an expert review group to obtain their opinion on technical or scientific aspects of a dispute. Panels have frequently sought input from experts particularly in relation to scientific matters.[21] For example, in all disputes to date concerning the SPS Agreement,

---

17 Appellate Body Report, *EC-Hormones* [133].

18 Panel Report, *Argentina-Footwear (EC)* [121].

19 DSU Article 13.1 provides: 'Each panel shall have the right to seek information and technical advice from any individual or body which it deems appropriate. However, before a panel seeks such information or advice from any individual or body within the jurisdiction of a Member it shall inform the authorities of that Member. A Member should respond promptly and fully to any request by a panel for such information as the panel considers necessary and appropriate. Confidential information which is provided shall not be revealed without formal authorization from the individual, body, or authorities of the Member providing the information.'

20 Appellate Body Report, *Canada-Aircraft* [1.85].

21 DSU Article 13.2 provides: 'Panels may seek information from any relevant source and may consult experts to obtain their opinion on certain aspects of the matter. With respect to a factual issue concerning a scientific or other technical matter raised by a party to a dispute, a panel may request an advisory report in writing from an expert review group. Rules for the establishment of such a group and its procedures are set forth in Appendix 4.'

panels have requested expert evidence over and above evidence provided by the parties.[22] Accordingly, panels have not hesitated to expand the factual record where necessary in order to fully appreciate the issues in dispute. This power was described by the Appellate Body in *US-Shrimp* as an 'ample and extensive authority to undertake and to control the process by which it informs itself both of the relevant facts of the dispute and of the legal norms and principles applicable to such facts.'[23] These fact-finding rules are supplementary in nature and support the basic proposition that panels must have sufficient evidence before them to properly discharge their duties.

4.2.2 The Requirement to Conduct a Comprehensive Review

In the previous section it was proposed that the factual record should be sufficiently wide in order for panels to properly fulfil their review function. In this section, the active or substantive element of the general standard of review is described. This limb of the general standard of review is referred to as the 'comprehensive review' test. The detailed criteria as to what constitutes a comprehensive review will vary under the different WTO Agreements due to significant differences in the subject matter being reviewed. However, as with any form of adjudicative review, there are two basic aspects to the review process that panels undertake. There is the analysis of factual and legal issues followed by the making of findings. The analysis aspect will involve panels assessing and appreciating material before them and conducting a reasoning process in order to frame the issues in dispute. The reaching of findings is perhaps best expressed as the final stage or purely deductive aspect of adjudication. For WTO panels it is the phase in which the issues are drawn together to determine whether a measure is consistent with WTO obligations.

The 'comprehensive review' test requires panels to conduct a thorough and searching review of factual and legal questions raised in disputes. As with the 'all available and sufficient evidence' test, panels are directed to take a practical but highly intensive approach to the review task. The key principle that panels ought to adhere to is to ensure that the review process is, as a whole, sufficient for them to competently determine whether a violation of WTO obligations has occurred. This principle of sufficiency, as with the formulation of the factual record, is crucial to panels being able to properly discharge their duties prescribed under the DSU. The 'comprehensive review' test is therefore

---

22 These panel decisions are: *EC-Hormones*, *Australia-Salmon*, *Japan-Agricultural Products II* and *Japan-Apples*. See also Scott, *The WTO Agreement on Sanitary and Phytosanity Measures*, above n 7, 133–6.

23 Appellate Body Report, *US-Shrimp* [106].

also a test that sets out a minimum standard, and it is essentially concerned with ensuring that the standard of panel review is of the highest quality. In general terms, a sufficient level of review will involve a panel setting out in its report matters such as a summary of the facts and provisions in issue, the arguments of the parties (and third parties), a detailed analysis of its reasoning, and its findings.[24] The analysis undertaken by panels should be measured by reference to its accuracy and the extent of a panel's appreciation of the evidence. Accuracy will generally involve a high degree of logic, detail and consistency within the analysis. In reviewing the adequacy of panel findings, the important consideration is for panels to ensure that their findings are consistent with the analysis undertaken. All of these indicia are concerned with ensuring a high quality review process. As with the 'all available and sufficient evidence' test, a beneficial way of conceiving this part of the general standard is to consider it as a minimum requirement of due process that panels must adhere to.

The panel review process will always require panels to make difficult factual and legal assessments.[25] There is often controversy over whether a panel has given adequate consideration to the issues, whether its reasoning is logical and coherent, or whether it has attached the correct weight or importance to particular pieces of evidence.[26] Further, panels are required to make findings on legal questions as to whether the facts fall within the scope of WTO provisions, and in doing so, seek to clarify the meaning of WTO provisions. These aspects necessarily involve an element of subjective assessment by panels. The review task of panels is therefore complex and it is impossible for panels to avoid criticism that they have 'over' or 'under' reviewed disputes.[27] The 'comprehensive review' test does not seek to reduce panel discretion by requiring panels to meet particular analytical criteria in each case. It is contended that panels should retain their discretion to appreciate evidence, so long as their review is sufficiently comprehensive in an overall sense.

---

[24] See DSU Article 12.7 which sets out the basic requirements of a panel report. For further information on the process in reaching a final report see Duane Layton and Jorge Miranda, 'Advocacy before World Trade Organization Dispute Settlement Panels in Trade Remedy Cases' (2003) 37(1) *Journal of World Trade* 69.

[25] Tania S. Voon and Alan Yanovich, 'The Facts Aside: The Limitation of WTO Appeals to Issues of Law' (2006) 40(2) *Journal of World Trade* 251 and 258.

[26] See for example Appellate Body Report, *US-Countervailing Duty Investigation on DRAMS* [144]–[158], [188] which is discussed in Ross S. Becroft, 'The Standard of Review Strikes Back: the US-Korea DRAMS Appeal' (2006) 9(1) *Journal of International Economic Law* 207.

[27] The question of applying an overly-intensive standard of review is dealt with by applying a specific standard of review which is discussed in Chapter 5.

If the 'comprehensive review' test prescribed a list of mandatory criteria for panels to satisfy, it would significantly reduce the panel's subjective field of analysis and its overall discretion. This prescriptive type of approach to the standard of review would have a number of negative consequences, such as creating more definitional problems and disputes about whether the standard has been fulfilled. It would also lead to further allegations that panels are being directed to conduct a *de novo* review of measures. Whilst no specific degree of deference is required for the review process, the 'comprehensive review' test is less intrusive than *de novo* review, primarily due to the narrower scope of the factual record discussed in the previous section. Further, panels would be held to account through the application of the second limb of the new standard of review proposed in this book, in which deference may be required based upon the rights and obligations of the parties expressed in the WTO Agreements.

It would not be difficult for the Appellate Body to adopt the 'comprehensive review' test. This test (and the whole general standard of review) is based upon the review task that panels must fulfil and it does not involve the introduction of new legal concepts. In addition, the way in which the objective assessment test has been developed by the Appellate Body has resulted in a general movement towards a form of comprehensive review. In a number of decisions, the Appellate Body has described the standard of review as being highly intensive in nature.[28] The type of language used by the Appellate Body could have been employed as part of the definition of the 'comprehensive review' test. It is recalled that in *EC-Hormones* the Appellate Body identified the standard of review as being that of objective assessment under DSU Article 11, and this assessment in part involved 'an obligation to consider the evidence presented to a panel and to make factual findings on the basis of that evidence.'[29] This language is similar to the two parts of the general standard and emphasizes adherence to due process, but it does not provide qualitative guidance on the nature of the review.

Subsequent Appellate Body decisions do provide some further guidance in relation to how panels must conduct their review. In *US-Lamb*, the Appellate Body stated that a panel can only fulfil its obligation to assess a safeguard measure if it has critically examined the explanation of a domestic agency in depth.[30] This approach was extended in *US-Cotton Yarn*, when the Appellate Body set out a detailed description of what an objective assessment involves

---

[28] See for example: Appellate Body Report, *US-Cotton Yarn* [74]; Appellate Body Report, *US-Countervailing Duty Investigation on DRAMS* [188].

[29] Appellate Body Report, *EC-Hormones* [133].

[30] Appellate Body Report, *US-Lamb* [148].

in relation to safeguard measures.[31] Panels were directed to assess whether the domestic agency has examined all relevant factors and provided an adequate explanation of its findings.[32] The explanation must address the nature and complexities of data and respond to plausible interpretations of data. This requirement for a detailed and critical assessment is, in some respects, akin to the 'comprehensive review' test.[33] This approach was developed further in decisions such as *US-Countervailing Duty Investigation on DRAMS* and *US-Softwood Lumber VI (Article 21.5-Canada)* when the Appellate Body has overturned panel findings due to the panel's lack of appreciation of evidence or excessively deferential approach.[34] Over time, the Appellate Body has developed a more intensive standard of review that requires a panel to accurately analyse and appreciate evidence and draw consistent findings.[35] This goes beyond merely determining whether some elementary reasoning process was carried out by the panel.

A major benefit of introducing the 'comprehensive review' test is that it would provide clearer guidance for panels about their basic standard of review obligations under all of the WTO Agreements. The general standard sets out the parameters of the review task in a manner that reflects the basic model of panel adjudication. By comparison, the objective assessment test has provided an inadequate framework for the development of the standard of review. This problem stems from the use of Article 11 of the DSU as the source of a general standard of review. An ordinary reading of this article discloses its purpose as an aspect of due process that is concerned with avoiding bias.[36] This is also how the Appellate Body applied Article 11 in *EC-Hormones* when it equated a panel's duty under that Article with a requirement to review disputes in good faith.[37] The requirement to examine a matter in good faith is a very different proposition from prescribing how panels are to undertake the review task.[38] The objective assessment test therefore gives panels no guidance as to the nature or intensity of a review. Whilst the trade remedy cases have greatly

---

31 Appellate Body Report, *US-Cotton Yarn* [74].

32 *Ibid.*

33 *Ibid.*

34 Appellate Body Report, *United States-Countervailing Duty Investigation on DRAMS* [144]–[148], [188]; Appellate Body Report, *US-Softwood Lumber VI (Article 21.5-Canada)* [93].

35 Matthias Oesch, 'Standards of Review in WTO Dispute Resolution' (2003) 6(3) *Journal of International Economic Law* 650 and 652. The one exception to this approach is in Appellate Body Report, *US-Continued Suspension* [590].

36 See Chapter 2, Section 2.4.2.

37 Appellate Body Report, *EC-Hormones* [133].

38 See Andrew D. Mitchell, 'Good Faith in WTO Dispute Settlement' (2006) 7(2) *Melbourne Journal of International Law* 339.

contributed to the development of the current standard of review, there has continued to be ambiguity in the absence of overriding principles being applied. In many ways the Appellate Body has been forced to articulate a standard of review which reflects the language of the agreement being contested because the objective assessment test does not provide any real framework for review. Without the introduction of the general standard of review, there is therefore a risk that the standard will continue to be applied in an unnecessarily ad hoc manner, or that it will continue to split into different WTO agreement-specific standards because of inadequate guidance from the objective assessment test.

4.2.3 Treatment of Facts and Law

The issue that this section addresses is whether the general standard of review discussed in sections 4.2.1 and 4.2.2 should be applied equally for facts and law. It is recalled from section 1.2.5 of Chapter 1 that, in various legal systems, a different standard of review is frequently applied to factual as opposed to legal questions. There is often some degree of deference exercised by courts to factual findings of lower courts or domestic agencies on the basis of expertise of the original decision-maker, for efficiency reasons, or based on some other policy grounds.[39] By contrast, there is often limited or sometimes no deference exercised by courts in domestic legal systems in relation to the review of legal questions, due to factors such as the need to ensure a consistent interpretation of laws. Whilst the approach to facts and law differs between various legal systems, this basic distinction between the treatment of facts and law is generally observed.

The distinction between factual and legal questions is not always clear in any jurisdiction. In the WTO context, the dichotomy was illustrated by the Appellate Body in *EC-Hormones* when it stated that:

> Determination of the credibility and weight properly to be ascribed to (that is, the appreciation of) a given piece of evidence is part and parcel with the fact finding process and is, in principle, left to the discretion of panels as triers of facts. The consistency or inconsistency of a given fact or set of facts with the requirements of a given treaty provision is, however, a legal characterization issue. It is a legal question.[40]

---

[39] Jeffrey Waincymer, *WTO Litigation: Procedural Aspects of Formal Dispute Settlement* (Cameron May, 2002) 348.

[40] Appellate Body Report, *EC-Hormones* [132]. The Appellate Body also stated in the same paragraph that 'Whether or not a panel has made an objective assessment of the facts before it, as required by Article 11 of the DSU, is also a legal question which, if properly raised on appeal, would fall within the scope of appellate review.'

In *EC-Hormones*, the Appellate Body held that the objective assessment test under Article 11 applied both 'in respect of both the ascertainment of facts and the legal characterizations of such facts under the relevant agreements'.[41] The test therefore applies to panel review of factual findings and legal interpretations. There have been very few statements by the Appellate Body reconfirming this approach.[42] However, for legal questions, the Appellate Body has made it clear that panels must also apply the customary rules of interpretation of public international law.[43] This is a reference to Articles 31 and 32 of the VCLT, which require international treaties to be interpreted in good faith based on the ordinary meaning of the treaty provisions and consistently with their object and purpose. These provisions aim to create a consistency in the interpretation of international treaties, and accordingly, they support the idea of panels not deferring to interpretations of WTO members.[44]

It is contended in this book that the Appellate Body has taken the correct approach on this issue and that the general standard of review should apply equally to facts and law. It is recalled that the standard of review of facts concerns the establishment of facts, whereas the standard of review of law relates to whether the measure (and the facts upon which the measure is based) comply with the WTO Agreements. Whilst applying a legal standard is frequently a more confined exercise, some degree of induction and analysis is required and no deference should be given in comparing a domestic measure with a WTO obligation. Two major practical reasons are given for a common factual and legal standard. First, if a panel was required to separate its analysis into factual and legal issues, then there is the potential to unnecessarily increase the complexity of the review process. The current WTO standard of review is already very complex, and there are a number of difficult issues that panels must deal with, including the requirement to apply a separate standard for anti-dumping disputes, and the progressive fragmentation of the objective assessment test into agreement-specific standards. Further, in their review of measures, panels must often examine a wide variety of laws, such as domestic laws or regulations, or international laws. If a separate legal standard was

41 Appellate Body Report, *EC-Hormones* [116].

42 In *Argentina-Footwear (EC)* at paragraph 122 the Appellate Body stated that 'In addition to "an objective assessment of the facts", we note too, that part of the "objective assessment of the matter" required of the panel by Article 11 of the DSU is an assessment of the "applicability of and conformity with the relevant covered agreements." Consequently, we must also examine whether the Panel correctly interpreted and applied the substantive provisions of Articles 2 and 4 of the *Agreement on Safeguards*.'

43 Appellate Body Report, *EC-Hormones* [118].

44 Matthias Oesch, *Standards of Review in WTO Dispute Resolution* (Oxford University Press, 2003) 42 and 87.

applied, there would be the potential for this standard to further fragment into discrete standards for different categories of law.

A second reason why the general standard of review should not differentiate between facts and law is that it serves no useful function where the standard of review is highly intensive in relation to factual questions. The traditional dichotomy in domestic systems is usually based upon the requirement for the original decision-maker to afford some degree of deference in respect of earlier factual findings.[45] Under the general standard, panels would be required to satisfy two limbs: to examine all available and sufficient evidence, and to perform a comprehensive review of both factual and legal matters. No specific deference towards legal or factual issues concerning a measure is mandated. In relation to legal questions, such as whether a measure is in conformity with a WTO provision, a comprehensive review will therefore usually involve no deference to member interpretations of WTO provisions. This approach does not result in a separate more intensive, and arguably *de novo* standard of review for questions of law as some scholars have suggested.[46] Rather, it may be characterized as applying the general standard of review in conjunction with the relevant VCLT provisions to ensure a consistent and unified approach to treaty interpretation. Any emerging differences between the interpretation of facts and law are, in any event, unlikely to be controversial, as the membership has in the past expressed more concern at the way in which panels have conducted their assessment of facts.

4.3 JUSTIFICATIONS FOR A NEW GENERAL STANDARD OF REVIEW

In this section, I will discuss four major justifications for adopting the general standard of review. Firstly, I will explore the legal basis for introducing this new standard. In particular, I will focus on how the general standard may be justified based upon a purposive interpretation of the DSU. Secondly, I will assert that this is an acceptable basis of interpretation and that it would not be contrary to the Uruguay Round outcomes. Thirdly, I will discuss the extent to which the general standard satisfies the principles identified in Chapter 3, and I will then highlight its advantages over the objective assessment test and other approaches. Finally, I will determine how the general standard might operate

---

45 See Chapter 1, Section 1.2.3.

46 Oesch, *Standards of Review in WTO Dispute Resolution*, above n 44, 174. He suggests that both panels and the Appellate Body have consistently engaged in *de novo* review by interpreting WTO provisions pursuant to the methods provided for in the VCLT and they have not deferred to legal interpretations of national agencies.

in conjunction with Article 17.6 of the Anti-Dumping Agreement, and in this regard, I will conclude that these two standards can function in relative harmony.

4.3.1 The Legal Basis for Developing a New Standard of Review

In understanding the legal basis for a new general standard of review, it is important to appreciate the way in which the Appellate Body has justified the introduction of the objective assessment test. The Appellate Body was careful to adhere to a textual approach in respect of the objective assessment test, perhaps in order to minimize the suggestion that it had somehow exceeded its authority. I have argued earlier in this book that Article 11 of the DSU does not disclose any sort of standard of review and it is, at best, a provision that sets out minimum due process standards.[47] It is therefore necessary, when justifying the general standard of review, to move away from a textual approach and to look to whether this new standard of review is consistent with the purpose of key WTO provisions and the WTO Agreements as a whole. This is necessary because, in reality, there is no textual basis within the WTO Agreements for any particular standard of review, other than under Article 17.6 of the Anti-Dumping Agreement.

In order to determine the legal basis for taking a purposive approach in justifying a standard of review, it necessary to refer to the second sentence of Article 3.2 of the DSU, that provides:

> The Members recognize that it [*the dispute settlement system*] serves to preserve the rights and obligations of Members under the covered agreements, and to clarify the existing provisions of those agreements in accordance with customary rules of interpretation of public international law. (Emphasized text added)

This part of Article 3.2 both sets out the central purpose of the dispute settlement system, and provides a basis upon which panels may interpret the WTO Agreements. In this regard, the reference to customary rules of interpretation of public international law is a reference to Articles 31 and 32 of the VCLT, in which rules of international treaty interpretation have been codified.[48] The

---

47 See Chapter 2, Section 2.4.2.

48 VCLT Articles 31 and 32 provide:

Article 31
General rule of interpretation

1. A treaty shall be interpreted in good faith in accordance with the ordinary meaning to be given to the terms of the treaty in their context and in the light of its object and purpose.

Appellate Body has confirmed this available recourse to the VCLT and has identified Article 31(1) of the VCLT as a 'general rule of interpretation'.[49] This Article provides that 'a treaty shall be interpreted in good faith in accordance with the ordinary meaning to be given to the terms of the treaty in their context and in the light of its object and purpose'. It therefore permits treaty interpretation by reference to a treaty's context, object and purpose, and not merely by examining the ordinary meaning of treaty wording.[50] Further, it is not necessary for treaties to be interpreted in a hierarchical way, whereby the purpose and context may only be considered after determining ambiguity with the wording of the treaty text.[51]

It is important to recognize that the VCLT is primarily concerned with the method of interpretation of particular treaty provisions, rather than broader legal doctrines, such as the standard of review.[52] There is, however, no reason why the interpretive rules of the VCLT cannot be used to evince the meaning of various DSU provisions, which may in turn support the introduction of the

---

2. The context for the purpose of the interpretation of a treaty shall comprise, in addition to the text, including its preamble and annexes:
(*a*) any agreement relating to the treaty which was made between all the parties in connection with the conclusion of the treaty;
(*b*) any instrument which was made by one or more parties in connection with the conclusion of the treaty and accepted by the other parties as an instrument related to the treaty.
3. There shall be taken into account, together with the context:
(*a*) any subsequent agreement between the parties regarding the interpretation of the treaty or the application of its provisions;
(*b*) any subsequent practice in the application of the treaty which establishes the agreement of the parties regarding its interpretation;
(*c*) any relevant rules of international law applicable in the relations between the parties.
4. A special meaning shall be given to a term if it is established that the parties so intended.

Article 32
Supplementary means of interpretation
Recourse may be had to supplementary means of interpretation, including the preparatory work of the treaty and the circumstances of its conclusion, in order to confirm the meaning resulting from the application of article 31, or to determine the meaning when the interpretation according to article 31:
(*a*) leaves the meaning ambiguous or obscure; or
(*b*) leads to a result which is manifestly absurd or unreasonable.

49 Appellate Body Report, *US-Gasoline* [17].
50 Appellate Body Report, *Japan-Alcoholic Beverages II* [11], [12].
51 Panel Report, *Canada-Autos* [10.21].
52 See Panel Report, *US-Shrimp* [114] discussed in Mitsuo Matsushita, Thomas J. Schoenbaum and Petros C. Mavroidis, *The World Trade Organization: Law, Practice and Policy* (Oxford University Press, 2nd ed, 2006) 32.

general standard of review. Moreover, as panels may look to the structure and wording of WTO Agreements as a whole to determine the meaning of specific provisions, it is useful for a new standard of review to be justified by reference to the object and purpose of the DSU as a whole.[53]

Having established that the purpose of the DSU can be an appropriate basis for justifying a new standard of review, it is appropriate to identify the major purposes of the DSU and to determine if the general standard of review is consistent with these purposes. It is clear from Article 3.2 that the central purposes are to preserve the rights and obligations of members and to clarify the meaning of the WTO Agreements. DSU Article 3.4 requires panels to provide rulings that are in accordance with member rights and obligations, and DSU Article 19.2 directs panels to ensure that rulings do not add to or diminish rights and obligations under the WTO Agreements. The Appellate Body, in *US-Wool Shirts and Blouses*, confirmed this 'enforcement of negotiated outcomes approach' and stated:

> Given the explicit aim of dispute settlement that permeates the DSU, we do not consider that Article 3.2 of the DSU is meant to encourage either panels of the Appellate Body to 'make law' by clarifying existing provisions of the WTO Agreement outside the context of resolving a particular dispute.[54]

It is clear therefore that the DSU provisions focus on the maintenance of the Uruguay Round outcomes, and more broadly, on the provision of security and predictability in the multilateral trading system.[55]

The general standard of review is consistent with and supportive of the objectives of the DSU. It does not seek to create new rights and obligations or alter existing ones. It is formulated with the direct purpose of ensuring that the substantive WTO obligations are met and it places heavy emphasis on the contractual nature of the WTO Agreements.

Many scholars have argued that a more highly intensive or comprehensive standard of review will in fact alter existing member rights because it is giving panels greater authority than was agreed to in the DSU. For reasons given in the preceding paragraphs, I do not agree with this proposition. However, even if this were true, there are two related secondary arguments that support the introduction of the general standard. Firstly, there is the argument that panels do and ought to possess an inherent jurisdiction over

---

53 Panel Report, *Guatemala-Cement I* [7.7].

54 Appellate Body Report, *US-Wool Shirts and Blouses* [19].

55 The first sentence of Article 3.2 of the DSU provides: 'The dispute settlement system of the WTO is a central element in providing security and predictability to the multilateral trading system.'

their subject matter.[56] In other words, there is a jurisprudential need for an adjudication body to be able to develop rules and procedures that may assist it in fulfilling its dispute settlement task. This is perhaps even more the case in an institutional environment such as the WTO, where it is difficult for any formal rule changes to be made to improve dispute settlement processes. In other words, inherent jurisdiction can be used as a necessary means of fulfilling stated objectives in international treaties, subject to certain limitations.[57] It is the use of the Appellate Body's inherent jurisdiction that has, in conjunction with the DSU provisions, assisted to resolve many procedural issues that have arisen to date, such as the competence to deal with *amicus curiae* briefs.[58] The standard of review I am arguing for may be justified on this basis and would not be contrary to the existing use of inherent jurisdiction. Secondly, there is a basic need for any adjudicator to employ and develop procedures that seek to attain a significant level of due process. That is, procedures that appropriately emphasise qualities such as the impartiality and workability of the dispute settlement process.

4.3.2 Assessment Against Relevant Standard of Review Principles

A useful way of judging the new general standard of review is to analyse it against the major principles identified in Chapter 3. Three principles were identified: whether a standard supports the key WTO objectives, whether it promotes or maintains adjudicative legitimacy, and finally, whether it operates in conjunction with appropriate dispute settlement procedures. It is recalled from Chapter 3 that these three principles were distilled from a critique of the current objective assessment test and other theoretical approaches.

---

56 Chester Brown, *A Common Law of International Adjudication* (Oxford University Press, 2007) 55–82; Andrew D. Mitchell and David Heaton, 'The Inherent Jurisdiction of WTO Tribunals: The Select Application of Public International Law Required by Judicial Function' (2010) 31 *Michigan Journal of International Law* 561.

57 Mitchell and Heaton argue that three basic limitations should apply to the use of inherent jurisdiction by WTO Tribunals, being first, that the application of an international law rule be necessary for the proper exercise of an adjudicative function; second, that the rule in question must have no substantive content of its own; third, its application must not be inconsistent with the WTO Agreements. See Mitchell and Heaton, 'The Inherent Jurisdiction of WTO Tribunals: The Select Application of Public International Law Required by Judicial Function', above n 56, 563.

58 Andrew Mitchell, 'Fair Crack of the Whip: Examining Procedural Fairness in WTO Disputes Using an Australian Administrative Law Framework' in *Ten Years of WTO Dispute Settlement: Australian Perspectives* (Commonwealth of Australia, 2006), 65–8.

Dealing with these three issues in turn, I contend that the new general standard of review is extremely supportive of the key aims of the WTO dispute settlement system. It is designed with this very objective in mind. As discussed in Chapter 3, the objectives identified in DSU Article 3.2 are the maintenance of security and predictability of the trading system, preservation of member rights and obligations, and clarification of the meaning of WTO provisions.[59] These objectives emphasize the need for the preservation of the outcomes of the Uruguay Round. It is therefore important for panels to have ample authority to make authoritative decisions about the conformity of measures with the WTO Agreements. The rigorous and due process orientated approach contemplated by the general standard seeks to ensure that panel review is sufficient to determine whether a member has complied with its WTO obligations. The standard is intensive and undeferential in nature and emphasizes the need for sufficient review to determine substantive obligations. Critically, the general standard provides WTO stakeholders with a clear model of review, which would enable members to more easily determine whether a panel has exceeded its review task or whether the review has resulted in a distortion of negotiated rights and obligations. In other words, I contend that the general standard would result in panels having an even higher level of accountability to properly discharge their functions, and it would also provide clearer guidance for the Appellate Body when reviewing panel decisions.

Adjudicative legitimacy is ultimately concerned with the confidence of the WTO membership in the functioning of the dispute settlement system.[60] As discussed in Chapter 3, common indicia for measuring adjudicative legitimacy include the relative ability of a dispute settlement system to ensure that a defendant accedes to the jurisdiction and that a defendant complies with any adverse ruling. The adoption of the general standard of review is unlikely to result in a reduction in adjudicative legitimacy.[61] With its focus on due process and panels maintaining rigorous review standards, I contend that members are more likely to hold the dispute settlement process in higher regard should the general standard be introduced. Indeed, if certain members were to complain about panels overreaching their authority in conducting a thorough review, then it is likely that the grievance is not with the review process itself, but with

---

[59] See Chapter 3, Section 3.3.2.

[60] This is the case irrespective of whether this conception is derived from the idea of the collective will of States or from broader notions of legitimacy. See World Trade Organization, *The Future of the WTO: Addressing institutional challenges in the new Millennium – Report by the Consultative Board to the Director-General Supachai Panitchpakdi* (World Trade Organization, 2004) [108]–[143]; David Beetham, *The Legitimation of Power* (MacMillan, 1991) 20.

[61] See Chapter 3, Section 3.3.3.

the complex and difficult issues that those members must now deal with as part of the WTO dispute settlement system.[62] For example, there may be difficult domestic political or economic considerations that mean that a member cannot accept the role and competency of WTO panels in certain situations. To put it another way, even if the standard of review was quite deferential to domestic measures, parties would potentially complain that the review was inadequate in some way. Complainants would argue that there has been inadequate review, and respondents would still argue that the review was less deferential than is required. The best way to ensure adjudicative legitimacy is to create a 'hard but fair' system where member measures are tested, but within the confines of a system that aims to preserve negotiated outcomes.

The third principle identified in Chapter 3 was the need for a standard of review to be complementary to other dispute settlement procedures.[63] In other words, does the standard of review promote (and not undermine) other important procedures? The procedures identified were the scope of fact-finding, expertise, efficiency of decision-making and procedural fairness. It is contended that the general standard of review is, on the whole, supportive of these aspects of procedure. In grouping these aspects, it is most obvious that the general standard of review, by virtue of its rigour and intensive nature, promotes a broad scope of fact-finding and the employment of expertise. Procedural fairness is also promoted as the faithful application by panels of the 'all available and sufficient evidence' and 'comprehensive review' tests will necessarily require the use of basic elements of procedural fairness, such as an absence of bias, providing a fair hearing and issuing written reasons. Of course, other aspects of procedural fairness, such as adequate time frames for procedural steps, are not directly connected with any particular standard of review. With regards to efficiency, in recent years there has certainly been an issue with the time taken by some panels to consider complex issues and to prepare reports.[64] However, a more intensive review process does not necessarily equate to less decision-making efficiency, and there are various other reforms that could be taken up by panels before the standard of review was

---

[62] See discussion of the general legal rigour of the DSU in Robert E. Hudec, 'Broadening the Scope of Remedies in WTO Dispute Settlement' in Freidl Weiss and Jochem Weirs (eds), *Improving WTO Dispute Settlement Procedures: Issues and Lessons from the Practice of Other International Courts and Tribunals* (Cameron May, 2000) 345, 345–51. The author notes: 'If the author's description of the political attitudes underlying the adoption of the new WTO Dispute Settlement System is correct, it must be recognized that the WTO legal system serves a reluctant government clientele.'

[63] See Chapter 3, Section 3.3.4.

[64] See for example, Panel Report, *EC-Approval and Marketing of Biotech Products* which took well in excess of the DSU timeframes for publication and was more than 1000 pages long.

compromised. For example, the more frequent use of the principle of judicial economy to avoid having to address claims that are inconsequential to a dispute outcome.[65]

4.3.3 Brief Assessment Against Other Standards of Review

In this section, I briefly examine how the objective assessment test and the alternative approaches discussed in Chapter 3 compare with the new general standard of review by reference to standard of review principles and any other relevant considerations. Unlike the general standard, it is difficult to determine to what extent the objective assessment test promotes or maintains the integrity of the principles discussed in the previous section. Arguably, it was the intention of the Appellate Body to create a malleable and ambiguous basis for the standard of review so that it could be developed as seen fit, and it would avoid major controversy.[66] If this is the case, then the Appellate Body has placed significant emphasis on maintaining adjudicative legitimacy. However, I contend that the 'trade off' in adopting the objective assessment test is that it does not adequately support the key WTO aims, or the development of appropriate procedures. The major problem with the objective assessment test is that its textual reliance is misplaced, and the Appellate Body has been required to develop the doctrine in a haphazard way in order for a meaningful standard to be applied in disputes arising under different Agreements. Part of the rationale for proposing a new general standard of review is not only that it will improve the quality of decision-making by panels, but also that stakeholders will have a clear understanding of the standard that is in fact being applied.

Unlike the general standard, the alternative approaches examined in Chapter 3 invariably do not adequately satisfy the standard of review principles, and many of them suffer from a misconception as to the function of a standard of review. Most of the alternative approaches involve the trading off of the need to support key WTO aims and the need for adjudicative legitimacy. The misconception maintained with these approaches is that they frequently attempt to mediate systemic or substantive issues through the lens of the standard of review. A standard of review based on a deliberation test is a case in point.[67] If

---

65 See Layton and Miranda, 'Advocacy before World Trade Organization Dispute Settlement Panels in Trade Remedy Cases', above n 24, 89.

66 See Matsushita, Schoenbaum and Mavriodis, *The World Trade Organization: Law, Practice and Policy*, above n 52, 130, where the authors note: 'Panels and the Appellate Body have taken a middle-of-the-road approach and applied a test that is a mixture of these two principles depending upon the particulars of the case concerned.' The two principles referred to are that of *de novo* review and deference.

67 See Chapter 3, Section 3.2.2.

we recall, it is argued that more deference is justified where the formulation of domestic measures has involved significant levels of public deliberation.[68] Aside from the obvious complications with defining this test, such an approach would carve out large areas of domestic policy from being subject to WTO review. This would make it more difficult for WTO dispute settlement to meaningfully preserve the rights and obligations of the membership. This approach is also ultimately seeking to ensure that the WTO is sensitive to domestic policy considerations. It is therefore trying to use the standard of review as a mediating factor in determining what is and is not within a panel's purview. The most direct way for these concerns to be addressed is for changes to be made to the WTO commitments.[69] However, even if this is not possible, a better approach to remaining sensitive to the policy environment of the membership is for the DSB to clarify the meaning of substantive WTO obligations or exceptions rather than to attempt this through the standard of review.

The reasonable regulator test advocated by Button is subject to similar difficulties.[70] This test is perhaps not as aggressive as the deliberation test in seeking to carve out domestic decisions from WTO review. Nonetheless, it does seek to add some type of qualitative condition to the panel review process. A panel would need to determine whether any measure made by a domestic regulator was reasonable.[71] Button's test does have a surface appeal, partly because of the familiarity of the concept of reasonableness. Further, it is asserted that reasonableness is already referred to in a number of WTO Agreements.[72] This may be the case, but in the context of the standard of review, unlike those references found in substantive provisions, reasonableness is used as an overarching concept that is inevitably going to add a layer of complexity to a panel's review task.[73] It may also in fact erode adjudicative legitimacy as well as risking core dispute settlement aims because the membership may sense that only modest or substantial compliance with WTO commitments is necessary. Therefore, it would not sufficiently satisfy the standard of review principles, and it is unlikely to enhance the dispute settlement system.

The same types of problems are to be found with respect to the other approaches examined in Chapter 3. Any standard of review that requires panels to apply new and unfamiliar concepts is going to suffer from these

---

68 *Ibid.*

69 For discussion about progress of the Doha Round of negotiations see William J. Davey, 'The WTO: Looking Forwards' (2006) 9(1) *Journal of International Economic Law* 3.

70 See Chapter 3, Section 3.2.3.

71 Catherine Button, *The Power to Protect: Trade Health and Uncertainty in the WTO* (Hart Publishing, 2004) 218.

72 *Ibid* 220.

73 See Chapter 3, Section 3.2.3.

kinds of difficulties. Concepts such as 'margin of appreciation' or 'rational relationship' are either going to potentially change the nature of the WTO commitments, or make the standard of review overly complex, or both.

The only standard of review that is arguably somewhat similar to the new general standard is that of *de novo* review. A *de novo* standard has the major apparent advantage of not having any form of qualifying criteria that panels must apply and therefore panels would simply be required to fully review a dispute to determine the question of compliance.[74] Panels would arguably be spared the task of having to review a dispute through the prism of the 'all available and sufficient evidence' and 'comprehensive review' criteria. However, even the application of a *de novo* standard of review would not necessarily lessen scrutiny and complaints by parties. Members may, for example, assert that a panel has failed to conduct a sufficiently thorough review to meet a *de novo* standard. Another major difficulty is that a *de novo* standard may lead to a diminution of adjudicative legitimacy that panels presently enjoy. It is essential that a procedurally-based test, such as the new general standard, be adopted in order for panels to avoid criticism that they have exceeded their DSU Article 3.2 mandate.

4.3.4 The Relationship with Article 17.6 of the Anti-Dumping Agreement

In justifying the general standard of review, it is important to determine its relationship with Article 17.6 of the Anti-Dumping Agreement. It is recalled from Chapter 2 that the anti-dumping standard is the only standard of review that was specifically prescribed in the Uruguay Round Agreements.[75] Article 17.6(i) requires panels to determine that the establishment of facts by domestic authorities was proper and that their evaluation was unbiased and objective.[76] Article 17.6(ii) requires panels to interpret the Anti-Dumping Agreement in accordance with the customary rules of interpretation of public international law. It was also suggested in *US-Hot-Rolled Steel* that there is unlikely to be any conflict between Article 17.6(i) and the objective assessment test.[77]

[74] *De novo* review would not impose any procedural obstacles to determining compliance. See Waincymer, *WTO Litigation: Procedural Aspects of Formal Dispute Settlement,* above n 39, 349, where the author notes: 'Notions of standard of review have become important in those cases where there appears to be substantial compliance by the domestic bureaucracy with the procedures set out in the WTO Agreements but where the ultimate conclusion may not appear to be the most appropriate one on the evidence available.'

[75] See Chapter 2, Section 2.4.4.

[76] *Ibid.*

[77] Appellate Body Report, *US-Hot Rolled Steel* [55].

The relationship between the anti-dumping standard and the general standard may be conceived in two basic ways. Firstly, the general standard may apply to all WTO Agreements other than the Anti-Dumping Agreement. Alternatively, the general standard may operate cumulatively with the anti-dumping standard. In this latter scenario, panels would first need to satisfy the general standard, and then they would also need to satisfy the anti-dumping standard. This latter scenario is consistent with the two-stage test that I am proposing in this book. Accordingly, the anti-dumping standard set out in Article 17.6 could effectively become part of the new standard of review. In this way, the general standard would operate as a 'gateway' standard before the agreement-specific standard of review is applied. There is an element of duplication with the use of both the general standard and the anti-dumping standard given that the anti-dumping standard was intended to be a discrete standard of review. This is, however, unavoidable given that the anti-dumping standard is a unique product of the Uruguay Round negotiations.[78]

Even if the general standard and the anti-dumping standard were not adopted cumulatively, and the general standard was applied to all WTO Agreements except the Anti-Dumping Agreement, the standards would work quite consistently and are unlikely to create many major distortions in dispute settlement outcomes. Indeed, in many ways the new general standard is more textually consistent with Article 17.6(i) than the objective assessment test. If we examine the wording of Article 17.6(i) more closely, it states that 'the panel shall determine whether the authorities' establishment of the facts was proper and whether their evaluation of those facts was unbiased and objective.' To a significant extent, this mirrors the two parts of the general standard comprising the need to examine 'all available and sufficient evidence' and to perform a 'comprehensive review'. It is, however, acknowledged that the second sentence of Article 17.6(i) is more likely to engender deference because the panels are only required to examine whether an authority's evaluation was unbiased and objective. There is no direction for panels to conduct a thorough analysis to determine if compliance has been achieved. The Appellate Body's statement that the language of Article 17.6(i) closely reflects that of Article 11 and that an active review of anti-dumping measures is required, perhaps adds confusion to the meaning of Article 17.6(i).[79] Therefore, arguably if the new general standard was adopted cumulatively, then the deferential approach contemplated by Article 17.6(i) could be embraced.

---

78 See Chapter 2, Section 2.4.4.

79 Appellate Body Report, *US-Hot Rolled Steel* [55].

Article 17.6(ii) has not to date generated any deference to panels because of the approach taken in practice that the VCLT does not permit more than one interpretation of a treaty.[80] This renders the second sentence of Article 17.6(ii) unworkable, and the first sentence's requirement to abide by the VCLT goes no further than Article 3.2 of the DSU, and does not create a different legal standard for anti-dumping cases. The legal standard of review under the general standard would therefore be no different from the legal standard under the anti-dumping agreement. As suggested above, a more faithful reading of the anti-dumping standard could be achieved if the general standard is adopted, but it would still be very difficult for panels to circumvent the VCLT to arrive at more than one permissible interpretation along the lines contemplated by the *Chevron doctrine*.[81]

4.4 CONCLUSION

In this chapter, I have provided a definition for a new general standard of review. The new general standard is divided into two parts: the requirement for panels to examine all available and sufficient evidence, and the requirement for panels to conduct a comprehensive review. I have sought to demonstrate that the new general standard is a clearer and more principled standard of review than the current objective assessment test. Further, its introduction would not require a major change in the approach of the Appellate Body and panels to the standard of review issue. In the second part of this chapter, I have explored some of the major reasons for adopting a new general standard, and I dealt with various anticipated criticisms. I have sought to establish that the general standard is justified via principles of public international law, and it is consistent with underlying principles that should inform the construction of the WTO standard of review. It has been contended that the general standard is a more advantageous model for WTO jurisprudence than the objective assessment test and alternative approaches that have been proposed. There is,

80 For articles on the deference and the anti-dumping standard of review see: James Durling, 'Deference but only when due: WTO Review of Anti-Dumping Measures' (2003) 6(1) *Journal of International Economic Law* 125; J. Greenwald, 'WTO Dispute Settlement: An exercise in Trade Law Legislation?' (2003) *Journal of International Economic Law* 6, 113; Lee Hamilton, 'US Antidumping Decisions and the WTO Standard of Review: Deference or Disregard?' (2003) 4 *Chicago Journal of International Law* 265. See also Chapter 2, Section 2.4.4.

81 See discussion of the legal standard of review in Chapter 2, Section 2.4.4. See also Asif H. Qureshi, *Interpreting WTO Agreements* (Cambridge Univesity Press, 2006) 218–9.

accordingly, a strong case for its introduction and application in future WTO cases. In Chapter 5, I will be putting forward the second aspect of the new standard of review, which is flexible in nature and takes into account the different obligations imposed upon members in the WTO Agreements.

5. Modification of the general standard of review

5.1 INTRODUCTION

In Chapter 4, a new test for a general standard of review was described and arguments for its adoption were given. This general standard advantages stakeholders in WTO disputes in that it provides a clear and uniform approach to the panel review process. It is also relatively intrusive and undeferential, thereby ensuring that panels are not prevented from being in a position to determine whether measures comply with WTO obligations. In short, the general standard is an appropriate form of review to apply in many WTO disputes. However, the WTO Agreements deal with very diverse subjects, and the measures under review, as well as the procedures giving rise to them, are also extremely diverse.[1] This suggests that a general standard of review may not be appropriate in all cases.

There are aspects of this diversity of subject matter that support the idea that there should be some kind of 'tailoring' of the standard of review. From a practical standpoint, panels may not have the resources to examine the veracity of raw or technical evidence in certain trade remedy matters in order to satisfy the general standard.[2] Further, the general standard may not be appropriate in cases where it may duplicate scrutiny that has already been carried out by a domestic authority.[3]

There are also broader policy questions about the need for differential approaches to review for agreements that deal with 'core' issues like tariff reductions versus agreements that provide for newer types of obligations, such as in the case of the TRIPS Agreement.[4] These kinds of issues lead to the

---

[1] Tania S. Voon and Alan Yanovich, 'The Facts Aside: The Limitation of WTO Appeals to Issues of Law' (2006) 40(2) *Journal of World Trade* 251.

[2] Matthias Oesch, *Standards of Review in WTO Dispute Resolution* (Oxford University Press, 2003) 58. The issue of adequate judicial resources often discussed with related issues such as the efficiency of the judicial process and expertise and experience of different judicial bodies.

[3] *Ibid.*

[4] See Chapter 3, Section 3.2.6.

proposition that WTO panels should apply a flexible standard of review depending upon the nature of the WTO obligations being assessed.[5] Various tests, such as a 'reasonableness' standard, that have been previously advocated, have also been so advocated with a flexible subject matter in mind.[6]

In this chapter I will argue for the introduction of a different standard of review in circumstances where the structure or wording of the WTO Agreements makes it more appropriate for there to be a change in the review process undertaken by panels. I will refer to this as a specific standard of review. It is not contended that this specific standard of review will be constructed and applied independently of the general standard of review. Nor is it envisaged that a specific standard would lead to a separate two-stage test whereby panels must apply the general standard followed by a different specific standard of review. Rather, what is proposed is that the specific standard would be a variation to the general standard, with the latter still applying in its own right in many cases.[7] Accordingly, the general standard of review would still either be fully applied or it would be applied to a greater or lesser degree where the criteria for its modification are met. A specific standard of review will not therefore be a uniform standard but it will vary depending upon the WTO Agreement and obligations in issue.

The general standard is therefore the starting point for developing a specific standard of review and it would be applied fully unless it is varied under the test put forward in this chapter. A specific standard of review would be the result of applying the general standard of review and then modifying that general standard to suit the structure and wording of particular WTO Agreements. The type of changes to the general standard will vary from agreement to agreement, but it is likely that a modified standard will place some degree of limitation on the panel review process.

The threshold issue for the introduction of a specific standard of review is to determine the criteria for its application. Following this step, it is necessary to identify the method by which the general standard of review may be modified to arrive at a new standard of review. When this methodology is applied across the various WTO Agreements, it is likely to generate different standards of review. These different standards will be discussed in more detail in Chapters 6 and 7. The first part of this chapter therefore focuses more on the

---

5 Claus-Dieter Ehlermann and Nicolas Lockhart, 'Standard of Review in WTO Law' (2004) 7(3) *Journal of International Economic Law* 491.

6 See Chapter 3, Section 3.2.3 for a description of the reasonable regulator test.

7 A specific standard of review is also referred to in this book as a modified standard of review or a flexible standard of review. Modified standard of review is more descriptive of this standard's relation to the general standard of review. Flexible standard of review is more descriptive of the way the specific standard may be applied.

basic issues of when a specific standard of review should apply, and, if so, how.

It will be argued that the catalyst for moving from the general standard of review to a specific standard should be when a WTO Agreement provides for members to retain particular jurisdictional competencies to carry out or maintain WTO obligations. The expression 'jurisdictional competencies' in this context refers to processes or decisions that are left up to the membership to carry out or make.[8] This will usually involve the WTO Agreements setting out some kind of special role for domestic authorities. In practical terms, this refers to a situation where a domestic decision-maker has been given some responsibility or discretion in carrying out or safeguarding WTO obligations. The general standard of review may therefore be varied in a number of ways, depending upon the specific competencies that are retained by the membership. It will be the nature and extent of the change in this allocation of responsibility that leads to the creation of different standards.

Once the threshold criterion is set out, I will then deal with the methods by which panels would modify the standard of review. I will argue that the question of how different standards of review may be formulated will also depend upon the nature and extent of the jurisdictional competencies retained by members. These competencies require analysis to determine the more precise contours of the standard. However, there will be common approaches under WTO Agreements that deal with similar subject matters and processes. In many instances, there will be a narrowing of the general standard of review by restricting the type of facts or findings that may be reviewed, or alternatively, by restricting how intensively matters may be scrutinized. A specific standard of review is therefore likely to generate some degree of deference towards member measures. However, I will also contend in this chapter that the specific standard is unlikely to be as deferential as other standards, such as the reasonable regulator test.[9]

In the final section I will discuss the major arguments for and against the introduction of a specific standard of review. I will contend that there is a compelling basis for its introduction as compared with merely retaining the general standard of review. Common criticisms of a standard of review that is flexible in nature include that such a standard may be overly complex to apply, or that it may protect dubious measures from proper scrutiny by panels.[10] A specific standard is unlikely to over complicate the standard of review as it would not be framed very differently when applied in respect of a number of similar agreements, such as the trade remedy agreements. It is also unlikely to

8 See Chapter 5, Section 5.2.1.
9 See Chapter 3, Section 3.2.6.
10 See Chapter 3, Section 3.2.5.

result in a major diminution in panel scrutiny or any consequential weakening of the dispute settlement system. More than anything, it is about recognizing the primacy of domestic processes and decision-making in the system, and determining how the panel system may be improved over time.

5.2 THE APPLICATION OF A SPECIFIC STANDARD OF REVIEW

5.2.1 The Threshold Test for the Modification of the General Standard of Review

This section discusses the threshold test for determining when the general standard of review should be modified. The threshold test will distinguish the circumstances when the general standard rather than the specific standard of review should be applied. What is proposed is that panels should apply a specific standard of review where a WTO Agreement stipulates that WTO members are to retain jurisdictional competencies in connection with the issuing and enforcing of measures. The threshold test therefore focuses on the concept of allocation of jurisdictional competencies between the WTO and the membership.

The expression 'jurisdictional competency' does not have a definitive meaning. It can be broadly described as the delimitation of a boundary within which a body has the authority and expertise to make decisions or otherwise exert its influence. It may mark the division of responsibility between different courts within a judicial system or, in an international setting, it may refer to the ability of an international organization to adjudicate in relation to the conduct of states.[11] The term 'jurisdiction' conveys the meaning of some kind of authority or power to make decisions or otherwise deal with a particular subject matter. It has been described as 'the right, power or authority to administer justice by hearing and determining controversies'.[12] Jurisdiction may be exercised within a geographic territory and it may be restricted to particular

---

11 See for example, a discussion regarding the jurisdictional competency of States and the International Criminal Court to prosecute crimes in Timothy L.H. McCormack and Sue Robertson, 'Jurisdictional Aspects of the Rome Statute for the New International Criminal Court' (1999) 23 *Melbourne University Law Review* 635.

12 *The Macquarie Dictionary* (Macquarie, 5th ed, 2009) 906 which provides: 'Jurisdiction: 1. The right, power or authority to administer justice by hearing and determining controversies. 2. Power; authority; control. 3. The extent or range of judicial or other authority. 4. The territory over which authority is exercised.'

disciplines or be limited in other ways.[13] It is often difficult to define in a practical sense because it is seen as part of the distribution of power within a legal system, and is therefore subject to change or manipulation.[14] In public international law the concept of jurisdiction is connected with the notion of sovereignty of states. It is often used to describe the lawful power of a state to define rights and duties and control the conduct of natural and juridical persons.[15]

Competence, in a legal sense, frequently refers to the capacity or fitness of a person to enter into legal relations or give evidence.[16] In the context of an institution having competency, the term relies more on the plain English definition. The Macquarie Dictionary defines 'competent' as: '1. properly qualified; capable. 2. fitting, suitable, or sufficient for the purpose; adequate.'[17] The emphasis upon the adequacy of the qualifications of an institution is the aspect of this term that is most relevant to international law. However, sometimes competency is not used to refer such qualities, but rather to the ability of an institution to assert its jurisdiction.[18] This equates competency with a kind of

---

13 *Butterworths Australian Legal Dictionary* (Butterworths, 1997) 651 which provides: 'Jurisdiction: The scope of the court's power to examine and determine facts, interpret and apply the law, make orders and declare judgment. Jurisdiction may be limited by geographic area, the type of parties who appear, the type of relief sought, and the point to be decided.'

14 See Sir Franklin Berman, 'Jurisdiction: The State', in Patrick Capps, Malcolm Evans and Stratos Konstadinidis (eds), *Asserting Jurisdiction, International and European Legal Perspectives* (Hart Publishing, 2003) 3, 3 where the author states that '"Jurisdiction" is a protean concept. Its contours are not readily definable and change over time. They change both in terms of what States wish to do (or would like to be able to do) in the exercise of power externally, and in terms of the willingness of the system of international law to recognize their exercise.'

15 Bernard H. Oxman, *Jurisdiction of States*, Max Planck Encyclopedia of Public International Law, available at http://www.mpepil.com, last accessed 31 March 2012.

16 See *Butterworths Australian Legal Dictionary* (Butterworths, 1997), 352 which provides: 'Competence: In relation to evidence, a witness's capacity or capability to testify in a legal proceeding.' See also *The Macquarie Dictionary*, above n 12, which provides: 'Competent: 3. Law (of a witness, a party to a contract, etc.) having legal capacity or qualification. [Latin competens, present participle,being fit].'

17 *The Macquarie Dictionary*, above n 12, 352. See also *The Oxford English Dictionary* (Oxford University Press, 2nd ed, 1989) 604, which defines 'Competent' as: '6. *Law* Legally qualified or sufficient. a. of a judge, court etc.: possessing jurisdiction or authority to act; b. of a witness, evidence etc.: capable of being brought forward, admissible; c. of a case etc.: within the jurisdiction of a court.'

18 In a private international law context see Michael Pryles, 'The Basis of Adjudicatory Competence in Private International Law' (1972) 21 *International & Comparative Law Quarterly* 61.

power or authority.[19] There is therefore a significant amount of overlap in the way the expressions jurisdiction and competency may be defined. Competency, in particular, is prone to feature within definitions of jurisdiction, as is exemplified below:

> 'Jurisdiction' is a form of legal power or competence. In a Hohfeldian sense, this means that jurisdiction concerns a competence to control and alter the legal relationships of those subject to that competence via the creation and application of legal norms.[20]

> When jurisdiction is considered to be the delimitation of competence, it is helpful to think of it as the distribution of *authority* (as distinguished from power) among different legal institutions and separate political entities. It is a formalistic description of the legal order within any social system.[21]

Despite the interwoven nature of the usage of these terms, it is important to view jurisdiction as conveying the idea of authority, and competency distinctly focussing on expertise. This is a major reason why the expression 'jurisdictional competency' is used in preference to the expression 'jurisdiction'. That is, the composite expression goes beyond the notion of an institution merely having formal authority and it suggests that an institution has an expertise to deal with the relevant subject matter. It may also connote some kind of responsibility for a body to deal with matters that have been assigned to it.[22] In addition, as jurisdictional competency may relate to a distribution of authority, then it may also be a pragmatic response in order to express a preference for particular institutions, (such as international versus domestic) to deal with different issues.

In the context of the WTO, at its broadest jurisdictional competency refers

---

[19] In some contexts, such as under French law, competency is also understood to mean the right of a court to exercise jurisdiction in a particular case. See Renata Szafarz, *The Compulsory Jurisdiction of the International Court of Justice* (Kluwer Academic Publishers, 1993) 2.

[20] See Patrick Capps, Malcolm Evans and Stratos Konstadinidis (eds), *Asserting Jurisdiction, International and European Legal Perspectives* (Hart Publishing, 2003) ix. The expression 'Hohfeldian' refers to Wesley Hohfeld, a Harvard law professor in the early part of the 20th Century, who developed an analytical framework for understanding interests in property. Hohfeld developed terms that are arranged as either 'correlatives' or 'opposites' in order to structure the internal relationships among the different fundamental legal rights. For example: 'Right' versus 'no-right' are known as jural opposites and 'right' and 'duty' as jural correlatives.

[21] Richard Falk, *The Role of Domestic Courts in the International Legal Order* (Syracuse University Press, 1964) 21.

[22] Renata Szafarz, *The Compulsory Jurisdiction of the International Court of Justice*, above n 19, 1.

to the scope of the authority of the WTO to regulate the multilateral trading system.[23] This authority is a product of the 'collective will' of the WTO membership in that individual members have relinquished authority to the WTO in specific policy areas in order to achieve certain agreed objectives.[24] In turn, this may generate ongoing tension between the interests of states and the interests of a centralized body like the WTO.[25] However, the expression jurisdictional competency in the context of this book concerns the role of dispute settlement panels, and their relationship with domestic bodies that carry out similar decision-making functions. These bodies are usually government departments or agencies exercising significant administrative decision-making powers.[26] More rarely they are domestic Courts or Tribunals that are reviewing administrative decisions.[27] The question to be resolved is whether a particular issue should be decided by a panel or by a domestic body, or if there is some kind of division of responsibility, where that point lies.

In some WTO Agreements, members are charged with the initial responsibility of determining whether WTO obligations have been complied with.[28] In many cases, this involves members setting up investigation and dispute settlement mechanisms at a domestic level to determine whether compliance has occurred.[29] Within some disciplines, there is therefore an allocation or division of responsibility between the WTO and the membership. This delineation of

---

[23] The status and authority of the World Trade Organization is prescribed in number of provisions of the Marrakesh Agreement Establishing the World Trade Organization. Article II(1) states that 'The WTO shall provide the common institutional framework for the conduct of trade relations among its Members in matters related to the agreements and associated legal instruments included in the Annexures to this Agreement.'

[24] The Final Act Embodying the Results of the Uruguay Round of Multilateral Trade Negotiations embodies the outcome of collective negotiations by the contracting parties to the GATT 1947. Article 4 of this Act only permitted acceptance of the Agreements as a whole. This arrangement is often referred to as the 'single undertaking'. This approach evidences the fact that members are required to compromise their trade objectives for a unified set of outcomes, including the appointment of the WTO as a centralized body to administer these outcomes.

[25] See Deborah Cass, *The Constitutionalization of the World Trade Organization* (Oxford University Press, 2005), 211–12.

[26] See Sharif Bhuiyan, *National Law in WTO Law: Effectiveness and Good Governance in the World Trading System* (Cambridge University Press, 2007) 207–9.

[27] *Ibid.*

[28] Major examples include Articles 3 and 4 of the Safeguards Agreement, Article 3 of the Anti-Dumping Agreement, Articles 11 and 15 of the SCM Agreement, and special safeguards referred to in Article 5 of the Agreement on Agriculture and Article 6 of the ACT.

[29] Note that domestic bodies will frequently be reviewing domestic regulation, which incorporates a member's WTO obligations.

jurisdictional competencies will also vary between the WTO Agreements because each Agreement has a different way of assigning adjudicative scrutiny of compliance due to its unique subject matter. Depending upon one's own theoretical perspective, the relationship between panels and domestic bodies may nonetheless to some degree be viewed as an example of wider constitutional relationship between international organizations and nation states.[30]

The expression 'jurisdictional competencies' was discussed by the Appellate Body in *EC-Hormones*. In that decision, the Appellate Body applied this expression in the following way:

> The standard of review applicable in proceedings under the *SPS Agreement,* of course must reflect the balance established in that Agreement between the jurisdictional competencies conceded by the Members to the WTO and the jurisdictional competencies retained by the Members for themselves. To adopt a standard of review not clearly rooted in the text of the *SPS Agreement* itself, may well amount to changing that finely drawn balance; and neither a panel nor the Appellate Body is authorized to do that.[31]

In this extract, the Appellate Body refers to jurisdictional competencies in terms of the broad framing of these competencies in the WTO Agreements and the institutional role undertaken by the WTO. However, in the second sentence, there is also a direct reference to the ability of panels or the Appellate Body to, in effect, change the division of jurisdictional competencies set out in the WTO Agreements by applying a different standard of review. Further, by implication, the Appellate Body is making reference to the relationship between panels and domestic authorities because, under many WTO Agreements, these authorities have a particular role that is set out in the text of the Agreements.

The above reasoning of the Appellate Body therefore supports the proposition that when panels are reviewing measures, they should apply a standard

---

[30] See Cass, *The Constitutionalization of the World Trade Organization: Legitimacy, Democracy and Community in the International Trading System*, above n 25, 15–18; Sabino Cassese, 'Administrative Law Without the State? The challenge of Global Regulation' 37 (2005) *New York University Journal of International Law and Politics* 680.

[31] Appellate Body Report, *EC-Hormones* [115]. It is recalled that this issue was raised by the Appellate Body in rejecting an argument by the European Communities that a new 'deferential reasonableness' standard of review should be applied in 'all highly complex factual situations'. The Appellate Body was rejecting the imposition of a new standard of review that imported new adjudicatory concepts, such as one based on reasonableness. In adopting a standard of review derived from Article 11 of the DSU, the Appellate Body was taking a textual approach, and it could also be applied in a somewhat flexible way that could take account of any differences in jurisdictional competencies within each Agreement.

that takes into account jurisdictional competencies retained by members in the WTO Agreements. Panels should therefore, in broad terms, give due recognition to the role of a domestic authority prescribed under the relevant agreement. For example, if the measure is the result of an investigation and published findings that is contemplated by an agreement, then this should be taken into account in the panel review. To use the words of the Appellate Body in *EC-Hormones*, the standard of review ought to be 'clearly rooted' in the text of the WTO Agreements in order for panels to be faithful to the preservation of rights and obligations agreed to by the membership.[32] This recognition of jurisdiction competencies involves more than merely applying the terms of the WTO Agreements. It may include modifying the standard of review itself in order to accommodate the division of jurisdictional competencies.

Whilst no other WTO Tribunal decisions expressly make reference to jurisdictional competencies, it was relied upon by Australia in its submissions in the case of *Australia-Apples*.[33] Australia contended that the extent of deference to be shown by a panel can be ascertained by examining the distribution of decision-making authority between members and the WTO enshrined in the SPS Agreement.[34] Australia argued that these jurisdictional competencies will usually be evidenced by some form of limitation on the nature of panel scrutiny in a panel's assessment of factual matters in relation to particular obligations, such as when reviewing SPS risk assessments.[35]

Further, various WTO cases implicitly deal with this issue when they discuss the need for a standard of review to be partly drawn from the text of the relevant agreement or when they emphasize the importance of the role of a domestic authority. This has occurred in a number of trade remedy decisions. In *US-Lamb*, the Appellate Body stipulated that a panel's review obligations stemmed in part from Article 11 of the DSU, and in part from requirements of Article 4.2 of the Safeguards Agreement.[36] In *US-Cotton Yarn*, the Appellate Body confirmed that the principles relevant to the review of safeguards, and in particular the investigatory role of the competent authority, applied for cases concerning the safeguard provisions of the ATC.[37] The Appellate Body, in *US-Countervailing Duty Investigation on DRAMS*, echoed this more forcefully in determining that 'Article 11 of the DSU must be understood in the light of the

---

32 *Ibid.*

33 *Australia-Apples*, First Written Submissions of Australia [184]–[187]. See further discussion of *Australia-Apples* in Chapter 2, Section 2.4.3.

34 *Ibid.*

35 *Ibid* [185].

36 Appellate Body Report, *US-Lamb* [105].

37 Appellate Body Report, *US-Cotton Yarn* [76].

obligations of the particular covered agreement.'[38] More significantly, in *US-Continued Suspension*, the Appellate Body found that the panel had not applied a sufficiently deferential standard of review in examining whether a member's risk assessment complied with Article 5.1 of the SPS Agreement.[39] The above decisions highlight the fact that there is considerable authority within existing WTO jurisprudence to develop a standard of review that is more formally based on the division of jurisdictional competencies between panels and domestic authorities under the WTO Agreements.

The above discussion of WTO cases raises the issue of how panels might decide when jurisdictional competencies will affect the standard of review that they apply. In other words, how would a panel know whether to apply the general standard of review, as described in Chapter 4, or a modified standard? The starting point is to determine whether there is a division of jurisdictional competencies between the WTO and members in relation to measures that may be subject to panel review. If the relevant agreement does not nominate a role for a domestic authority in decision-making processes concerning measures, then it is less likely that there would be any division of jurisdictional competencies, and in which case the general standard of review would be applied. Conversely, if the role of a competent authority is provided for in the Agreement, then this would signify the *prima facie* requirement to apply a different standard of review.

It is necessary, however, to go beyond the mere identification of the role of a domestic authority in the relevant agreement. In order to satisfy this threshold test, at least one of two further relevant factors will need to be met. Firstly, it is critical that the role of the competent authority involves a formal review of the measures, or at least the formal investigation of facts and matters giving rise to the measures.[40] That is, it is still necessary to examine the text of the WTO Agreements to determine whether the domestic authority has been granted the primary role as the reviewer or investigator of matters that are now before a panel. Evidence of this role would include factors such as the powers granted to the authority, any procedures it must follow and the level of discretion to reach findings. Secondly, it is also relevant to determine whether the particular WTO obligations that are in dispute are required to be satisfied through the involvement of a domestic authority. The trade remedy agreements set out a more formal role for domestic authorities, whereas other types of regulation, such as those dealt with under the SPS and TBT Agreements, are

38 Appellate Body Report, *US-Countervailing Duty Investigation on DRAMS* [184].

39 Appellate Body Report, *US-Continued Suspension* [590]. See discussion in Chapter 2, Section 2.4.3.

40 This is because in some cases the authority is not the issuer of the measures.

more likely to prescribe substantive obligations without mandating the domestic processes that will satisfy those obligations.[41] Therefore, if in practice, a formal domestic process needs to be undertaken prior to the adoption of a measure, then such a process must be taken into account even if it is not referred to in the WTO Agreements. In this situation there is still cause to depart from the general standard of review. It is the role undertaken by domestic authorities, whether directly prescribed, or incorporated by reference to WTO obligations that signifies the retaining of jurisdictional competencies by the membership.

Another way of conceiving this threshold or condition precedent for a modification to the standard of review is to determine whether, and if so, to what extent, a panel would be acting as a second tier of review following the processes that are carried out at a national level. If the role of a panel is more in the nature of revisiting domestic authority findings than reviewing a measure for the first time, then it is likely that the panel should be applying a modified standard of review. This distinction can be put in the following terms: 'the role of a panel is to review, not redo, what has been done at a national level'.[42] For disputes litigated under the trade remedy agreements, the invoking of a modified standard of review is likely to be relatively self-evident, but it may be less obvious with regards to, for example, an SPS measure that was based on a government-commissioned scientific report.[43] It is, therefore, possible to view individual WTO Agreements across a spectrum in which the jurisdictional competencies are wholly with the WTO at one end, and wholly with the domestic authority at the other. Each WTO Agreement may be placed along this spectrum depending upon the extent and nature of the obligations that must be carried out by a domestic authority. Where there are obligations that are necessary to be carried out by a domestic authority, then this will act as a signal for panels to modify the general standard of review. Whilst these obligations may not be easy to identify in the first instance, it would not be difficult for panels to develop short-form conventions as to which WTO obligations would give rise to a specific standard of review, and similar obligations could be grouped accordingly.

---

41 Articles 2.2, 5.1 and 5.5 of the SPS Agreement and Articles 2.1 to 2.8 of the TBT Agreement are examples of substantive obligations that may be formally carried out by a domestic authority.

42 See Ehlermann and Lockhart, 'Standard of Review in WTO Law', above n 5, 508. The expression 'review not redo' is discussed in the context of the operation of the Agreement on Safeguards and the SCM Agreement.

43 For example, Panel Report, *EC-Hormones (US)* [8.108]–[8.111]; Panel Report, *Japan-Apples* [4.138]–[4.140] where the evidentiary basis of particular SPS measures in dispute are discussed.

The use of jurisdictional competencies as a variable to construct new standards of review will mean that the nature of panel review will be more closely aligned with the type of measure being reviewed. This makes it an obvious and practical 'trigger point' for panels being required to adjust the standard of review that they apply. In other words, if scrutiny of a measure or of the issues giving rise to the measure has occurred domestically, then panels can compensate for this in their own analysis of the case before them. This will mean that, from a practical point of view, panels may be better able to appropriately identify their review task depending upon the evidence and the processes that have occurred prior to the panel being established.[44] The allocation of jurisdictional competencies between a panel and a domestic authority does not, however, of itself set the exact contours as to how panels would need to modify the standard of review. A specific standard of review requires further criteria to more accurately define such contours. In the next section, I will seek to set forth the criteria for applying a specific standard of review.

5.2.2 The Method of Construction of a Specific Standard of Review

The previous section dealt with the issue of when the general standard of review should be modified. It was argued that the retaining of jurisdictional competencies by members should signify a change in approach by panels, and that the nature and extent of these competencies retained should give some guidance as to the type of standard used. This section concerns the question of how panels might, in practice, modify the way in which they review cases. To put it another way, how might a panel go about modifying the standard of review when it is assessing cases that have already been scrutinized by a domestic authority?[45] This section will discuss how panels ought to adjust their approach in the light of the subject matter under review. Panels require more detailed guidance as to types of factors that would evidence the need for a specific standard of review, and, in turn, the way in which they would adjust their approach. The general proposition that more responsibility given to a national authority will result in a less intensive standard of review needs to be explored in further detail.

---

44 See Stephen Croley and John H. Jackson, 'WTO Dispute Procedures, Standard of Review and Deference to National Governments' (1996) 90(2) *American Journal of International Law* 211. Some of the practical aspects of a modified standard of review are discussed by the authors in the context of analysing the anti-dumping standard of review under Article 17.6 of the Anti-Dumping Agreement.

45 The domestic review processes being discussed are not intended to include legislative processes for implementing WTO obligations. These processes would not warrant changing the standard of review. Jurisdictional competencies retained by members are usually evidenced by separate domestic processes, in which a member examines whether WTO obligations have been complied with.

A specific standard of review represents a change in the general standard of review that was described in Chapter 4. The general standard is therefore the starting point for determining how panels are to approach their review task where members have retained jurisdictional competencies. When applying the general standard, panels must satisfy its two limbs: the requirement to examine all available and sufficient evidence, and the requirement to conduct a comprehensive review.[46] These limbs do not place many restrictions on the review process. Accordingly, the way in which panels should apply a specific standard of review is by narrowing these two limbs. This will occur, firstly, by narrowing the extent of the fact-finding processes carried out by panels, and secondly, by lessening the intensity of the review process. Regarding the first limb, a panel would, for example, in a safeguards dispute, focus on the factual record of the investigating authority and perform little or no independent fact-finding. It is, of course, much easier for panels to adjust the first limb, being the formal process of review, as opposed to the second limb, which concerns the manner of substantive review. The question then becomes more one of how panels are to be guided as to the intensity of their review. This may be quite a subjective exercise for panels and it is not easy to address.[47]

Broadly, it is argued that the major determinant of the specific standard of review is the extent of formality of procedures carried out by a domestic authority, either in accordance with WTO provisions, or otherwise in order to satisfy WTO obligations. The formulation of a specific standard of review, like the threshold issue of moving to a specific standard, is therefore based upon the division of jurisdictional competencies. However, once the threshold issues have been met, it is the *extent* to which jurisdictional competencies have been retained which becomes critical. Panels should, accordingly, adopt a less intensive standard of review where the WTO Agreements clearly set out or contemplate a role for domestic authorities in the review or issuing of measures. Domestic authorities such as government departments, instrumentalities, courts and tribunals may be involved in carrying out these processes. The extent to which these types of domestic authorities are performing WTO-related competencies may be evidenced by factors including the nature of any investigation, review or adjudication, and whether the reasoning and findings have been published.

Ehlermann and Lockhart divide domestic procedures into three categories.[48] The first category is the trade remedy agreements, which prescribe

---

[46] See Chapter 4, Sections 4.2.1 and 4.2.2.

[47] See for example, Appellate Body Report, *US-Countervailing Duty Investigation on DRAMS* [189]–[190] where the Appellate Body found that some aspects of the panel's review amounted to a *de novo* review.

[48] Ehlermann and Lockhart, 'Standard of Review in WTO Law', above n 5, 503.

very formal procedures. The second category is the non-trade remedy agreements that impose some procedures on members, and the third category is those WTO Agreements that give members the complete freedom as to the manner in which they implement their WTO obligations.[49] Based on this classification, it is likely that the trade remedy agreements will involve the greatest modification to the general standard of review. The second category would include the SPS and TBT Agreements. Disputes under these agreements usually concern measures that have already been subject to some level of scrutiny by domestic authorities, but these Agreements do not set out formal procedures and obligations of members in any detail. Panel review of a number of obligations under these Agreements would result in a lesser change in the standard. By contrast, the third category, which would include the GATT and a number of other WTO Agreements, involves the direct imposition of WTO obligations and no mediating role for domestic authorities. Disputes under these Agreements would not involve any modification to the general standard of review.[50]

The above framework represents a 'sliding scale' approach to the standard of review issue. More formal domestic processes will lead to a less intensive standard of review, and the reverse will also apply. It will mean that WTO Agreements containing a similar structure and obligations will produce like standards of review. It is therefore very unlikely that there would be any progressive fragmentation of the standard of review. Further, under this 'scale', the collective processes that are undertaken by domestic authorities and panels should result in adequate oversight of WTO obligations without any duplication of effort. To put this succinctly, oversight of WTO obligations will be either exclusively undertaken by panels or in combination with domestic processes occurring with appropriate WTO supervision.[51]

This approach does not, however, identify specific criteria for panels to use in the review process. In seeking to set out the contours of a specific standard of review, it is important to note that it is all but impossible to design a meaningful standard of review that completely disposes of panel subjectivity. For example, it is difficult for a panel to assess the bureaucratic and scientific issues that have been dealt with at a domestic level to determine if there is a lawful basis for SPS measures. The most significant consideration is for panels

---

49 *Ibid.*

50 Various WTO Agreements and the major obligations that would affect the standard of review are further explored in chapters 6 and 7. Examples of Agreements falling into this category include the Agreement on Import Licensing Procedures or the Agreement on Implementation of Article VII of GATT 1994, which deals with customs valuation.

51 See Bhuiyan, *National Law in WTO Law*, above n 26, 146.

to focus on the overall quality of the review process that has been conducted by the domestic authorities. General criteria that a panel ought to use when examining domestic processes might include:

1. whether the domestic review is based upon the best available and reliable evidence (including the use of expert evidence, where applicable);
2. whether the domestic review contains adequate reasoning and analysis and that any conclusions drawn are consistent with such evaluation;
3. what, if any, limitations exist in the domestic procedures;
4. the extent of transparency in the domestic processes;
5. whether any distinct methods of interpretation were used by domestic authorities.[52]

It is noted that all of the above points concern the formal aspect of review at a domestic level. That is, they relate to the way in which the domestic processes have been carried out. However, some of these points also inevitably go further and deal with the substantive review undertaken by domestic authorities. This is particularly the case for point 2, and to some extent for points 4 and 5. It is, of course, more difficult to set down guidelines for how panels are to apply these three criteria because, in assessing whether these criteria are met, panels are forced to make more subjective assessments due to the unique circumstances of each case.

In linking the above criteria to the need for a specific standard of review, what is proposed is for panels to develop frameworks which match these criteria with the competencies retained in the particular WTO Agreement under review. This aspect of the new test will be dealt with in detail in Chapters 6 and 7. However, to demonstrate this aspect, one such framework that might be applied, where formal processes or obligations are left for members, might comprise the following directives:

1. in examining the veracity of evidence, it is not necessary to evince new evidence unless there is a lack of evidence or unless the evidence is impugned by a lack of good faith;
2. in assessing the adequacy of the reasoning and conclusions, it is necessary to ensure that a high degree of consistency is present, but the testing of each proposition relied upon is not required;
3. in examining limitations existing in domestic procedures, determine only

52 Tracey Epps, 'Reconciling Public Opinion and the WTO Rules under the SPS Agreement' (2008) 7(2) *World Trade Review* 359, 381. In this article, Epps draws up a similar list of criteria for panels in the context of the review of SPS measures.

whether such limitations are likely to affect the domestic authority findings that are now in dispute;[53]

4. determine whether minimum standards of transparency have been met, such as the publication of reasons;
5. identify whether any distinct methods of interpretation have been used that would affect the outcome.

The above list of points is, in many respects, less complex and controversial than it superficially suggests. Panels should, for instance, be entitled to make judgments about the integrity of domestic processes in circumstances where there may be an absence of due process, good faith, or at the extreme end of the spectrum, possible corruption. Further, in reference to point 5, it is well recognized that panels have the competency to examine questions of interpretation concerning measures, which are frequently identified as legal rather than factual issues.[54]

In this section, I have been arguing that a specific standard of review would involve firstly, panels modifying the general standard of review to reflect any jurisdictional competencies retained by WTO members, and secondly, panels examining the quality of domestic processes giving rise to the measures so as to verify that the competencies exercised by members are WTO-consistent. The more precise 'contours' of the standard of review are therefore a combination of the delineation of jurisdictional competencies in the WTO Agreements and the task of panels to determine the substantive legal question in issue. On this basis, panels will still need to determine, in each case, how narrowly or widely they define their review task using the above criteria. The overarching determinant of a panel's approach to these criteria is the nature of the obligations or processes that have been retained by members under the WTO Agreements. As a general proposition, the greater the extent to which members have retained jurisdictional competencies, the less rigorously panels will be required to investigate domestic processes and decision-making. The more subtle determinant of the standard of review will be the specific WTO obligations in issue and the legal question that a panel is required to answer.

---

53 This is to be contrasted with 'as such' claims where a member's laws are challenged for being WTO inconsistent (see for example: Appellate Body Report, *Dominican Republic-Import and Sale of Cigarettes* [107] which discusses panel jurisdiction in respect of as such claims).

54 A good example of the WTO mandate on questions of interpretation is to be found in the various Zeroing cases. The clearest statement by the Appellate Body regarding this practice is in *US-Continued Zeroing* [299]–[313]. Zeroing concerns the controversial practice of the United States in anti-dumping investigations of not including any negative dumping margins in determining whether dumping had occurred.

Since *EC-Hormones* panels have attempted to adjust the standard of review through the lens of the objective assessment test, but based upon the type of measures being reviewed. Panels have therefore to some extent self-regulated the standard of review and, at times, have applied a standard that is similar to the test that is being proposed in this book. The difficulty with this approach is that there is no guidance for panels to identify and apply an appropriate standard of review. What has occurred several times with panel decisions is that panels have tried to identify a standard that is partly based on Article 11 of the DSU and partly based upon the text of the relevant WTO Agreement, but they have ended up generally applying a standard that is in fact much more intensive and closer to *de novo* review.[55] Accordingly, providing panels with more direct instruction about how they should review particular WTO obligations in light of jurisdictional competencies retained by members would assist panels to fulfil their function and it would also demonstrate a more balanced approach to dispute settlement.

5.2.3 The Treatment of Facts and Law

With the treatment of facts and law, a flexible standard of review does provide for a review of facts that is different from that of the general standard. The approach of panels to facts is likely to involve less scrutiny of facts than with respect to the general standard. There may, for instance, be more panel acceptance of the way in which facts were gathered or appraised by domestic authorities. This approach by panels is usually couched in terms of the degree of deference that a panel demonstrates towards the member whose measures are under review.[56] The standard of review will therefore change in relation to an assessment of facts, depending upon the extent of the panel's movement away from the general standard of review.

By contrast, whether a set of facts or a measure complies with the text of a WTO Agreement is a legal question.[57] It is entirely proper for legal questions to be the complete preserve of panels and panels should not be required to

[55] In Appellate Body Report, *US-Lamb* [106] the Appellate Body advocated a highly intensive standard of review that goes a considerable way towards *de novo* review and findings of whether the domestic authority was 'right' or 'wrong' in the first instance. See also Appellate Body Report, *Japan-DRAMs (Korea)* [134], in which the Appellate Body found that the panel's failure to conduct an active review of evidence was inconsistent with Article 11 of the DSU, and this arguably shifts the standard closer to *de novo* review.

[56] For further discussion of the principle of deference see Chapter 1, Section 1.2.1 and Chapter 3, Section 3.3.

[57] Appellate Body Report, *EC-Hormones* [132] with the relevant extract set out in Section 4.2.3 of Chapter 4.

soften their approach to these questions.[58] Therefore, it is advocated that a non-deferential standard of review be applied to questions of law, irrespective of whether the general standard or any specific standard has been applied in reviewing facts. This approach will mean that there will usually be a difference between the standard of review of facts and law where a specific standard is applied, and this differs from the general standard, where the approach to facts and law is very similar.

In Chapter 4, I gave reasons as to why a standard of review that was the same for facts and law was more attractive.[59] One of the major advantages of a uniform approach is to avoid entering into definitional disputes about whether the question under review is legal or factual in nature. Indeed, some questions arising under particular WTO Agreements may be regarded as mixed questions of fact and law, which arguably can make a panel review more difficult.[60] This criticism is acknowledged and, in principle, it would be more advantageous to design a standard of review that was uniform for questions of fact and law. However, it is contended that a standard that examines factual and legal matters differently does not necessarily impose additional burdens upon panels. As with many domestic courts and tribunals, it is well within the competency of panels to distinguish between issues of fact and law. In many cases where a domestic authority decision is under review, all aspects of such a decision may be categorized as factual issues, as opposed to the ultimate consideration of whether the decision is WTO consistent, which is a legal question.[61]

In cases where it may be difficult to distinguish between factual and legal questions, the Appellate Body safeguards this distinction when reviewing panel findings. This is necessary because the Appellate Body must determine what constitutes a legal question when exercising its jurisdiction under Article 17.6 of the DSU.[62] In *US-Stainless Steel (Mexico)*, the Appellate Body stated that:

---

58 Oesch, *Standards of Review in WTO Dispute Resolution*, above n 2, 173–4.

59 Chapter 4, Section 4.2.3.

60 For example, under the Anti-Dumping Agreement, panels may be required to review a domestic authority's determination of whether a particular set of facts constitutes injury pursuant to Article 3. It may be difficult to separate the facts relied upon by the authority from the issue of whether the decision made under domestic legislation conforms to the requirements of the Anti-Dumping Agreement.

61 In the analytic tradition this draws the distinction between the *factum probandum* (the ultimate fact in issue) and *facts probantia* (the facts adduced to prove or disprove that ultimate fact). For a discussion of this distinction see Mark Aronson, 'Unreasonableness and Error of Law' (2001) *University of New South Wales Law Journal* 26. See also Appellate Body Report, *India-Patents (US)* [66]–[68].

62 See for example Appellate Body Report, *Canada-Periodicals* [22]. For further discussion of this point see Voon and Yanovich, 'The Facts Aside: The Limitation of WTO Appeals to Issues of Law', above n 1, 239.

> The creation of the Appellate Body by WTO Members to review legal interpretations developed by panels shows that Members recognized the importance of consistency and stability in the interpretation of their rights and obligations under the covered agreements.[63]

There have been a number of decisions where the Appellate Body has made findings of whether a matter before it was factual or legal in nature.[64]

It is also important to bear in mind that the overall structure of a specific standard of review is more important than the need for uniformity in the standard. In other words, the level of scrutiny of measures is the most important consideration. It is essential that the legal standard of review is not deferential, and there are strong arguments in favour of tailoring the factual standard as argued in this chapter. Both of these separately outweigh the desirability of uniformity. Despite this, there is unlikely to be any discernable difference in the intensity of review between the legal and factual standards applied under many of the WTO Agreements where few, if any, jurisdictional competencies have been retained. In these situations, the general standard of review or a standard very close to the general standard would be applied. In the next section I will examine the legal and policy basis for a specific standard of review.

5.3 JUSTIFICATIONS FOR A SPECIFIC STANDARD OF REVIEW

In this section, I will discuss the major justifications for adopting a specific standard of review in the manner described in section 5.2 above. I will introduce section 5.3 by identifying some of the major arguments for and against a specific standard of review. In the second part of this section, I will explore the legal basis for introducing this new standard. I will argue that a specific standard of review in the form I have advocated may be justified based upon general rules of interpretation and various principles of public international law, and upon the existing body of WTO case law, which has already accommodated this type of approach. In the final two parts of this section, I will discuss the extent to which the test for a specific standard of review satisfies the principles identified in Chapter 3 and highlight its advantages over other theoretical approaches.

---

63 Appellate Body Report, *US-Stainless Steel (Mexico)* [145].

64 See for example, *US-Softwood Lumber V* [160]–[163]; *US-Upland Cotton (Article 21.5-Brazil)* [383]–[385].

5.3.1 General Arguments For and Against a Specific Standard of Review

A specific standard of review represents a movement away from the general standard in particular circumstances. Arguments about the appropriateness of this standard will inevitably focus on the issue of whether any form of deference towards the practices and interpretations of members in meeting their WTO obligations may be desirable. It is unlikely that a specific standard of review would confer an unjustified degree of deference towards WTO members.[65] For example, there may be a case to suggest that a standard based around the delineation of jurisdictional competencies is largely giving effect to the text of the WTO Agreements, and it would, if anything, prevent the WTO from overreaching in its authority.[66] For present purposes, it is assumed that a specific standard of review will result in some degree of deference, depending upon how far this standard deviates from the general standard.

The first argument in favour of a specific standard of review is that WTO Agreements will be interpreted and applied more effectively. This is because the standard of review would be made more appropriate in relation to the types of measures that are being disputed. It would also provide panels with more precise guidance as to how they should conduct the review process. The Appellate Body and panels would over time develop standards of review under various WTO Agreements taking into account the different subject matter of the Agreements. The panel review task would therefore become more practically focussed.

Opponents of this position would contend that a standard of review that is applied differently for different agreements is likely to be too complex for panels to apply.[67] This may in turn arguably lead to discrete ways of inter-

---

65 Robert Howse and Kalypso Nicolaidis, 'Enhancing WTO Legitimacy: Constitutionalization or Global Subsidiarity?' (2003) 16(1) *Governance* 73, 87 where the authors note that 'institutional sensitivity is not *mere* deference: it is consistent with strict scrutiny of national compliance with general trade regime norms such as non-discrimination, and especially procedural norms such as transparency and due process in the formulation and implementation of policies.'

66 Another interpretive approach is to argue that a modified standard of review is giving effect to 'constitutional' relationship between the WTO and members based on the principle of subsidiarity. However, it is not agreed by scholars that the principle of subsidiarity applies in WTO law and even if it did deference to non-WTO institutions is likely to be a necessary element in the definition of subsidiarity. See also Matthew Windsor, 'A Fine Balance? Delegation, Standards of Review, and Subsidiarity in WTO Dispute Settlement' (2008) 14 *Auckland University Law Review* 41.

67 Spamann discusses this complexity in relation to the use of intermediate standards of review. See Holger Spamann, 'Standard of Review for World Trade Organization Panels in Trade Remedy Cases: A Critical Analysis' (2004) 38(3) *Journal of World Trade* 533–4.

preting different WTO Agreements that could potentially diminish the uniformity in the application of fundamental WTO principles, such as non-discrimination and most favoured nation treatment.[68] This position is not sustainable as a basis to prevent the adoption of a variable standard of review per se. Panels already have to apply a separate standard of review in anti-dumping cases, and this procedural step of identifying and applying a specific standard in particular cases would not be beyond the competency of panels.[69] Further, Article 17.6 could be incorporated into the specific standard of review without the need for amendment to the WTO Agreements.[70]

A second major argument advanced in support of a specific standard of review is that it will introduce an element of institutional sensitivity to the review process.[71] This is obviously an important consideration in furthering the legitimacy of the WTO as an institution, and it would go some way towards avoiding the charge from domestic agencies and policy-makers that the WTO dispute settlement process has exceeded its mandate. Opponents of this argument would point out that any form of institutional sensitivity that leads to judicial deference by panels may result in the undermining of the DSB's authority. However, this proposition is far from made out given that the effective functioning of the DSB still relies upon cooperation from WTO members, and that the authority of the DSB is not solely a product of any formal powers exercised by the DSB.

There are various other arguments canvassed in support of, or in opposition to a standard of review that is flexible in nature. By way of example, a specific standard of review may lead to the better use of the expertise of domestic authorities in trade remedy matters. However, equally critics may point to the potential for a specific standard to lessen reliance on the expertise of WTO panels. These arguments tend to follow the traditional analysis for justifying standards of review in domestic jurisdictions, which focus on questions of

---

68 See GATT 1994, arts I, III. See Spamann, 'Standard of Review for World Trade Organization Panels in Trade Remedy Cases', above n 67, 559–60, where the author suggests that interpretations that give WTO members flexibility in complying with WTO obligations could result in the erosion of free trade benefits and he notes: 'If negotiators wish to preserve a certain margin of freedom for Members, they should do so through agreement on the substantive conditions included in the agreements'.

69 Whilst the anti-dumping standard has not to date been applied clearly and consistently (see section 2.4.4 of this book), these difficulties predominantly derive from the drafting of Article 17.6 rather than from the manner of its application by panels.

70 This is discussed in further detail in Chapter 6, Section 6.3.

71 Howse and Nicolaidis, 'Enhancing WTO Legitimacy: Constitutionalization or Global Subsidiarity?', above n 65, 87.

efficiency, delegation of powers as well as expertise.[72] It is difficult to assess a specific standard of review in relation to these policy considerations given the problems of comparing domestic institutions with the WTO.[73] However, it is extremely unlikely that a specific standard would impose additional burdens on the WTO or its members in these policy areas given that it would largely represent a shift in doctrine that matches existing panel practice.

5.3.2 The Legal Basis for a Specific Standard of Review

In Chapter 4 the legal basis for the development of a new general standard of review was articulated. It was established that a new standard has strong legal foundations, due primarily to the role of Article 3.2 of the DSU. Article 3.2 emphasizes the need to preserve the rights and obligations within the WTO Agreements, and permits provisions to be interpreted in accordance with the 'customary rules of interpretation of public international law'. This expression is understood to refer to Articles 31 and 32 of the VCLT, which incorporates both a textual and purposive approach to treaty interpretation. It was also argued that panels may develop some of their own procedures and rules based upon their inherent jurisdiction over the subject matter. A standard of review is both a method of interpretation and a tool of procedure.[74] I contend that the same argument exists for a specific standard of review as that which applies for the general standard of review. It is recalled that a specific standard of review is only applied in particular circumstances when a member's jurisdictional competencies are retained. Both of these standards are consistent with recognized sources of international law.

It is arguable that there is more justification for a specific standard of review based on international law than there exists for the general standard of review. There are a number of reasons in support of this proposition. Firstly, international law emphasizes the wording of the treaty or other 'constituent instrument' as a primary means of interpretation.[75] A specific standard of review has more of a textual foundation in the WTO Agreements than does the general standard. This is because a specific standard largely derives its char-

---

72 See Croley and Jackson, 'WTO Dispute Procedures, Standard of Review and Deference to National Governments', above n 44, 206.

73 *Ibid.*

74 Asif H. Qureshi, *Interpreting WTO Agreements* (Cambridge University Press, 2006) 224.

75 See Statute of the International Court of Justice, art 38(1), June 26, 1945, 59 Stat. 1055, 3 Bevans 1179 discussed in Ian Browlie, *Principles of Public International Law* (Oxford University Press, 7th ed, 2008) 3 and in Chester Brown, *A Common Law of International Adjudication* (Oxford University Press, 2007) 36.

acter from the division of jurisdictional competencies that are reflected in the wording of the WTO Agreements. This is to be contrasted with the general standard which is purely doctrinally based and does not rely upon the text of the WTO Agreements.

Secondly, the way in which WTO case law has evolved strongly suggests that a specific standard of review is already being applied, despite the absence of any formal doctrine giving recognition to it.[76] It is open to the Appellate Body to identify such a doctrine based upon prior dispute settlement practice.[77] In *Japan-Alcoholic Beverages II* the Appellate Body held that panel reports do not constitute subsequent practice for treaty interpretation under Article 31(3) of the VCLT,[78] and are accordingly not binding. However, despite this, there have been a significant number of panel and Appellate Body decisions that have stated that previous rulings are strongly persuasive in nature.[79] This was firmly expressed by the Appellate Body in *US-Stainless Steel (Mexico)* in stating that:

> the legal interpretation embodied in adopted panel and Appellate Body reports becomes part and parcel of the acquis of the WTO dispute settlement system[80]

and

> ensuring 'security and predictability' in the dispute settlement system implies that, absent cogent reasons, an adjudicatory body will resolve the same legal question in the same way in a subsequent case.[81]

Thirdly, whilst the VCLT expresses customary rules of interpretation of international law,[82] it does not contain an exhaustive list of principles that may be utilised to interpret the WTO Agreements.[83] There are a number of general international law principles that may be relied upon as a legal basis for a modified

---

76 See Chapter 2, Section 2.4.3.

77 Mitsuo Matsushita, Thomas J. Schoenbaum and Petros C. Mavroidis, *The World Trade Organization: Law, Practice and Policy* (Oxford University Press, 2nd ed, 2006) 111–12.

78 Appellate Body Report, *Japan-Alcoholic Beverages II* [13]–[14]. See Chapter 2, Section 2.4.1.

79 See for example, Panel Report, *US-Continued Suspension* [7.338]; Panel Report, *Canada-Continued Suspension* [7.338]; Appellate Body Report, *US-Stainless Steel (Mexico)* [145]–[162]; Panel Report, *EC-Salmon* [7.69]; Panel Report, *US-Shrimp (Thailand)* [7.32]–[7.35].

80 Appellate Body Report, *US-Stainless Steel (Mexico)* [145].

81 *Ibid.*

82 See Panel Report, *EC-Bananas III (Article 21.5-US)* [7.93].

83 Brown, *A Common Law of International Adjudication*, above n 75, 43.

standard of review. The principle of effectiveness is one such example. This principle of effectiveness assumes that the parties to a treaty intended its provisions 'to have a certain effect, and not to be meaningless'.[84] It has been employed by international courts to confirm that international organizations have powers and capacities other than those expressly conferred upon them, and to ensure the effective exercise of their own functions.[85] The principle of effectiveness was recognized by the Appellate Body in *US-Shrimp* in the context of interpreting Article XX(g) of the GATT 1994.[86] Another example is the principle of inherent jurisdiction which is discussed in Section 4.3.1 of Chapter 4.[87] Whilst caution must be exercised in applying principles to develop new standards of review, it is noteworthy that the WTO, mainly through the agency of the Appellate Body, has already employed a number of legal principles in its interpretation and application of the WTO Agreements in an effort to develop the multilateral trading system.[88] Some principles, such as the need to take an 'evolutive approach' to treaty interpretation, are more likely to be embraced,[89] whereas other more distinct principles, including proportionality and subsidiarity will be more difficult to incorporate into WTO law.[90]

5.3.3 Assessment Against Relevant Standard of Review Principles

In Chapter 4, the general standard of review was assessed against three principles: whether a standard supports the key WTO objectives, whether it promotes adjudicative legitimacy, and whether it operates effectively in conjunction with procedural aspects of dispute settlement. It was argued that the general standard is consistent with all three standards of review principles. The issue for consideration is whether a specific standard of review would

---

[84] See Sir Robert Jennings and Sir Arthur Watts (eds), *Oppenheim's International Law* (Pearson Higher Education, 9th ed, 1992) referred to in Brown, *A Common Law of International Adjudication*, above n 75, 43.

[85] *Ibid* 44.

[86] Appellate Body Report, *US-Shrimp* [131].

[87] See Andrew D. Mitchell and David Heaton, 'The Inherent Jurisdiction of WTO Tribunals: The Select Application of Public International Law Required by Judicial Function' (2010) 31 *Michigan Journal of International Law* 561.

[88] For example, the principle of good faith, referred to in Appellate Body Report, *US-Shrimp* [158]. For a list of general principles utilized in WTO law see Meinhard Hilf, 'Power, Rules and Principles – which orientation for WTO/GATT law?' (2001) 4(1) *Journal of International Economic Law* 111.

[89] Brown, *A Common Law of International Adjudication*, above n 75, 46.

[90] Axel Desmedt, 'Proportionality in WTO law' (2001) 4(3) *Journal of International Economic Law* 441.

similarly operate consistently with these principles. It is recalled that a specific standard of review is a *modification of the general standard*, and therefore the results of any analysis are unlikely to be radically different. However, what is sought to be demonstrated is that the adoption of a flexible standard of review applying either the general standard or a variant of this achieves a more ideal balancing of these principles.

It is contended that a specific standard of review would still be supportive of the key aims of WTO dispute settlement, despite there being the likelihood of more deference being conferred on members in particular disputes. This can be understood by examining it against the three elements of DSU Article 3.2, being the maintenance of security and predictability of the multilateral trading system, preservation of rights and obligations, and clarification of the meaning of WTO provisions.[91] Opponents of any deference would argue that it weakens the multilateral trading system by leading to different interpretations of WTO provisions. This is not the case because a specific standard of review does not apply to legal interpretations of WTO provisions, and only applies to the assessment of facts. Further, in assessing facts, panels would be ascribing an appropriate level of review to a review of facts under different WTO Agreements. There would still be a sufficient level of rigour in factual review by panels, and it would promote 'predictability' because it would provide guidance to panels and members as to the way in which factual assessments are conducted. Finally, there would not be any alteration in the rights and obligations of members because a specific standard is aligning the standard of review with WTO obligations. In other words, it is creating a standard of review that recognizes the rights and obligations of members precisely so that the standard of review does not vary these rights and obligations.

One can argue strongly that a specific standard of review will promote adjudicative legitimacy within the WTO. This is because whilst a specific standard is still a rigorous standard, it would generate a degree of institutional sensitivity towards members.[92] Therefore, in principle, there would both be a high level of confidence in the system as well as recognition of the role played by domestic authorities in the system. Legitimacy is a difficult concept that is a product of the complex relationships between the WTO and

---

[91] See Chapter 4, Section 4.3.1. Further, by promoting the objectives of dispute settlement, the broader WTO objectives concerning trade liberalization are also advanced.

[92] Howse and Nicolaidis, 'Enhancing WTO Legitimacy: Constitutionalization or Global Subsidiarity?', above n 71, 89; Croley and Jackson, 'WTO Dispute Procedures, Standard of Review and Deference to National Governments', above n 44, 211–13.

the membership.[93] It is very much a case of balancing the rights of members with the central authority of the WTO. Whilst the influence of a new standard of review in institutional terms is modest, it is an important step in modernizing the WTO to circumvent some of the criticisms that the WTO has exceeded its mandate or that it needs to somehow democratize its processes.

It is important to acknowledge that a specific standard of review may pose procedural challenges as well as offering benefits. On the positive side, in some cases, it would reduce the burden on panels in the areas of fact-finding and factual analysis. It would also arguably lead to more efficiency in that panels may be able to deal with cases more quickly and publish shorter rulings. By contrast, common criticisms of this standard are that it is overly complex, that it usurps panel expertise and that it is procedurally unfair in that it advantages respondents over complainants.[94] In answer to these claims, it is without doubt that a specific standard is likely to be somewhat complex to apply in the first instance. However, panels would soon have the benefit of common interpretive approaches to those provisions that are frequently litigated. Secondly, a modified standard would not result in panels being divested of their expertise as they will still be required to critically review measures. This same point applies in defence of the claim that respondents will be advantaged. Recognizing the role of domestic authorities does not equate to favouring the decisions made by those authorities. Overall, a specific standard of review is likely to generate an approach to dispute settlement that is faithful to the DSU objectives, and which advances the legitimacy of the WTO without sacrificing the integrity of the dispute settlement system.

5.3.4 Brief Assessment Against Other Standards of Review

In this section, I briefly examine how the objective assessment test and the alternative approaches discussed in Chapter 3 compare with a specific standard of review by reference to standard of review principles and any other relevant considerations.

The model proposed for a specific standard of review does bear some resemblance to the way in which the objective assessment test has been devel-

---

93 Robert Howse, 'Adjudicative Legitimacy and Treaty Interpretation in International Trade Law: The Early Years of WTO Jurisprudence' in Joseph Weiler (ed), The *EU, the WTO and the NAFTA: Toward a Common Law of International Trade* (Oxford University Press, 2000) 35.

94 The reverse is also true in that the perception of a more intrusive standard of review has led to a high number of appeals by respondents claiming that a panel failed to correctly apply Article 11 of the DSU. See Matthias Oesch, 'Standards of Review in WTO Dispute Resolution' (2003) 6(3) *Journal of International Economic Law* 635 and 658 for further discussion on this point.

oped by the Appellate Body. Like the specific standard, the objective assessment test has evolved using a general standard in the form of Article 11 of the DSU, which is then varied based upon the substantive provision under review. However, the objective assessment test suffers from the fact that it has no jurisprudential framework to dictate its functioning or how it may develop in the future.[95] Article 11 is incapable of embodying a more generalized standard of review, and it is unclear when and to what extent the objective assessment test should be varied to be read in conjunction with substantive WTO obligations. The objective assessment test is confusing and relies upon a close reading of many Appellate Body decisions in order to appreciate how it may operate. Whilst the objective assessment test may have been developed as a way of relating legal principles to the WTO texts and thus pursuing adjudicative legitimacy, it has failed in this endeavour given the frequent criticism that it has created a standard of review that is very similar to *de novo* review.[96]

When examining a specific standard against alternative standards of review it is apparent that the alternative approaches are either too extreme or they involve the introduction of new legal principles that may have difficulty being applied or accepted. The deliberation test is an example of a test that is too extreme in that it would require panels to add, as a consideration in their review, whether a measure has undergone some kind of public deliberative process.[97] This approach overemphasizes adjudicative legitimacy at the expense of achieving a strong dispute settlement regime. The reasonable regulator test is less radical, but it does introduce the administrative law concept of reasonableness as a threshold test for interpreting measures.[98] Aside from difficulties in determining what is reasonable in particular cases, there is the problem of introducing legal principles to WTO dispute settlement that have neither a connection to the WTO texts, nor an obvious linkage to the inherent jurisdiction of WTO panels. A specific standard of review has neither of these major flaws: it would operate with some sensitivity towards a member's actions without it being a radical departure from the current approach, and it basis is firmly rooted in the texts and within the authority of the WTO.

---

[95] See Chapter 2, Section 2.4.5.

[96] See Appellate Body Report, *US-Softwood Lumber VI (Article 21.5-Canada)* [93] where the Appellate Body sets out a comprehensive description of the standard of review that requires a careful and thorough examination of domestic trade remedy measures.

[97] Chapter 3, Section 3.2.2.

[98] Chapter 3, Section 3.2.3.

5.4 CONCLUSION

The purpose of this chapter was to set out the test for a specific standard of review and to advance arguments as to why it should be adopted. It would provide a sound framework for reviewing the various WTO Agreements, and, over time, panels would develop standardized approaches for assessing different Agreements. A specific standard is likely to generate a degree of deference towards some member measures. This will be based upon the obligations carried out by domestic authorities in relation to the review of facts, but not for questions of law. Based on the criteria for a specific standard, it is unlikely that there would be any deference towards measures assessed under the GATT, and little or no deference for SPS or TBT measures. By contrast, there is likely to be a greater degree of deference in the case of measures reviewed under the Anti-Dumping, SCM and Safeguards Agreements. Further, there is unlikely to be any need for deference under many other WTO Agreements such as those dealing with Customs Valuation and Import Licensing which prescribe per se measures.

In some ways, the use of the concept of deference can oversimplify matters, but it is a useful means to understand the relationship between the WTO and its members. A specific standard of review is not primarily formulated from any constitutional or administrative law principles such as those involving issues of the allocation of power, subsidiarity or proportionality. It is based around jurisdictional competencies that are derived from the text of the WTO Agreements, and could be implemented in a practical manner. It would not require renegotiation of the agreements and it could be simply embraced doctrinally by the Appellate Body.[99] The application of a specific standard of review to various WTO Agreements will be covered in Chapters 6 and 7.

---

[99] Bhuiyan, *National Law in WTO Law*, above n 26, 156.

6. The application of a new standard of review to the Trade Remedy Agreements

6.1 INTRODUCTION

In Chapters 4 and 5 of this book I advanced a theoretical alternative to the current WTO standard of review. Broadly, a two-stage test is proposed, whereby a general standard applies universally to the WTO Agreements, subject to its modification to a specific standard in particular disputes. The general standard centrally concerns the need for sufficient panel scrutiny in panel hearings, whereas the specific standard is a product of the general standard and recognition of the demarcation of responsibilities of the WTO and its members under the WTO Agreements.

Chapters 6 and 7 deal with how the new standard of review would apply to various WTO Agreements. This chapter describes how the new standard of review would apply to measures contested under the Anti-Dumping, SCM and Safeguard Agreements. The focus will be on trade remedy measures, but I also deal with subsidies. I also briefly refer to the safeguard mechanisms within the Agreement on Agriculture and the now defunct ATC.[1] In Chapters 6 and 7 it is my intention to provide a brief survey of how the new standard of review may be characterized in the selected disciplines, but there is no scope to analyse specific obligations in detail to provide a comprehensive 'map' of the standard of review.

The Trade Remedy Agreements are important in the development of a new standard of review because they generally involve the assumption of more responsibility by members for the carrying out of WTO obligations. Therefore, pursuant to the new test, the general standard of review in many cases may not apply, and each trade remedy agreement could potentially give rise to a specific standard of review. However, the application of the new standard of

[1] These trade remedy agreements are both part of Annex 1A to the Marrakesh Agreement establishing the World Trade Organization titled 'Multilateral Agreement on Trade in Goods'. The Agreement on Textiles and Clothing expired on 31 December 2004.

review to Trade Remedy Agreements may also lead to common approaches given that there are major similarities in the obligations and processes contained in these agreements. The Trade Remedy Agreements are also significant in the context of the WTO standard of review because more than thirty per cent of the total number of WTO complaints filed to date have involved disputes about anti-dumping, countervailing and safeguard measures.[2] This significant representation of trade remedies in WTO dispute settlement could potentially justify the use of a unique standard of review for panel review of trade remedy measures.

The survey of the new standard in relation to the Trade Remedy Agreements will proceed as follows. Firstly, I will briefly discuss the issue of panels distinguishing factual and legal questions in trade remedy reviews. Secondly, in the major part of this chapter, I will summarize the major concepts and obligations under each agreement and then describe how the new standard for reviewing facts would be applied to the Trade Remedy Agreements. When dealing with the Anti-Dumping Agreement, I will also set out how the Article 17.6 standard of review could be applied in conjunction with the new standard. Thirdly, I will briefly examine how the new standard of review compares with the current approach of WTO Tribunals, and speculate on whether the new standard may result in different dispute outcomes.

This chapter seeks to demonstrate that there is a need to apply the new standard of review to the Trade Remedy Agreements. It is likely to lead to common approaches in reviewing issues that are factually contentious and therefore create better guidance for panels and members in the future. Further, the new standard could be applied without great difficulty because it is already partially reflected in recent WTO case law.[3]

---

[2] See http://www.worldtradelaw.net.ezp.lib.unimelb.edu.au/database/agreementcount.asp, last accessed 31 March 2012. As at March 2012, 141 out of 430 complaints filed have involved disputes concerning Anti-Dumping Duties, Countervailing Duties and Safeguard Measures. The number of individual complaints expressed as a percentage of the total number of WTO complaints filed is 21 per cent for the Anti-Dumping Agreement, 6 per cent for countervailing duty disputes under the SCM Agreement and 9 per cent for the Agreement on Safeguards. This results in an aggregate of 36 per cent of the total number of WTO complaints but some disputes have involved more than one of these types of measures.

[3] See Chapter 2, Section 2.4.3.

6.2 FACTUAL AND LEGAL ISSUES IN REVIEWING TRADE REMEDIES

A standard of review of facts that differs from the legal standard of review would require panels to separate factual and legal issues in their analysis. This may pose particular challenges for panels in trade remedy disputes, where it is not always easy to assign the issues into factual and legal 'boxes'. The Trade Remedy Agreements frequently involve a complex assessment of whether a set of facts satisfies criteria that permits the imposition of a trade remedy. This is more likely to generate mixed questions of fact and law than assessments made under other WTO Agreements. For example, a panel may be required to answer the following question: does a surge in excess domestic inventories mean that the local industry has suffered injury in accordance with Article 15.4 of the SCM Agreement? It may be possible to separate the factual assessment from its application to the legal criteria. However, a panel is sometimes required to make a judgment that inseparably combines an appreciation of the facts with an interpretation of the relevant agreement. It is often the injury and causation findings, being a feature of the Trade Remedy Agreements, that have the propensity to generate mixed questions of fact and law because of the way panels must apply economic data to legal criteria.[4] Other issues, such as for example, whether a claim for countervailing measures has the requisite support of a local industry, might simply involve an interpretation of facts, with their application to the agreement posing no difficulty.[5]

In responding to this difficulty, it is contended that panels should, where possible, separate their factual analysis from the application of factual conclusions to the Trade Remedy Agreements. If this is not possible, then panels should apply a more intensive standard of review to mixed questions of fact and law than would apply to a purely factual question. This is because it is important to avoid deferential interpretations of the Trade Remedy Agreements that would potentially result in the inconsistent application of their provisions. Therefore, in those instances where mixed characterization questions are unavoidable, panels would be required to apply the factual standard of review and to also ensure that the domestic measures do not create an interpretation of the particular provisions that is likely to lead to difficulties in the way they are applied in the future. This would potentially result in a standard of review that is more intensive than the factual standard, but less intrusive than the legal standard. It is a practice that panels, to some degree, have

---

4 See Anti-Dumping Agreement arts 3, 5; SCM Agreement, arts 11, 15; Safeguards Agreement, art 4.

5 SCM Agreement, art 11.4.

already applied when they review national level measures. For example, in *Mexico-Olive Oil*, the panel was clearly concerned about systemic problems created if complaining parties had to demonstrate the direct passing through of subsidy benefits in every investigation.[6] This additional requirement is not, in effect, requiring panels to apply a legal standard to mixed questions, but rather it is designed to ensure that there is sufficient uniformity in interpreting key trade remedy provisions.

It is also important to consider how the new standard of review may relate to 'as such' and 'as applied' claims.[7] In an 'as such' claim, provided that the measure at issue is clear, then the conformity of the measure to the WTO Agreements will be a legal question, and accordingly, the general standard of review will apply. By contrast, an 'as applied' case, particularly involving the trade remedy disciplines, is more likely to involve factual matters. As will be discussed in this chapter, this is more likely to give rise to a specific standard of review. The distinction between 'as such' and 'as applied' is not itself determinative of the standard of review argued for in this book, but rather the major determinate is the jurisdictional competencies in the WTO Agreements, which frequently are evidenced by the role of domestic authorities in issuing measures in 'as applied' cases.

6.3 THE ANTI-DUMPING AGREEMENT

6.3.1 Key Concepts and Obligations

The Anti-Dumping Agreement sets out the rules for members to lawfully impose anti-dumping duties on imports.[8] This Agreement is based on Article VI of the GATT and first appeared as a discrete agreement following the Kennedy Round of negotiations.[9] The dumping of goods into foreign markets is often referred to as price discrimination between markets.[10]

---

6 Panel Report, *Mexico-Olive Oil* [7.144].

7 See discussion on 'as such' and 'as applied' disputes in Chapter 1, Section 1.3.1.

8 The full title of this Agreement is 'Agreement on the Implementation of Article VI of the General Agreement on Tariffs and Trade 1994'.

9 Agreement on the Implementation of Article VI of the General Agreement on Tariffs and Trade, 30 June 1967, GATT BISD, 15th Supplement, 1968, 24.

10 Petros C. Mavroidis, Patrick A. Messerlin and Jasper M. Wauters, *The Law and Economics of Contingent Protection in the WTO* (Elgar International Economic Law, 2008) 7.

Anti-dumping duties, like all trade remedies, in principle run counter to the major objective of the WTO of reducing barriers to international trade.[11] However, these agreements are often seen as integral to the multilateral trading system because they arguably act to discourage trade distorting practices or are treated as necessary exceptions to free trade principles. In the case of dumping, the economic argument is that dumping may injure local industries and prevent them from competing 'on a level playing field', which if left unchecked, may lead to monopolistic behaviour on the part of exporters.[12]

Disputes concerning the Anti-Dumping Agreement account for more than 20 per cent of the total number of cases that commenced in the WTO to date.[13] This is the highest proportion of cases for a single WTO discipline.[14] Dumping cases also often generate controversy. One major argument for this is that in an era of historically low general tariff barriers, trade remedies are often viewed as a contingent 'lever' that members may use to protect domestic

---

[11] See for example, Article 2 of the Marrakesh Declaration which provides 'Ministers affirm that the establishment of the World Trade Organization (WTO) ushers in a new era of global economic cooperation, reflecting the widespread desire to operate in a fairer and more open multilateral trading system for the benefit and welfare of their peoples. Ministers express their determination to resist protectionist pressures of all kinds. They believe that the trade liberalization and strengthened rules achieved in the Uruguay Round will lead to a progressively more open world trading environment. Ministers undertake, with immediate effect and until entry into force of the WTO, not to undertake any trade measures that would undermine or adversely affect the results of the Uruguay Round negotiations or their implementation.'

[12] Mavroidis, Messerlin and Wauters, *The Law and Economics of Contingent Protection in the WTO*, above n 10, 10–11, where the argument is put in the following terms: 'Anti-dumping supporters invoke three reasons which, in their view, present dumping as unacceptable pricing behaviour, or, at least, as a behaviour to be limited by anti-dumping measures. First, dumping is a predatory pricing strategy with a strong anti-competitive, monopolizing goal. Second, dumping is a discriminatory pricing practice which generates distortion among markets. Lastly, dumping reflects asymmetrical conditions in the exporting and importing markets which give an unfair strategic advantage to the foreign exporter(s) over the import-competing firms.' These economic arguments are not particularly strong. See Alan Sykes, 'Comparative Advantage and the Normative Economics of International Trade Policy' (1998) 1(1) *Journal of International Economic Law* 49, 80–81. Arguably the sanctioning of trade remedies is more of a result of politics, and particularly the role of domestic vested interests.

[13] See http://www.worldtradelaw.net.ezp.lib.unimelb.edu.au/database/agreementcount.asp, last accessed 31 March 2012. To March 2012 there have been 91 anti-dumping complaints out of a total number of 430 WTO disputes.

[14] The SCM Agreement accounts for a similar number of cases as compared with the Anti-Dumping Agreement but the majority of SCM cases to date have dealt with subsidies rather than countervailing measures. The most litigated discipline is the GATT, although cases concerning the GATT only and not more specific disciplines account for a modest 51 out of 427 cases to date.

industries.[15] Those who advocate for further access to markets claim that anti-dumping measures are a backward step in the overall trade liberalization process, whereas proponents of anti-dumping measures argue that they are necessary to ensure fairness in the international trading system.[16]

The Anti-Dumping Agreement requires domestic authorities to investigate whether anti-dumping duties should be levied against exporters of goods consequent upon a complaint being lodged by a domestic industry.[17] The Agreement also sets out how the investigation should proceed and what is relevant to an authority's deliberations. Therefore, authorities are granted a high level of independence to make findings and it is these findings that are usually the subject of panel review. Accordingly, panels are frequently the second tier of review of anti-dumping measures.

In order for a member to lawfully impose anti-dumping duties, it is necessary to satisfy two core criteria. A complaining party must first show that goods are being dumped in the relevant market. Dumping occurs where goods are exported at less than the normal value of sale in the country of export.[18] This is often referred to as the dumping margin. Secondly, it must be established that the domestic industry producing like goods is suffering economic injury that has been caused by the dumping.[19] Once these requirements are met, subject to detailed procedural requirements, authorities may levy duties up to the dumping margin, which is usually based on the difference between the export price and the price at which the domestic industry is deemed to be suffering harm.[20]

---

[15] Philip A. Akakwam, 'The Standard of Review in the 1994 Anti-Dumping Code: Circumscribing the Role of GATT panels in reviewing national anti-dumping determinations' (1996) 5 *Minnesota Journal of Global Trade* 272, 282 where the author states 'anti-dumping laws are often captured by protectionist forces and turned into de facto instruments of protection.'

[16] Mavroidis, Messerlin and Wauters, *The Law and Economics of Contingent Protection in the WTO*, above n 10, 7; Thomas J. Prusa, 'Comments on "Antidumping: Overview of the Agreement"' in Kyle W. Bagwell, George A. Bermann, Petros C. Mavroidis (eds), *Law and Economics of Contingent Protection in International Trade* (2010) 257, 258.

[17] There are a number of articles in the Anti-Dumping Agreement that describe the role of the domestic authorities. There is no clause that summarizes these obligations. However, Article 5.3 provides: 'The authorities shall examine the accuracy and adequacy of the evidence provided in the application to determine whether there is sufficient evidence to justify the initiation of an investigation.'

[18] Anti-Dumping Agreement, art 2.1. There are other methodologies for determining dumping (for example, based on selling at below cost) set out in the Anti-Dumping Agreement.

[19] Anti-Dumping Agreement, art 3.1.

[20] Anti-Dumping Agreement, art 9.3.

6.3.2 The Role of Article 17.6

The application of the new standard of review to the Anti-Dumping Agreement requires unique analysis because of the existence of Article 17.6 of that Agreement. It is recalled from Chapter 2 that Article 17.6 sets out a discrete standard of review that only applies to anti-dumping disputes.[21] This raises a number of issues that need to be addressed. The threshold question is whether Article 17.6 should be part of the new standard of review. Relevant to this question is whether the text of the WTO Agreements applies to the exclusion of, or in priority to, broader standard of review principles that may be relied upon by WTO Tribunals. Assuming that Article 17.6 ought to still apply, it is then necessary to determine how this provision might operate as part of the new standard of review.

It is without question that Article 17.6 must be applied by WTO Tribunals.[22] This provision is part of the applicable law that a WTO Tribunal is required to apply, irrespective of the fact that this provision is procedural in nature.[23] This is made clear in DSU Article 7.1, which sets out the standard terms of reference for WTO disputes as being the relevant provisions in the Agreements cited by the parties to a dispute.[24] Further, the subject-matter jurisdiction, which defines the types of claims that may be brought, is limited in DSU Article 1.1 to 'disputes brought pursuant to the consultation and dispute settlement provisions of the agreements listed in Appendix 1'.[25]

Given the importance placed on the text of the WTO Agreements, it is also uncontroversial that the wording of the Agreements will take priority over general principles of law.[26] This is supported by DSU Articles 3.2 and 19.2, which function to ensure the primacy (but not necessarily exclusivity) of the WTO texts. Both of these provisions confirm that WTO Tribunals may not add to or diminish from the rights and obligations set out in the WTO Agreements.[27] However, this rule is not as indefeasible as these provisions

---

21 See Chapter 2, Section 2.4.4.

22 Article 17.1 of the Anti-Dumping Agreement, which deals with the application of Article 17, provides: 'Except as otherwise provided herein, the Dispute Settlement Understanding is applicable to the consultations and the settlement of disputes under this Agreement.'

23 Lorand Bartels, 'Applicable Law in WTO Dispute Settlement Proceedings' (2001) 35(3) *Journal of World Trade* 499.

24 *Ibid.*

25 *Ibid* 502.

26 See, for example, Joost Pauwelyn, *Conflict of Norms in Public International Law* (Cambridge University Press, 2003) 444.

27 Bartels, 'Applicable Law in WTO Dispute Settlement Proceedings', above n 23, 507.

suggest. The distinction between the application of the WTO Agreements and principles is not always clear as often provisions may be based on, or interpreted by reference to, broader international legal principles.[28] In addition, WTO Tribunals may also have some scope for interpretation in cases by virtue of their inherent jurisdiction over the subject matter.[29] This frequently serves the purpose of fulfilling necessary functions where procedural issues have not been fully articulated in the WTO Agreements, and issues such as *amicus* briefs and burden of proof have been dealt with in this way.[30]

Having established that Article 17.6 should be part of the standard of review applied in anti-dumping disputes, and that it should take priority over the new standard, it remains to determine how Article 17.6 may be integrated with the new standard. The most obvious approach, which is advocated here, would be to identify Article 17.6 as an example of a specific standard of review. Article 17.6 sets out the standard of review for both factual and legal issues that is ostensibly more restrictive that the general standard of review. It may be viewed as 'legislative' recognition of the role undertaken by domestic authorities in dumping investigations. However, it is still important for the new standard of review to be a basis for interpreting Article 17.6. This is especially the case in light of the difficulties that WTO Tribunals have had in arriving at a settled meaning of Article 17.6. For example, the requirement under Article 17.6(i) for panels to determine if the establishment of facts was 'proper' and an evaluation was 'unbiased' and 'objective' may be better interpreted by reference to other criteria that determine the adequacy of the review process. This would be similar to what has occurred to date where WTO Tribunals have frequently interpreted Article 17.6(i) in conjunction with the objective assessment test.[31] Therefore, panels would apply Article 17.6, but interpret this provision by reference to the new standard of review. In this way, the anti-dumping standard would be applied in a manner that is arguably more faithful to its original design, and it would operate as part of a broader standard of review applied to all WTO Agreements.

The existence of Article 17.6 makes the development of the new standard of review more complex in relation to anti-dumping disputes. However, it is not feasible for this unique standard to be made redundant when developing a new standard. What is being advocated is for Article 17.6 to become part of

---

[28] Andrew D. Mitchell, *Legal Principles in WTO Disputes* (Cambridge University Press, 2008) 80.

[29] See VCLT, arts 31, 32.

[30] Bartels, 'Applicable Law in WTO Dispute Settlement Proceedings', above n 23, 515–17.

[31] Appellate Body Report, *US-Hot-Rolled Steel* [55]–[56]; Panel Report, *US-Steel Plate* [7.1]–[7.7].

the new standard. The challenge will be for WTO Tribunals not to further erode the intention of Article 17.6.[32] Arguably, a new standard that is based upon the idea of giving recognition to the role of domestic authorities may in fact reduce the scope of this problem.

6.3.3 The Application of the New Standard to the Anti-Dumping Agreement

Anti-dumping measures are contingent in nature and the Anti-Dumping Agreement stipulates that it applies to situations where members have taken action under anti-dumping legislation or regulations.[33] This sets the parameters of this agreement in that measures may only be adopted following an investigation conducted at a national level by a domestic authority.[34] The role contemplated for domestic authorities is therefore central to the operation of the agreement. The Anti-Dumping Agreement contains detailed rules concerning what an authority shall consider in its investigation and how the investigation shall proceed. For example, the agreement prescribes when an authority may commence an investigation, when it must terminate an investigation, what criteria exist for determining injury and dumping, as well as how the process and outcomes must be publicized.[35] Overall, there are fairly rigorous obligations imposed upon domestic authorities to only impose dumping measures once various procedural and substantive criteria have been satisfied.

In light of the prominent role of domestic authorities, it is clear that a specific standard of review ought to be applied by WTO panels when reviewing the facts of a case. The Anti-Dumping Agreement identifies various major competencies that are the responsibility of members, as opposed to being that

---

[32] Gary N. Horlick and Peggy A. Clarke, 'Standards for Panels Reviewing Anti-Dumping Determinations under the GATT' in Ernst-Ulrich Petersmann (ed), *International Trade Law and the GATT and WTO Dispute Settlement System* (Kluwer Law International,1997) 302 and commentary in Chapter 2, Section 2.4.4.

[33] Anti-Dumping Agreement, art 1.

[34] This is usually a government department (e.g. Customs department) or a specialized agency. In the United States the International Trade Commission is responsible for investigating whether there is any material injury to domestic industries whereas the Department of Commerce investigates whether dumping is occurring.

[35] Relevant provisions include Article 5.1, requiring an investigation to be initiated upon written application by or on behalf of the domestic industry. Article 5.2 sets out minimum information that must be contained in an application for anti-dumping measures. Article 5.8 stipulates that authorities must terminate an investigation if there is not sufficient evidence of either dumping or of injury to justify proceeding with the case. Article 2 sets out methodologies for determining dumping. Article 3.4 sets out criteria for determining injury. Article 4 defines domestic industry to determine standing. Article 6 sets out general procedural and evidentiary requirements.

of WTO panels, which would entitle a panel to move away from a general standard of review.[36] However, as foreshadowed in the previous section, Article 17.6 of the Anti-Dumping Agreement should be applied prior to developing a specific standard that is derived from other provisions of this agreement. It is therefore contended that Article 17.6 is not an exhaustive statement on the anti-dumping standard of review, and that a specific standard may provide broader guidance for its application.[37] This is not a contentious matter because the wording of Article 17.6 to a large degree already reflects the new standard of review articulated in this book. Further, given the interpretive problems associated with Article 17.6, the introduction of the new standard of review may promote a more consistent approach by panels and demonstrate an appropriate degree of deference.

Article 17.6(i) prescribes the standard of review of facts in anti-dumping disputes. This provision makes it clear that a panel must review the investigation and findings of domestic authorities rather than to conduct a *de novo* review of its own.[38] Panels must examine two issues, being first whether the establishment of the facts was proper, and second, whether the evaluation by authorities was unbiased and objective.[39] If these criteria are satisfied, then the panel must not overturn the findings of the domestic authority. There is obviously a degree of contentiousness about the key expressions 'proper', 'unbiased' and 'objective' in that they are open to be interpreted as conferring greater or lesser degrees of intrusion in the review of anti-dumping investigations.[40] However, despite this ambiguity, it is clear from a complete reading of Article 17.6, that panels must nonetheless ensure that investigations are of a sufficiently high standard.[41] The design of Article 17.6(i) is therefore

---

36 It is common for this delineation in competencies to manifest in the domestic authority being the adjudicator at first instance.

37 The use of the specific standard of review of facts may be similar to that of the Article 17.6 and Article 11 of the DSU. In *US-Hot Rolled Steel* the Appellate Body stated at paragraph 55 that these provisions were not in conflict and that Article 17.6 may be viewed as supplementing rather than replacing Article 11.

38 This was affirmed in Panel Report, *Guatemala-Cement II* [8.17]–[8.19] and supported by decisions such as Appellate Body Report, *US-Hot Rolled Steel* [55] in which it was stipulated that Article 17.6 is to be read in conjunction with Article 11.

39 In *Thailand-H-Beams*, the Appellate Body elaborated on the aim of Article 17.6(i) at paragraph 116, stating that its function is to 'prevent a panel from "second guessing" a determination of a national authority when the establishment of the facts is proper and the evaluation of those facts is unbiased and objective.'

40 See Chapter 2, Section 2.4 for a discussion of cases interpreting Article 17.6(i).

41 See Catherine Li, 'In quest of the proper standard of review in WTO trade remedy cases' in Mitsuo Matsushita, Dukgeun Ahn and Tain-Jy Chen (eds), *The WTO Trade Remedy System: East Asian Perspectives* (Cameron May, 2006) 93, 107–8.

extremely similar to the new standard of review in that it both emphasises the primacy of the domestic processes, and it also charges panels with the responsibility of safeguarding the quality of domestic investigations. Further, whilst it is impossible to completely avoid panel interpretations that move in the direction of *de novo* review, the existence of the new standard of review doctrine would underpin future interpretations of Article 17.6(i). Panels would be required to focus on issues such as the rigour of domestic processes or the strength of the reasoning, rather than whether the authority has reached the 'correct' decision.[42]

It is clear from the above discussion that Article 17.6 may remain as a specific example of the new standard of review of facts, and that the anti-dumping standard can be informed by the way the new standard may be applied to other trade remedy agreements. When applying the new factual standard in trade remedy cases panels should, at all times, consider whether there is adequate logic and analytical rigour in the domestic level investigation.[43] Panels will need to test the reasoning and conclusions of domestic authorities, (but without panels themselves 'reinvestigating' the matter or testing each and every proposition). Such a distinction should engender a moderate degree of deference. This approach by panels is the key to ensuring adequate oversight of the quality of the domestic review, and it involves at its core an examination of the rationality of the domestic decision-making process. The credibility of the domestic decision-making process will also be informed by factors such as whether relevant evidence has been taken into account, a proper explanation of the decision is provided or the decision may be materially affected by procedural errors or differing interpretations.[44] The resulting standard of review of facts would also be informed by the precise provisions of the Anti-Dumping Agreement that are being examined by panels but such standard would be fairly similar for most provisions.

Article 17.6(ii) sets forth the standard of review for legal questions. There are two parts to this provision. Firstly, panels must interpret the Anti-Dumping Agreement in accordance with the customary rules of interpretation of public international law.[45] Secondly, where a finding of a domestic authority is a 'permissible interpretation' of an anti-dumping provision, then panels are directed to not disturb those findings. The first aspect of this standard has been accepted as referring to articles 31 and 32 of the VCLT, which enshrines

---

42 This approach would be reinforced by the fact that it would also be mirrored in respect of similar obligations in other WTO Agreements.

43 As a separate task, panels must then determine the legal question of whether the measure is inconsistent with any WTO obligations.

44 See Chapter 5, Section 5.2.2.

45 See Chapter 2, Section 2.4.4.

methods of treaty interpretation.[46] The second criterion is unique to the Anti-Dumping Agreement, but it has largely been ignored by the Appellate Body due to the fact that interpretation under the VCLT is designed to result in only one correct interpretation.[47] Article 17.6(ii) therefore, in practice, has allowed panels to arrive at their own legal interpretations of provisions without any deference to the interpretations of domestic authorities.

As with Article 17.6(i), the language of Article 17.6(ii) bears a strong similarity to the new legal standard of review put forward in this book. It has been argued in this book that legal questions should be governed by the general standard of review, rather than a specific standard adapted to each Agreement.[48] The general standard is highly intensive in nature and is the equivalent of *de novo* review for determining legal questions.[49] This, in turn, is entirely consistent with Articles 31 and 32 of the VCLT, which require the interpreter of a treaty to reach the correct interpretation based on the interpretive rules, and without deference to other interpretations. The legal standard of review under 17.6(ii) is therefore, in substance, the same as that of the new standard of review, as well as the legal standard currently used in disputes concerning other WTO Agreements. The new standard of review may also clarify the arguably redundant nature of Article 17.6(ii) and confirm the unfettered prerogative of panels to interpret WTO provisions.

Having established that the new standard of review and Article 17.6 may be applied in a complimentary fashion, it is apt to provide some issue-based examples of how the new standard may be applied. It will be evident from the examples, that the new standard would not have necessarily altered the findings of the relevant WTO Tribunal. The central issues in anti-dumping disputes are the assessment of the dumping calculations and the local industry injury analysis. Many cases that have come before WTO Tribunals have concerned the composition or inclusion of figures or factors that influence

---

[46] See Appellate Body Report, *US-Gasoline* [16]–[17]; Appellate Body Report, *Japan-Alcoholic Beverages I*, [10]; Appellate Body Report, *India-Patents (US)* [43]–[46]; Panel Report, *US-Section 301 Trade Act* [7.21]–[7.22].

[47] WTO Tribunals have not to date invoked the second sentence of Article 17.6(ii). In *US-Hot Rolled Steel*, the Appellate Body admitted that is was open to be utilized in the future, but failed to identify how this may occur, Various commentators have criticised Article 17.6(ii). For example, J. Greenwald, 'WTO Dispute Settlement: An exercise in Trade Law Legislation?' (2003) *Journal of International Economic Law* 6, 114 in which the author has described this provision as a 'dead letter'.

[48] Chapter 5, Section 5.2.3. This is principally because panels must have full powers to review legal questions and no deference to domestic authorities is appropriate.

[49] In Chapter 4, the general standard was described as involving a comprehensive formal and substantive review of matters in dispute.

dumping or injury findings.[50] These issues are frequently contentious because they may affect the decision to impose or not impose duties. They are therefore useful for discussing the standard of review.

In *Mexico-Anti-Dumping Measures on Rice*, the panel determined that Mexico had acted inconsistently with Article 3 of the Anti-Dumping Agreement by choosing to base its injury determination on a period which ended over 15 months before the initiation of the investigation.[51] Further, in *US-Hot-Rolled Steel*, the Appellate Body upheld the panel's conclusion that the United States had acted inconsistently with Article 6.8 of the Anti-Dumping Agreement, by failing to include information supplied late by Japanese exporters in its determination of dumping margins.[52] Both of the above cases demonstrate that the panels were well within their powers of review because the issue concerned the establishment of the facts by a domestic authority, which was not deemed proper pursuant to Article 17.6(i). The application of the new standard of review would not have altered these findings in either case because the proper establishment of facts is clearly a procedural matter which panels must adjudicate on given that it affects the quality of domestic review process.

This is to be contrasted with a situation where the dispute concerns the reasoning of a domestic authority. For instance, under Article 3.2 of the Anti-Dumping Agreement, an authority must consider whether there has been a significant increase in dumped imports. The issue then is how closely a panel should analyse the authority's reasoning. Under the new standard, the panel would be required to determine whether the factual record and the reasoning undertaken by the domestic authority are sufficient to support a positive finding on this issue.[53] The sufficiency would be determined by the panel examining the quality of decision-making by the domestic authority against the claims made in respect of Article 3.2, but it would not involve a retrial of the

---

50 See James Durling, 'Deference but only when due: WTO Review of Anti-Dumping Measures' (2003) 6(1) *Journal of International Economic Law* 134, where the author lists major issues that are the subject of disputes under Articles 2 and 3 such as like goods, terms of sale, costs before resale or the definition of domestic industry.

51 Panel Report, *Mexico-Anti-Dumping Measures on Rice* [7.64].

52 Appellate Body Report, *US-Hot-Rolled Steel* [89]–[90]. Article 6.8 of the Anti-Dumping Agreement states that 'In cases where any interested party refuses access to or otherwise does not provide, necessary information within a reasonable period or significantly impedes the investigation, preliminary and final determinations, affirmative or negative, may be made on the basis of facts available. The provisions of Annex II shall be observed in the application of this paragraph.'

53 See Chapter 5, Section 5.5.2 for suggested criteria that panels might use to verify the quality of decision-making by domestic authorities.

original investigation. This potentially would require the panel to go further than merely examining whether the evaluation was 'unbiased and objective' but the intensity of panel review on this question would fall short of deciding the issue on the merits. The role of the panel in scrutinizing findings is to ascertain whether such findings are based upon positive evidence rather than on conjecture or theoretical possibility. The level of intrusion will vary slightly depending upon the nature and wording of the particular anti-dumping provision being examined, which may involve evidence of matters such as material injury (or the threat thereof), causation and economic indicators including production, inventory levels and pricing. It is conceivable that the new standard of review would be more intensive than the standard suggested by the wording of Article 17.6, but given the current expansive interpretation of Article 17.6, it may in fact result in a more deferential standard in practice.[54]

There is also likely to be a close similarity in panel findings resulting from the application of the legal standard of review under Article 17.6(ii) and the general standard of review. When examining the panel's injury findings, the Appellate Body in *Thailand-H-Beams* upheld the panel's determination that Article 3.4 (listing factors for assessing injury) requires a mandatory evaluation of all factors.[55] Regarding the legal standard as applied to dumping findings, the Appellate Body, in *EC-Bed Linen*, found that the practice of zeroing, as used in calculation of dumping margins, was inconsistent with Article 2.4.2.[56] In particular, this practice contravened the requirement for there to be a fair comparison for calculating dumping margins.[57] Further, zeroing was not found to be a permissible interpretation under the second sentence of article 17.6(ii).[58] Both of these cases highlight the need for WTO Tribunals to have complete authority to reach legal interpretations of WTO provisions, irrespective of the potential inconsistency between the first and second sentences of Article 17.6(ii). It is unlikely that the application of Article 17.6(ii) as part of the new standard of review would result in any change in legal interpretations.

---

54 The new anti-dumping standard may therefore be more consistent with the rationale for introducing Article 17.6.

55 Panel Report, *Thailand-H-Beams* [121]–[128].

56 Appellate Body Report, *EC-Bed Linen* [86]. There have been a number of WTO cases that have dealt with the practice of zeroing. The practice of zeroing is controversial and takes different forms. 'Simple zeroing' occurs where the margin of prices of imports which are higher than prices of foreign domestic sales are not included in the overall calculation of the dumping margin. Instead, these sales are treated as having a value of zero rather than a negative value in the dumping margin assessment. A good summary of zeroing may be found at Appellate Body Report, *EC-Bed Linen* [47].

57 See Anti-Dumping Agreement, art 2.4.

58 Appellate Body Report, *EC-Bed* Linen [63]–[66].

If anything, it would confirm the obsolescence of the notion of 'permissible interpretations'. Practices such as zeroing and the manner of injury assessment should not be treated deferentially given that they ultimately concern whether a member has complied with its WTO obligations. The new standard of review would therefore potentially assist to clarify the meaning of Article 17.6(ii).[59]

6.4 THE AGREEMENT ON SUBSIDIES AND COUNTERVAILING MEASURES

6.4.1 Key Concepts and Obligations

The SCM Agreement sets out disciplines regarding the use of subsidies and the rules for the imposition of countervailing measures in response to certain types of subsidies.[60] The basic distinction in economic terms that the Agreement attempts to make is between export and production subsidies, with the former viewed as having much more demonstrable net negative welfare impacts, both to domestic economies and world trade.[61]

The SCM Agreement provides two courses of action for members, the multilateral track and the unilateral track. The multilateral track involves initiating a complaint under the DSU to challenge the legitimacy of a subsidy per se. The unilateral track involves a national-level investigation conducted by domestic authorities to determine whether countervailing duties shall be imposed upon exporters from the country granting the subsidies.[62] If the investigation results in the imposition of countervailing duties against some or

---

[59] This is to be compared with the comments by the Appellate Body in *US-Hot Rolled Steel* at paragraph 61 that 'We cannot, of course, examine here which provisions of the *Anti-Dumping Agreement* do admit of more than one "permissible interpretation".' These interpretive questions can only be addressed within the context of particular disputes, involving particular provisions of the *Anti-Dumping Agreement* invoked in particular claims, and after the application of the rules of treaty interpretation in Articles 31 and 32 of the *Vienna Convention*. These comments leave open the possibility of permissible interpretations but without specifying how they may arise.

[60] The SCM Agreement was the successor to the Tokyo Round 'Agreement on the Interpretation and Application of Articles VI, XVI and XXIII.'

[61] Mavroidis, Messerlin and Wauters, *The Law and Economics of Contingent Protection in the WTO*, above n 10, 293.

[62] Members may not use the multilateral and unilateral procedures simultaneously in respect of injury to a member's domestic market, but there is no restriction on, for example, using the multilateral approach regarding injury to a member's export markets. It is important to acknowledge that the key difference between the multilateral and domestic processes is that the former is a state to state forum, whereas the latter is initiated by a local industry.

all exporters from a WTO member, then that member may seek to challenge that measure on the basis that it does not comply with the WTO rules. As with all domestic trade remedies, countervailing measures are not viewed as trade enhancing, but rather as a protectionist mechanism.

A subsidy is defined as a financial contribution by a government or a public body that involves the direct transfer of moneys or financial benefits such as tax credits, equity, favourable loans, guarantees or the provision of goods or services.[63] In addition, a subsidy must be specific to an enterprise or industry or a group of enterprises or industries.[64] The SCM Agreement does not seek to make all subsidies unlawful. Rather the SCM Agreement focuses on two main categories, prohibited subsidies and actionable subsidies.[65] Prohibited or 'red light' subsidies are subsidies that are contingent upon export performance or upon the use of domestic goods over imported goods.[66] These are not permitted under any circumstance. By contrast, actionable subsidies are subsidies that are not unlawful per se, but which will not be permitted should they cause injury to a domestic industry of another member, a nullification or impairment of benefits or serious prejudice to the interests of another member.[67] Prohibited and actionable subsidies may both be contested via the multilateral track. Despite the SCM Agreement providing a definition of subsidies, there have been a number of cases about the meaning of this provision.[68]

The unilateral track sets forth its own criteria, which to some extent overlaps with the multilateral track. The SCM does not limit the unilateral track to actionable subsidies, but presumably it would be necessary for members to prove injury, which is not required for the multilateral track. A successful application for countervailing duties will need to demonstrate the existence (and where possible the amount) of a subsidy, injury to domestic industry, and

---

[63] SCM Agreement, art 1.1. Note that prohibited subsidies are deemed to be specific under SCM art 2.3.

[64] SCM Agreement, art 2.

[65] Prohibited subsidies are dealt with in Articles 3–4 and actionable subsidies in Articles 5–7. A third category, non-actionable subsidies (Article 8), exempting narrowly defined research and development, environmental and regional initiatives, expired on 1 January 2000. It is also noteworthy that there are a number of rules and commitments in the Agreement on Agriculture concerning subsidies that take priority over the SCM Agreement.

[66] SCM Agreement, art 3.1.

[67] SCM Agreement, art 5. Serious prejudice has a separate definition in Article 6, which includes where the total *ad valorem* subsidization of a product exceeds 5 per cent.

[68] For example, see Appellate Body Report, *Canada-Aircraft* regarding conferred benefit (Article 1.1(b)), Appellate Body Report, *Canada-Autos* regarding specificity (Article 2), Appellate Body Report, *US-Countervailing Duty Investigation on DRAMS* regarding entrustment or direction (Article 1.1(a)(1)(iv)).

a causal link between the subsidised imports and injury.[69] If a countervailable subsidy exists, then the imposition of countervailing duty is designed to negate the effects of the subsidy and 'create a level playing field'.[70] These criteria to a large extent mirror those contained in the Anti-Dumping Agreement.[71] In particular, injury findings made by domestic authorities in countervailing duty cases and anti-dumping cases are based upon almost identical WTO Agreement wording and administrative processes. This supports the proposition that the standard of review under the SCM should be substantially the same as in respect of the Anti-Dumping Agreement.

The SCM Agreement sets out several provisions concerning how members are to conduct countervailing investigations.[72] Domestic authorities have a central role in administering such investigations. A domestic authority must review the accuracy and adequacy of evidence in the complaint prior to the initiation of the investigation as well as determine whether the complainants have proper standing.[73] There is also the requirement for consultations to take place prior to the investigation.[74] Once the investigation has commenced, there are a number of due process requirements for authorities to meet, such as the requirement to issue public notices of initiation and of preliminary and final determinations and to publish detailed explanations of determinations.[75] Further, once the requisite grounds are established, the imposition of countervailing duties is at the discretion of members, although many members have an additional public interest test within national legislation which must also be satisfied.[76]

6.4.2 The Application of the New Standard to the SCM Agreement

The most important distinction to make in SCM disputes for the purpose of applying the new standard of review is between cases that have come before the DSU via the multilateral route versus the unilateral route. It is very likely that panels would need to apply a different standard of review for those two types of cases. This is because, where parties take the multilateral route, it will

---

69 SCM Agreement, art 11.2.

70 SCM Agreement, art 10, note 36.

71 For example, the non-exhaustive list of factors constituting injury in SCM Agreement Article 15.4 is very similar to that contained in Article 3.4 of the Anti-Dumping Agreement.

72 SCM Agreement, arts 11–23.

73 SCM Agreement, arts 11.3, 11.4.

74 SCM Agreement, art 13.

75 SCM Agreement, art 22. Article 12 also deals with the right to be given information and confidentiality.

76 SCM Agreement, art 19.1.

generally be the first time that a matter is subject to adjudication, and the disputes will most commonly concern whether the subsidy is prohibited or actionable under Articles 3 to 7 of the SCM Agreement. By contrast, if the unilateral track is taken, then the dispute will be about whether a domestic authority has complied with obligations under Articles 10 to 22 of the SCM Agreement when imposing countervailing measures on imports. Parties may contest the lawfulness of subsidies by directly invoking WTO dispute settlement procedures, whereas countervailing cases are a response to another member using countervailing duties as a trade remedy.[77]

If the multilateral track is taken then it would be appropriate for panels to apply the general standard of review. In such cases, the panel is the adjudicator of first instance and would be determining whether a measure is permissible under the SCM Agreement. By way of example, in *Canada-Autos*, the panel was asked to determine whether a Canadian measure allowing exporters of motor vehicles to import vehicles duty-free was a subsidy contingent upon export performance.[78] In most cases there will be factual issues for panels to assess, such as how a subsidy scheme was administered, but there is no difficulty with panels applying a highly intensive standard of review to both factual and legal questions. The factual analysis can become more difficult for panels where they are examining actionable subsidies, because of the need for the complainant to prove injury, nullification or impairment of benefits or serious prejudice.[79] Despite the existence of a number of deeming provisions, it is still necessary in multilateral track cases for panels to review evidentiary matters, and there is no reason why panels should exercise judicial deference towards member measures.[80]

In countervailing duty cases, unlike in subsidy cases, it is advocated that panels should apply a specific standard of review that is more deferential in nature.[81] To do otherwise would be to treat the national level investigation process as merely part of the factual background of the matter, and it would ignore the important role given to domestic authorities in reviewing whether

77 Mavroidis, Messerlin and Wauters, *The Law and Economics of Contingent Protection in the WTO*, above n 10, 298.

78 Panel Report, *Canada-Autos* [10.201], affirmed by Appellate Body, *Canada-Autos* [108]–[109].

79 SCM Agreement, arts 5, 6.

80 There have been very few cases dealing with Articles 5 and 6. One example is *Indonesia-Autos* where the panel rejected evidence from the United States and the European Communities that their exports to Indonesia had been displaced or impeded as a result of Indonesian subsidies. See Panel Report, *Indonesia-Autos* [14.212]–[222].

81 The arguments supporting this proposition are very similar to those relevant to the Anti-Dumping Agreement: see Section 6.6.1 above.

grounds for the imposition of countervailing duties exist.[82] Article 10 of the SCM Agreement provides that 'Countervailing duties may only be imposed pursuant to investigations initiated and conducted in accordance with the provisions of this Agreement and the Agreement on Agriculture.'[83] To apply the general standard of review to countervailing measure cases would create the distinct risk of panels applying a *de novo* standard of review, and there has been evidence of this already occurring in some cases.[84]

There are a number of provisions in the SCM Agreement which evidence the competencies mandated for domestic authorities. Procedurally, authorities must screen applications for relief and, where a prima facie case is made out, they must conduct a public investigation process and follow various other procedural requirements.[85] Authorities must also determine the existence and the amount of the subsidy, and that through the effects of the subsidy, the subsidized imports are causing injury, before imposing countervailing duties.[86] These responsibilities allocated to domestic authorities mean that a specific standard of review that is more deferential ought to be applied by panels in cases concerning countervailing measures.

When a panel is examining most procedural criteria, such as whether major foreign exporters were sent questionnaires, there is generally not much factual controversy, and panels can therefore adopt more of a 'checklist' approach and simply determine whether a procedure was satisfied, without it repeating the full review task of the domestic authority. However, in countervailing cases, it is much more likely that a panel will need to undertake an analysis of substantive issues, such as whether there was a basis for the domestic authority to find that a subsidy has caused injury to a domestic industry. Under Article 15.4, authorities must evaluate all relevant economic factors and indices having a bearing on the state of the domestic industry. Therefore, there is certainly a role for the panel to review this evaluation.

In reviewing these substantive criteria, it is inappropriate for a panel to assess evidence as if it was the original decision-maker to see if it reaches the same conclusion as the domestic authority. Panels must provide adequate oversight of the membership by applying a factual standard that safeguards the

---

[82] Investigations are normally conducted by the Customs Department or specialized government authorities with similar powers.

[83] SCM Agreement, art 10, second sentence.

[84] See discussion of the current standard of review in Chapter 2, Section 2.4.3, and in particular statements of the Appellate Body in the following decisions: *US-Countervailing Duty Investigation on DRAMS*, *US-Continued Zeroing* and *US-Softwood Lumber VI (Article 21.5-Canada)*.

[85] SCM Agreement, arts 11.3, 12, 14 and 15.

[86] SCM Agreement, art 19. Less stringent criteria applies for provisional measures under Article 17.

quality of the original decision. By limiting the standard to one which looks at the quality of the decision, a *de novo* review may be avoided. The level of scrutiny applied in this type of case is nonetheless likely to require an analysis of the reasoning and conclusions of the domestic authority based on the original factual record. In other words, is the measure a rational result of the case put before the authority? WTO Tribunals have, in some instances, ably tried to find the 'middle ground' between a cursory review and a full *de novo* review. As discussed in section 6.2, in *Mexico-Olive Oil* the panel agreed with the Mexican authorities that it was not necessary to establish that a subsidy passed through from olive growers, who received the subsidy, to exporters, and that this decision was 'one that could be reasonably reached on the basis of the record evidence'.[87] By contrast, in *US-Lead and Bismuth II*, the Appellate Body affirmed a panel finding that the United States authorities erred in presuming that a subsidy passed through where the recipient of the subsidy had been sold.[88]

6.5 THE SAFEGUARDS AGREEMENT

6.5.1 Key Concepts and Obligations

This Agreement sets out the rules by which members may impose safeguard measures. The text is originally based upon Article XIX of the GATT, headed 'emergency action on imports of particular products'. The rationale for this trade measure is to allow members to impose some kind of trade restriction on imports as a 'safety value', where there are unforeseen developments that lead to a product being imported in such increased quantities that they cause or threaten serious injury to domestic producers.[89] Safeguards in recent years have mainly taken the form of tariff rate quotas, *ad valorem* tariff increases and general tariff increases.[90] Further, safeguards must be applied to all imports, irrespective of their source.[91] They may be imposed for up to four years, and extended for a total period of application of eight years.[92] Historically, there have been fewer safeguard measures imposed compared with anti-dumping measures, but there have

[87] Panel Report, *Mexico-Olive Oil* [7.165].
[88] Appellate Body Report, *US-Lead and Bismuth II* [63].
[89] GATT 1994, art XIX.
[90] Quotas or other quantitative restrictions are not now commonly used.
[91] Safeguards Agreement, art 2.2.
[92] Safeguards Agreement, arts 7.1, 7.3.

nonetheless been a number of significant WTO disputes dealing with safeguards.[93]

The criteria for the imposition of safeguards is for there to be an increase in imports of a product that causes or threatens to cause serious injury to a domestic industry producing like or directly competitive products.[94] In addition, the increase in imports must be as a result of unforeseen developments.[95] Serious injury is defined broadly as a significant overall impairment to the position of a domestic industry.[96] Some further guidance is given in Article 4.2(a) in listing indicia such as changes in the level of sales, production and profit.[97] There is no definition of causation and Article 4.2(b) merely stipulates that when factors other than increased imports are causing injury to the domestic injury at the same time, such injury shall not be attributed to increased imports. Predictably, most disputes under this Agreement have centred on the establishment of serious injury and causation. The criteria for determining injury under the Safeguards Agreement are also very similar to the criteria set out in the Anti-Dumping and SCM Agreements.[98]

The Safeguards Agreement does contemplate economic analysis by referring to relative and absolute increases in imports. For example, imports may have substantially increased as a result of increases in domestic demand and there may be no injury to domestic producers.[99] Finally, from a substantive point of view, members may only apply safeguards to the extent necessary to prevent or remedy serious injury and to facilitate adjustment.[100]

---

93 The number of safeguard cases have varied markedly over the years. It has been suggested that during the Uruguay Round, negotiators wanted to make the use of safeguards more attractive than anti-dumping measures because of the high use of anti-dumping measures during the 1980s and early 1990s. See Mavroidis, Messerlin and Wauters, *The Law and Economics of Contingent Protection in the WTO*, above n 10, 465.

94 Safeguards Agreement, art 2.1.

95 Appellate Body Report, *Argentina-Footwear (EC)* [83]–[84], [93]–[94]. This is based upon Article 1 of the Safeguards Agreement, which refers to GATT 1994, art XIX.

96 Safeguards Agreement, art 4.1(a).

97 Some factors listed in Article 4.2(a), such as the rate of increase of imports, do not provide direct evidence of injury and can only lead to this conclusion inferentially or in combination with other factors.

98 See Safeguards Agreement, art 4.2(a), Anti-Dumping Agreement, art 3.4 and SCM Agreement, art 15.5.

99 Mavroidis, Messerlin and Wauters, *The Law and Economics of Contingent Protection in the WTO*, above n 10, 479. Mavrodis refers to three basic components or curves that may influence an injury analysis, namely domestic demand, domestic supply and foreign supply. Note also that the Safeguards Agreement refers to serious injury as opposed to material injury in the Anti-Dumping Agreement, with this higher injury threshold perceived as requiring more elaborate evaluation methods.

100 Safeguards Agreement, art 5.1. There is also direction of the extent of the safeguard should quantitative restrictions be used.

The Safeguards Agreement requires members to only impose safeguards following an investigation by 'competent authorities'.[101] The Agreement contains a number of due process requirements, such as the issuance of public notices, making allowances for importers, exporters and other interested parties to present evidence and their views through public hearings or other appropriate means, and to publish a report setting out an authority's findings and reasoned conclusions.[102] There are also provisions allowing for provisional safeguards of up to 200 days following a preliminary determination that there is clear evidence of actual or threatened injury.[103] Overall, there is very little detail in the Safeguards Agreement about the procedural obligations for domestic authorities in conducting investigations.[104] However, the Appellate Body in *US-Wheat Gluten* has taken a practical approach and has read almost all of the procedural requirements in the Anti-Dumping and SCM Agreements into the Safeguards Agreement.[105]

There are also safeguard mechanisms contained in other WTO Agreements that, to a large degree, mirror the criteria set out in Articles 2 and 4 discussed above. These special safeguard provisions are contained in the Agreement on Agriculture and the Agreement on Textiles and Clothing, with the latter of these agreements having now expired.[106] There is also a special safeguard provision contained in the WTO Accession Protocol for China which is proving somewhat controversial.[107] Separate provisions were negotiated in relation to the Agreement on Agriculture and ATC because of the significant reforms undertaken in the textile and agriculture sectors, including large reductions in tariff rates and 'tariffication', whereby non-tariff barriers were converted to tariffs.[108] These Agreements also contain separate safeguard mechanisms such as specific price and volume triggers as conditions for introducing safeguards, restrictions on the maximum level of the safeguard, and different time periods

101 Safeguards Agreement, art 3.1.

102 *Ibid.*

103 Safeguards Agreement, art 6.

104 There is considerably more detail of this kind in the Anti-Dumping and SCM Agreements.

105 Appellate Body Report, *US-Wheat Gluten* [53]–[55].

106 See Agreement on Agriculture, art 5; ATC, arts 2.20, 6. The ATC expired on 31 December 2004.

107 *Accession of the People's Republic of China*, WTO Doc WT/L/432 (2001); *United States-Measures Affecting the Importation of Certain Passenger Motor Vehicle and Light Vehicle Tyres*, WTO Doc WT/DS299/1 (2009) (Request for Consultations). See also Panel Report, *US-Tyres (China)*; Appellate Body Report, *US-Tyres (China)*.

108 See for example the recitals and Article 20 of the Agreement on Agriculture and the recitals and Article 1.1 of the ATC.

for maintaining safeguards.[109] There have been very few cases concerning the safeguard provisions under these Agreements.[110] Any commentary and analysis concerning the standard of review would apply equally to any specialized provisions, although the requirement for the Textile Monitoring Body to review domestic textile and clothing measures prior to panel procedures being invoked may have had an impact on the standard of review in the case of the ATC.[111]

6.5.2 The Application of the New Standard to the Safeguards Agreement

The Safeguards Agreement, in some ways, provides the best example of how a new standard of review may be applied in trade remedy disputes. There is no distinct standard of review as applies to Anti-Dumping disputes, and unlike the SCM Agreement, there are no direct multilateral dispute procedures. The safeguard measures that come before a panel to review have almost invariably been previously examined by domestic authorities. The authorities have the responsibility of conducting a formal investigation in accordance with Article 3 and it is their findings of fact and law which panels must assess, rather than panels reviewing the issues on a *de novo* basis. Whilst the procedural provisions are much more truncated than in the Anti-Dumping and SCM Agreements, domestic authorities are given the jurisdictional competency to determine whether the measures have been lawfully imposed.[112] The Safeguards Agreement therefore will give rise to a specific standard of review that is more deferential than the standard that would apply to a non-trade remedy agreement.

As mentioned in the previous section, panels are likely to read due process requirements into the Safeguards Agreement.[113] Therefore, panels will look to see if domestic authorities have met these minimum procedural obligations. Whilst there is always concern about such 'gap filling' interpretations by panels, this may be seen as part of a similar standard of review being applied

---

109 See Agreement on Agriculture, art 5; ATC, arts 2.20, 6.

110 Cases litigated under these Agreements comprise Panel Report, *Chile-Price Band System* as modified by Appellate Body Report; *Columbia-Safeguard Measure of Imports of Plain Polyester Filaments from Thailand* WT/DS181 (settled through TMB process); Panel Report, *US-Underwear* as modified by Appellate Body Report; Panel Report, *US-Wool Shirts and Blouses* as modified by Appellate Body Report; Panel Report, *US-Cotton Yarn* as modified by Appellate Body Report.

111 See ATC, arts 6, 8.10.

112 Domestic authorities will of course determine the validity of measures in accordance with domestic regulation that incorporates WTO commitments.

113 Appellate Body Report, *US-Wheat Gluten* [53]–[55].

by panels to national level decisions in trade remedy cases. In terms of substantive obligations, the key issues that authorities must determine are whether serious injury exists, and whether such injury to a domestic industry has been caused by a rapid increase in imports. Such a determination will require compelling evidence from the local industry applying for safeguard protection. In many respects, a stronger case needs to be made out for establishing injury than in dumping cases, given the higher 'serious' rather than 'material' injury test.[114] The evaluative process for domestic authorities is therefore often complex and difficult, with a heavy reliance on economic and financial data.

All of this means that panels should exercise significant deference towards domestic authorities, but at the same time they should ensure that there is sufficient oversight of the quality of the domestic findings. Of course it still begs the question of how to regulate the intensity of review in safeguard disputes. This, again, requires panels to determine whether there is a rational basis for the findings of the domestic authority in light of the record evidence and legal criteria.[115] The issues under review by panels are therefore similar to those that arise in anti-dumping and countervailing duty disputes. The level of intensity of review will not always be straightforward in relation to substantive issues, such as serious injury and causation, because it involves more than a checklist approach, but less than a complete re-evaluation of the issues. For example, in determining serious injury, it is not just a matter of looking to see if the authority has examined production levels, loss of market share or any other indicia listed in Article 4.2. Some factors may be more relevant than others, and there may be other factors not listed in Article 4.2 that are influential. Panels must still exercise critical judgment and ascertain whether a measure is based upon positive evidence rather than mere assertion. Ultimately, the major consideration for panel scrutiny in respect of Article 4.2 is whether the domestic authority has established a strong rational relationship between the factual questions required to be answered in the national level investigation and the findings made by the authority.

---

114 See Safeguards Agreement, arts 2.1, 4; Anti-Dumping Agreement, art 4. The expressions 'serious injury' and 'material injury' are also found in GATT 1994, arts XIX, VI respectively.

115 Refer to the list of indicative criteria in Chapter 5, Section 5.2.2.

6.6 COMPARISON OF THE NEW STANDARD WITH THE CURRENT STANDARD APPLIED IN TRADE REMEDY DISPUTES

In this section, I will briefly examine how the new standard of review of facts compares with its treatment to date by WTO Tribunals under disputes brought under the Anti-Dumping, SCM and Safeguard Agreements. This comparison will demonstrate that the new standard would be more deferential and strike a better balance with the guiding principles discussed in earlier chapters. I will deal with each of the Trade Remedy Agreements in turn, but the issues are quite similar for each agreement, and this evidences the need for the adoption of a common approach.

6.6.1 The Anti-Dumping Agreement

The major difference between the new Anti-Dumping Standard and the current standard of review is the way in which Article 17.6(i) would be applied.[116] There are at least two main criticisms of the current usage of Article 17.6(i). Firstly, there is uncertainty about exactly how intensive this article requires panels to be in their factual review, and secondly, there has been a movement in the direction of *de novo* review. The language of Article 17.6(i) suggests that panels must only examine matters of procedure and due process. However, the Appellate Body's interpretation of this article as requiring an 'active examination' also suggests that panels must go further and examine the substantive issues in dispute.[117] For example, when determining that a domestic authority's establishment of facts was 'proper', a panel necessarily needs comprehensively to review the scope and appropriateness of the factual record.[118] Despite this, it is the reading of Article 17.6 in conjunction with Article 11 of the DSU that has arguably contributed more to an intrusive interpretation of Article 17.6(i). In a number of decisions WTO Tribunals have

---

[116] The legal standard of review pursuant to Article 17.6(ii) is not discussed in this section. Article 17.6(ii) as applied and the new legal standard proposed in this book are likely to be very similar. (See Section 6.3.3 above.)

[117] There have been some very sound attempts to interpret Article 17.6(i). In Panel Report, *Mexico-Corn Syrup* [7.95] the panel formulated a test described as 'objective sufficiency' when it noted that its role was to 'examine whether the evidence before the investigating authority at the time it initiated the investigation was such that an unbiased and objective investigating authority evaluating that evidence could have properly determined that sufficient evidence of dumping, injury and causal link existed to justify initiation.'

[118] Matthias Oesch, *Standards of Review in WTO Dispute Resolution* (Oxford University Press, 2003), 91.

stated that these two articles are complimentary and that Article 17.6 does not contain an exhaustible statement of the standard of review.[119] The effect of this is to incorporate some of the elements of the objective assessment test into the Anti-Dumping test.[120] Whilst it is clear that the drafters of Article 17.6 had a materially deferential standard in mind, the only certainty that has emerged is that WTO Tribunals have rejected *de novo* review in anti-dumping cases, but without articulating a consistent deferential interpretation.[121]

Overall, under the current standard of review, it is open to panels to apply Article 17.6(i) in such a way which accords less deference to domestic authority evaluations, and from a pragmatic point of view, such an interpretation is understandable given the possible perception of domestic authorities favouring their own local industries in anti-dumping investigations.[122] Whilst there can be no guarantees of panels no longer misapplying Article 17.6(i), the new standard would help to develop an interpretation that is in keeping with the design of the Anti-Dumping Agreement and similar agreements. The new standard would be more deferential because of the recognition of the extensive role carried out by domestic authorities. The new standard would also still account for potential bias in requiring panels to focus on the quality of decision-making, which would include oversight of most key procedural and substantive issues.

6.6.2 The SCM Agreement

In a number of decisions under the SCM Agreement, the Appellate Body has affirmed a standard of review that is almost indistinguishable from *de novo* review.[123] In *Japan-DRAMs (Korea)*, the Appellate Body determined that a panel erred in failing to examine whether the Japanese investigating authority's evidence supported a finding of entrustment or direction that was necessary to establish the existence of a subsidy under Article 1.1 of the SCM

---

119 See Appellate Body Report, *US-Hot Rolled Steel* [55]–[56], Panel Report, *US-Steel Plate* [7.1]–[7.7] and Appellate Body Report, *US-Softwood Lumber VI (Article 21.5-Canada)* [89]–[91].

120 *Ibid.*

121 See Horlick and Clarke, 'Standards for Panels Reviewing Anti-Dumping Determinations under the GATT', above n 32, 298; Oesch, *Standards of Review in WTO Dispute Resolution*, above n 118, 89. Anti-Dumping decisions where WTO Tribunals have rejected *de novo* review include Panel Report, *Egypt-Rebar from Turkey* [7.8]–[7.14]; Panel Report, *Guatemala Cement II* [8.17]–[8.19].

122 Oesch, *Standards of Review in WTO Dispute Resolution*, above n 118, 92.

123 It is as yet unknown whether the more deferential standard prescribed by the Appellate Body in the SPS case *US-Continued Suspension* will affect the standard applied in SCM and other trade remedy cases.

Agreement.[124] The panel had refrained from undertaking this analysis because it found that it was the role of the investigating authority to determine if the evidence supported a positive finding of entrustment or direction.[125] The Appellate Body found that the panel should have conducted the review itself to decide whether there was evidence sufficient to support such a determination. This followed a related decision of *US-Countervailing Duty Investigation on DRAMS*, where the Appellate Body also determined that a panel applied the incorrect standard of review, in that the panel did not review evidence in its totality.[126] In that case, the Appellate Body ironically found that the panel had engaged in *de novo* review, despite the Appellate Body, in faulting the panel's approach, requiring a similar standard to be exercised.

In *US-Softwood Lumber VI (Article 21.5-Canada)*, the Appellate Body considered the standard of review applied by a panel in reviewing an injury determination under both the SCM Agreement and Anti-Dumping Agreement.[127] In finding that the panel had not applied the correct standard of review under the SCM Agreement, the Appellate Body determined that it is the role of panels to conduct an in-depth examination of the explanations given by the authority and to test its reasoning against the evidence.[128] The Appellate Body gave particular examples of this such as the requirement for panels to review how individual pieces of evidence can reasonably be relied upon to support particular inferences, and how the evidence in the record may support a panel's factual findings.[129]

Both of the above decisions indicate that the Appellate Body is applying a near *de novo* standard of review. In doing so, it is casting a very high burden on panels to examine matters in acute detail and to prepare lengthy rulings detailing their analysis. Part of the rationale of the Appellate Body is that a lesser standard of review 'imposes an undue burden on the complaining party'.[130]

---

124 Appellate Body Report, *Japan-DRAMs (Korea)* [117]–[142].

125 Panel Report, *Japan-DRAMs (Korea)* [7.253].

126 Appellate Body Report, *US-Countervailing Duty Investigation on DRAMS* [188].

127 Appellate Body Report, *US-Softwood Lumber VI (Article 21.5-Canada)* [89]–[140].

128 Appellate Body Report, *US-Softwood Lumber VI (Article 21.5-Canada)* [93], [138].

129 Appellate Body Report, *US-Softwood Lumber VI (Article 21.5-Canada)* [98]–[99].

130 Appellate Body Report, *US-Softwood Lumber VI (Article 21.5-Canada)* [138]. This criticism of the panel was directed at the panel's repeated reliance on the test that Canada had not demonstrated that an objective and unbiased authority could not have reached the conclusion that the USITC did, which is at odds with the present standard of review.

This approach by the Appellate Body appears to 'swing the pendulum' too far towards *de novo* review. Under the new standard proposed in this book, the standard of review applied in relation to countervailing investigations would not be so intensive and panels would be charged with the task of looking at the overall quality of the domestic investigation. There would be more leeway given to domestic authorities to reach their findings and also more discretion accorded to panels in their review methodology. It is of course difficult to conclude whether or not the two decisions discussed above would have been decided differently had the new standard been applied. It is perhaps unlikely in the applicable softwood lumber decision because of the fact that it appears that the panel adopted a more obviously deferential standard closer to an 'arbitrary or capricious' standard.[131] In the two decisions concerning countervailing duties on DRAMS, the finding against the panels on the standard of review issue was directly relevant to the key question of whether 'entrustment or direction' was made out and a subsidy existed.[132] Although there were other grounds argued in the appeal, it is strongly arguable that this issue was pivotal in the result.

It is contended that the factual standard of review applied in respect of the countervailing provisions in the SCM Agreement ought to be more deferential than the general standard of review by virtue of the special role of the domestic investigating authorities. In applying a specific standard of review advocated in this book this would be the case. Cases on the legality of subsidies per se that are first litigated before a WTO panel should be subject to the general standard of review. The structure of the countervailing provisions in the SCM Agreement are very similar to those within the Anti-Dumping Agreement, and subject to any variance created by Article 17.6, should result in a reasonably uniform standard of review.

6.6.3 The Safeguards Agreement

The treatment of the standard of review issue by WTO Tribunals when deciding safeguard cases has been very similar to the treatment under other trade remedy agreements. Accordingly, very little can be added to the observations made in sections 6.6.1 and 6.6.2. In several safeguard cases, the Appellate Body has repeatedly stated that *de novo* review is to be avoided, whilst at the same time articulating a standard that is highly intensive and often indistin-

---

[131] See *Citizens to Preserve Overton Park Inc v Volpe* 401 US 402, 416 (1971) discussed in Chapter 1, Section 1.2.5.

[132] *US-Countervailing Duty Investigation on DRAMS* and *Japan-DRAMS (Korea)*. DRAMS is an acronym for dynamic random access memory semiconductors.

guishable from *de novo* review.[133] This is despite the fact that WTO Tribunals have importantly recognized that the factual standard is partially derived from the provisions of the agreement under review. In *US-Lamb* and *US-Cotton Yarn*, the Appellate Body stated that the precise nature of an examination conducted by a panel, in reviewing a claim under Article 4.2 of the Safeguards Agreement, stems in part from the obligations contained in Article 4.2, and in part from the obligation to conduct an objective assessment under Article 11.[134] This creates a contradiction in the approach of WTO Tribunals in that a standard of review founded on the obligations of the Agreement on Safeguards ought to lead to more judicial appreciation of the role carried out by those authorities. Thus, the standard that should be applied based upon current safeguard cases ought to be more deferential. It is intended that the new standard of review would go some way towards removing this contradiction between theory and practice.

6.7 CONCLUSION

In this chapter I have provided a description of how the new standard of review, as proposed in Chapters 4 and 5, might apply to the Trade Remedy Agreements. The application of the new standard of review would result in a movement away from the general standard of review to a more specific standard of review. This is principally a product of the role of domestic authorities as 'arbiters of first instance' in reviewing trade remedy complaints. This responsibility is enshrined in each of the trade remedy agreements. Accordingly, WTO panels would apply a standard of review that is more deferential than would otherwise apply. Effective oversight by panels would nonetheless still require them to review the quality of the domestic authority decision-making. This involves panels doing more than merely checking to see if the authorities have addressed the relevant legal criteria or carried out due process requirements. Panels will still need to examine whether the reasoning and conclusions of the domestic authorities are rational, based on the factual record. The exact level of scrutiny required of panels will vary depending upon the nature of the facts and obligations that are in issue. However, there is no question that panels would have the competency to deal with potential problems posed by

133 See for example, Appellate Body Report, *US-Cotton Yarn* [74].

134 Appellate Body Report, *US-Lamb* [105]; Appellate Body Report, *US-Cotton Yarn* [76].

domestic level investigations, such as a lack of due process or bias in favour of domestic producers.[135]

The proposed standard of review would be extremely similar for each Trade Remedy Agreement, despite the potential difficulties posed by Article 17.6 of the Anti-Dumping Agreement. This similarity in approach would make the new standard more straightforward to apply in future trade remedy cases.

In the Chapter 7, I will be using the same approach as employed in this chapter to examine how the new standard of review may be applied to a number of other WTO Agreements.

135 In this author's opinion, it is unlikely the proposed standard of review for trade remedies would undermine the power of WTO panels to rigorously enforce applicable WTO rules but of course it may alter individual case outcomes. Even if this approach did reduce the rigour exercisable by panels, arguably the proper interpretation of the WTO Agreements is a more important consideration.

7. The application of a new standard of review to selected non-trade remedy agreements

7.1 INTRODUCTION

In this chapter, I will be examining how the new standard of review will apply to three WTO Agreements: the SPS Agreement, the TBT Agreement and GATT 1994. The first major reason for selecting these agreements is that each of them involves differing levels of responsibility for members in the carrying out of their WTO obligations. This helps to demonstrate how the new standard would apply in different situations. The relation between these agreements may be described as a sliding scale, where the SPS and TBT Agreements and GATT 1994, in that order, prescribe a lesser degree of responsibility for domestic authorities to exercise any kind of oversight in relation to measures. This is to be contrasted with the trade remedy agreements, where formal review processes are required to be followed by domestic authorities. In addition, many of the other WTO Agreements, such as GATS, the Agreement on Customs Valuation or the Agreement on Import Licensing Procedures are quite similar to GATT 1994, in that they do not retain specific competencies for members to safeguard WTO commitments.[1]

[1] GATS, art VI (2)(a) does prescribe some generalized review obligations. The first sentence of this Article provides: 'Each Member shall maintain or institute as soon as practicable judicial, arbitral or administrative tribunals or procedures which provide, at the request of an affected service supplier, for the prompt review of, and where justified, appropriate remedies for, administrative decisions affecting trade in services.' This would not be a sufficient basis to depart from the standard of review applied in respect of GATT 1994 (see Section 7.5). In *Thailand-Cigarettes (Philippines) (Panel)* [7.99]–[7.100], in examining claims under the Agreement on Customs Valuation, the panel confirmed that the precise standard of review will depend upon whether the panel must conduct an analysis of the facts as the first trier of facts or as reviewer of factual determinations made by domestic authorities. However, as the role of domestic authorities is not prescribed in this Agreement the standard of review is unlikely to be very different in either scenario as was demonstrated in this case.

A second major reason for selecting these agreements is that a number of disputes concerning these agreements have generated controversy and debate in relation to the issue of whether the WTO is increasingly interfering in the domestic affairs of members, and is in some way overreaching its mandate.[2] The SPS Agreement, in particular, has been the subject of much scrutiny in cases such as *EC-Hormones*[3] and *EC-Approval and Marketing of Biotech Products*.[4] The *EC-Hormones* case is especially useful in a standard of review analysis. It was the decision that first identified DSU Article 11 as containing the standard of review, and it also discusses the need for there to be rational relationship between the measure and a national-level risk assessment.[5] Additionally, the Appellate Body, in its Article 21.5 compliance decision on *EC-Hormones* has since then signalled a more deferential approach to reviewing health and safety risk assessments carried out by domestic authorities.[6]

There will be a brief survey here of the new standard of review under the three subject agreements. For each, there will be an identification of the major obligations from which I will identify those obligations that may affect the standard of review. It will be shown that particular obligations should generate a specific standard of review of facts under the SPS and TBT Agreements, but that the standard of review for GATT 1994 disputes should be the general standard discussed in Chapter 4. In identifying the nature of the standard to be applied in TBT and SPS disputes, I will discuss how panels and domestic authorities might undertake their responsibilities in order to achieve a high quality review process within the framework of each agreement. Selected cases referenced in this chapter will help demonstrate how the new standard might operate and how deferential or intrusive the standard is likely to be.

---

2 This is particularly the case with SPS disputes, which may, for example, involve the protection of traditional agricultural industries or native animal species. As at March 2012, panel decisions in which the principal complaint concerned the SPS and TBT Agreements and the GATT 1994 accounted for approximately 30 per cent of all WTO cases. The breakdown of this figure is 9 per cent for SPS cases, 10 per cent for TBT cases and 11 per cent for GATT 1994 cases. (Note that approximately 78 per cent of all panel complaints filed to date involve claims of GATT inconsistency but this is usually in conjunction with claims by WTO members alleging contraventions of other WTO Agreements.) Source: http://www.worldtradelaw.net.ezp.lib.unimelb.edu.au/database/agreementcount.asp, last accessed 30 March 2012.

3 This case has been the subject of various rulings comprising: Panel Report, *EC-Hormones (US)*; Panel Report, *EC-Hormones (Canada)*; Appellate Body Report, *EC-Hormones*; Award of Arbitrator, *EC-Hormones*; Decision by the Arbitrators, *EC-Hormones (Canada) (Article 22.2-EC)*; Decision by the Arbitrators, *EC-Hormones (US) (Article 22.6-EC)*; Panel and Appellate Body Reports, *US-Continued Suspension*.

4 Panel Report, *EC-Approval and Marketing of Biotech Products*.

5 Appellate Body Report, *EC-Hormones* [116], [193].

6 Appellate Body Report, *US-Continued Suspension* [585]–[592].

Finally, in order to provide a contrasting illustration, at the end of this chapter I will briefly compare how the standard of review has been applied to date under each agreement.

This chapter will further demonstrate the need for a cohesive doctrine to properly develop the standard of review, particularly in light of the disparate subject matter of the WTO Agreements. There is justification for a principled approach that can, at the same time, be deployed by WTO Tribunals in a flexible manner. Current WTO jurisprudence, despite a 'mantra-like' reliance on the objective assessment test, evidences support for this approach. The focus of this chapter is to identify how the new standard might work in practice in the SPS, TBT and GATT 1994 contexts. However, by implication, it will also be instructive on how the new standard may be applied to other non-trade remedy agreements.

7.2 UNIFORMITY OF THE STANDARD OF REVIEW IN NON-TRADE REMEDY AGREEMENTS

An important threshold issue in applying the new standard of review to non-trade remedy agreements is the question of whether there will be a single standard for each agreement, or whether the new standard will apply to particular obligations within these agreements. This issue is not nearly as prominent in trade remedy agreements, where the obligations centre around a formal national level process, and the division of competencies between panels and authorities is more obvious. For non-trade remedy agreements, it is frequently the case that any specific responsibilities to be carried out by members may only relate to certain types of obligations, with other parts of the agreement containing more generalized rules. A good example is the SPS Agreement, where Article 2.2 provides that 'members shall ensure that any sanitary or phytosanitary measure is applied only to the extent necessary to protect human, animal or plant life or health…'. In contrast, Article 5.1 of the SPS Agreement requires members to base measures on a risk assessment, which is usually carried out by members prior to the measure being implemented.

The position I have adopted is that the new standard of review should not simply apply in a uniform fashion across all obligations, but that it should be applied to specific obligations. To do otherwise would be to undermine the new standard because it would be applied in situations where the Agreements have not contemplated particular tasks to be undertaken by members. Further, it also leads to more consistency in interpreting Agreements because similar provisions in different WTO Agreements would not be subject to different standards of review. For instance, there are a number of provisions in various WTO Agreements requiring members to ensure that measures are not more trade restrictive than necessary.[7] The exception to this position is that where obligations are to be read in conjunction with an obligation requiring a specific standard of review, then they should also be subject to the same specific standard. For example, the Appellate Body, in *EC-Hormones*, noted that Articles 2.2 and 5.1 of the SPS Agreement should be read together, as Article 2.2 informs the meaning of Article 5.1.[8] It is acknowledged that it will not always be clear which obligations are to be grouped for applying a particular standard of review, and this issue can only be determined in subsequent WTO Tribunal decisions.[9]

7.3 THE AGREEMENT ON SANITARY AND PHYTOSANITARY MEASURES

7.3.1 Key Concepts and Obligations

This Agreement concerns the regulation of sanitary and phytosanitary measures, which are defined as any measure that is applied to protect human, animal or plant life or health from various hazards such as pests, disease, toxins, or contaminants or disease causing organisms in food, beverages and feedstocks.[10] The Agreement essentially concerns the relationship between national health and safety and international trade.[11] Measures include all laws, regulations or procedures, but also processes and production methods, quarantine treatment and packaging and labelling requirements.[12] The key concept in the SPS Agreement is that such measures are permitted in order to protect human, animal or plant life or health. It is therefore a limitation on the objective of trade liberalization between WTO members. However, this right to maintain SPS measures is restricted on the basis that members may only apply SPS measures to the extent necessary to protect human, animal or plant life or health.[13] The terminology 'only to the extent necessary' could potentially

---

7 For example, SPS Agreement, art 5.6.

8 Appellate Body Report, *EC Hormones* [180]–[181].

9 For example, a least trade restrictive analysis may form part of an SPS risk assessment, and may therefore be subject to a different standard of review: see Chapter 7, Section 7.3.2.

10 SPS Agreement, Annex A, paragraph 1.

11 Catherine Button, *The Power to Protect: Trade Health and Uncertainty in the WTO* (Hart Publishing, 2004) 217, 1.

12 *Ibid.*

13 SPS Agreement, art 2.1. There is also the requirement for members to apply most favoured nation and national treatment obligations in Article 2.3.

leave the exact level of acceptable SPS measures quite uncertain. However, this Agreement is more exacting in that it requires members to ensure that SPS measures are based on scientific principles, and are not maintained without sufficient scientific evidence.[14] Members are also encouraged to harmonize SPS measures by basing them on international standards, guidelines or recommendations.[15]

The SPS Agreement attempts to prescribe some specific parameters for the determination of what is an appropriate level of SPS protection.[16] SPS measures must be based on a risk assessment as is appropriate to the circumstances.[17] Members must consider as part of their risk assessment, matters such as available scientific evidence, testing methods, quarantine treatments and the prevalence of specific diseases and pests.[18] Potential economic damage, rectification costs and the costs of alternative risk minimisation measures must also be taken into account.[19] Further, members are required to furnish reasons for maintaining SPS measures where another member believes that such measures are constraining or have the potential to constrain exports and where the measures are not based upon international standards.[20]

This Agreement seeks to articulate, so far as possible, the line to be drawn between free trade principles and the limited exception set out in Article XX(b) of GATT 1994.[21] Three major aspects of the Agreement have been the source of the majority of SPS disputes. Firstly, there is the requirement for measures to be based on sufficient scientific evidence.[22] Secondly, there is the requirement for measures to be not more restrictive than required in order to

---

14 SPS Agreement, art 2.2. See also Joanne Scott, *The WTO Agreement on Sanitary and Phytosanity Measures: A Commentary* (Oxford University Press, 2007) 3. Note also that Article 5.7 provides an exception to this rule by permitting members to provisionally adopt SPS measures where there is insufficient scientific evidence, provided that the measure is based upon available pertinent information and the member obtains additional information necessary for a more objective assessment of risk and reviews the SPS measure within a reasonable period of time.

15 SPS Agreement, art 3.1.

16 SPS Agreement, art 5.

17 SPS Agreement, art 5.1.

18 SPS Agreement, art 5.2.

19 SPS Agreement, art 5.3.

20 SPS Agreement, art 5.8.

21 GATT 1994, art XX(b) provides: 'Subject to the requirement that such measures are not applied in a manner which would constitute a means of arbitrary or unjustifiable discrimination between countries where the same conditions prevail, or a disguised restriction on international trade, nothing in this Agreement shall be construed to prevent the adoption or enforcement by any contracting party of measures: ... necessary to protect human, animal or plant life or health; ...'.

22 SPS Agreement, art 2.2.

achieve an appropriate level of SPS protection.[23] This obligation is not met where an alternative measure that achieves the appropriate level of SPS protection is available and is significantly less restrictive to trade.[24] Thirdly, SPS measures must be based upon a risk assessment carried out by a member maintaining the measure and the risk assessment must have taken into account factors listed in the SPS Agreement.[25]

Given the technical and scientific nature of SPS disputes, panels are encouraged to seek advice from experts who are chosen in consultation with the parties and, where appropriate, establish an advisory technical experts group or consult relevant international organizations.[26]

All of the above aspects are, in the end, about determining what is an appropriate level of risk that may justify maintaining SPS measures. It is now settled that members do not have the complete freedom to decide on what level of risk they may accept. The approach of the panel (as upheld by the Appellate Body) in *Japan-Apples* evidences that there must at least be more than a minimal risk.[27] There has, for some time, been concern that the SPS Agreement 'swings the pendulum' too far in favour of trade liberalization objectives by not giving national regulators sufficient discretion to assess the risks to protect health and safety.[28] The fact that the first three SPS cases were won by complainants has potentially increased these concerns.[29] Further, the Appellate Body has rejected the recognition of the precautionary principle as a general legal principle that may be applied by panels in assessing these types of cases.[30] This has meant that WTO Tribunals have had to find ways to mediate this tension

---

23 SPS Agreement, art 5.6.

24 Footnote to SPS Agreement, art 5.6.

25 SPS Agreement, arts 5.1–5.3. Note that a member may rely on a risk assessment carried out by an international organization or another member. See Appellate Body Report, *EC-Hormones* [189]–[190].

26 SPS Agreement, art 11.2.

27 Panel Report, *Japan-Apples*, [8.199, 8.222]; Appellate Body Report, *Japan-Apples* [160], [168].

28 Button, *The Power to Protect: Trade, Health and Uncertainty in the WTO*, above n 11, 3–4. The issue of health and safety is often used as an example of how the WTO may affect the national sovereignty of WTO members.

29 The first three cases were *EC-Hormones*, *Australia-Salmon* and *Japan-Agricultural Products*.

30 Appellate Body Report, *EC-Hormones* [123]–[124]. The Appellate Body noted that the precautionary principle did not override the ordinary principles and methods of treaty interpretation, but it did nonetheless suggest that the precautionary principle 'finds reflection' in Article 5.7 and 3.3 of the SPS Agreement. See also *EC-Approval and Marketing of Biotech Products* [7.87]–[7.89] where the panel refers to the Appellate Body's comments in *EC-Hormones* and confirms that the legal status of the precautionary principle is unsettled.

between trade liberalization and domestic health and safety objectives. The standard of review has been one such mechanism. This has been identified more recently by the Appellate Body in *US-Continued Suspension* in which it determined that the panel applied an overly intensive standard of review that did not respect the merits of the member's own risk assessment.[31] The impact of this case is significant as it demonstrates the use of a more deferential standard of review to reduce intrusion in contentious health and safety matters. In the next section, I will examine how the new standard of review may be applied to this issue of risk assessments and related matters.

7.3.2 The Application of the New Standard to the SPS Agreement

In this section, I will address the following matters concerning how the new standard of review may be applied in respect of SPS measures. Firstly, I will assess whether panels ought to apply the general standard of review as opposed to a specific standard to SPS measures. Secondly, if a specific standard is to be applied, I will need to define the characteristics of this specific standard by reference to particular obligations set out in the SPS Agreement. Assuming that a specific standard is to be formulated, I will also examine other issues that may inform the new standard, such as the overall quality of review by a panel, and the requirement for there to be a rational relationship between risk assessments and measures.

The threshold issue for applying the new standard is to determine whether the general standard should be applied without modification. The determinant of this is whether a member's jurisdictional competencies have, in some way, been retained by virtue of the drafting of the SPS Agreement. When examining the text of the SPS Agreement, it is not immediately clear whether or not members have retained any direct responsibilities to regulate SPS measures for the purposes of ongoing WTO compliance. The Agreement has the appearance of a set of rules over which members have little discretion. The key issues of scientific justification, least trade restrictive measures and risk assessments are simply referred to in the text and a line may be drawn via panel adjudication between measures that comply with the terms of the Agreement and those which do not. In other words, a panel's role would be to determine whether WTO obligations have been met, and in doing so, a panel would apply a more intensive standard of review. This is in direct contrast to the structure of the trade remedy agreements, which clearly mandate a high level of national control over trade remedy measures through administrative and judicial procedures.

---

[31] Appellate Body Report, *US-Continued Suspension* [585]–[615].

Despite the above, a closer examination of the SPS Agreement evidences the fact that members do retain jurisdictional competencies, albeit to a limited degree. The major determinant of this is the risk assessment provisions within Article 5, which require SPS measures to be based upon a risk assessment, with the scientific and economic factors that members shall take into account listed in that Article.[32] These competencies may also be construed more widely when they are read in conjunction with the scientific justification and least trade restrictive requirements set out in Articles 2.2, 3.3, 5.4 and 5.6. This shows that the WTO is not the sole agent in protecting rights and performing obligations pursuant to this Agreement. Members do participate in this process, and for this reason, it is not appropriate for panels to apply the highly intensive general standard of review. Under the SPS Agreement, it is the fact that members must actively participate in the instituting or maintaining of a contingent measure that means a specific standard ought to be applied.[33]

Given that the general standard ought to be excluded, it falls to determine the nature and scope of the specific standard that would apply in SPS disputes. It is recalled from Chapter 5 that the specific standard is also defined by reference to the allocation of jurisdictional competencies within the relevant WTO Agreement. The primary delineator of member competencies in the SPS Agreement are the obligations set out in Articles 5.1 to 5.3. The requirement for members to base their SPS measures on a risk assessment, as appropriate in the circumstances, and, in doing so, to take into account various scientific and economic criteria, constructs a regime whereby members must have some kind of domestic process to deal with the issuance and maintenance of SPS measures. This process needs to be able to justify SPS measures in accordance with the terms of the SPS Agreement. It will often be inadequate to benchmark SPS measures against international standards because the level of protection sought will be higher than the international standard, or the science concerning the risks is unclear.[34]

There are several requirements of a risk assessment that create obligations that members must fulfil when maintaining SPS measures. These requirements place an onus on members to show that SPS measures are justified and are not merely a disguised restriction on international trade.[35] Members must, first, be able to rely upon a risk assessment.[36] A risk assessment is defined in Annexure

---

32 SPS Agreement, arts 5.1, 5.2.

33 The specific standard of review applied will, in turn, be influenced by the quality of a member's participation in the issuing or review of the disputed measures.

34 See Scott, *The WTO Agreement on Sanitary and Phytosanity Measures*, above n 14, 5 where the author notes that '...the AB has been required to walk a line between international harmonization and respect for regulatory diversity.'

35 SPS Agreement, arts 2.3, 5.1 and 5.4.

36 SPS Agreement, art 5.1.

A as the evaluation of the likelihood of entry, establishment or spread of a pest or disease within the member's territory, its biological and economic consequences and potential adverse effects on human or animal health.[37] It would appear that it is insufficient for a member to simply rely upon generalized scientific studies, and where no specific studies exist, a member must conduct an active assessment that directly addresses the risks.[38]

Secondly, the risk assessment must disclose some actual risk of harm to human, animal or plant life of health. Governments must be responding to real identified risks and not 'knee-jerk reactions' to fears or purely hypothetical risks.[39] It is, however, still unclear from present WTO case law as to what minimum level of risk is necessary in order to maintain SPS measures. Findings as to the level of risk will be directly impacted upon by the quality of scientific research and the amount of consensus within the scientific community. Minority scientific opinion may also be taken into account by members in any risk assessment.[40]

Thirdly, pursuant to Article 5.1, SPS measures must be 'based upon' a risk assessment. This implies that measures need not be identical and may differ according to a member's own domestic circumstances. This terminology does, however, raise the problem of how strictly the measures must be based upon the risk assessment. The Appellate Body has determined that the expression 'based upon' refers to the objective and observable relationship between a risk assessment and a measure.[41] This test is otherwise referred to as the rational relationship test, and connotes that the measure must logically follow the reasoning and conclusions of the risk assessment. That is, there must be a matching of at least some of the scientific conclusions in the risk assessment and the scientific conclusions implicit in the SPS measures or reasonably supporting the measures.[42] This is clearly different from the requirement for there to be strict conformity.[43]

---

[37] SPS Agreement, Annex A, paragraph 4

[38] Appellate Body Report, *EC-Hormones* [189]–[190]. The Appellate Body overturned the panel's finding that a risk assessment must be taken into account before the measures were implemented.

[39] *Ibid.*

[40] See Appellate Body Report, *EC-Hormones* [194] wherein the Appellate Body states: 'Responsible and representative governments may act in good faith on the basis of what, at a given time, may be a divergent opinion coming from qualified and respected sources. This is also discussed in Appellate Body Report, *EC-Asbestos*, Section VII C1.

[41] Appellate Body Report, *EC-Hormones* [189].

[42] Appellate Body Report, *EC-Hormones* [192]–[193].

[43] Gavin Goh, 'Tipping the Apple Cart: The Limits of Science and Law in the SPS Agreement after *Japan-Apples*' (2006) 40 *Journal of World Trade* 669.

Fourthly, members must ensure that the level of SPS measures must be as least trade restrictive as possible.[44] This obligation may not be addressed in a risk assessment, but may be part of the implementation of the risk assessment at a later stage. It is very difficult for WTO Tribunals to assess whether there are more trade enhancing measures available to members because this is likely to involve difficult questions about a member's domestic priorities, resource allocation and its ability to pay for alternative measures. This is to be contrasted with, for example, more fundamental issues of whether a measure is discriminatory or is a disguised restriction on international trade.[45]

When the above obligations are considered in the aggregate, they disclose the contours of the new standard of review for SPS measures. What these obligations demonstrate is that members have a material degree of participation in the justification of SPS measures, and that the obligations are not prescribed through formal processes, nor are they extremely onerous on members. There is also a significant amount of discretion that members retain in relation to the carrying out of a risk assessment or an analysis of trade effects. This means that there is little basis for panels radically moving away from an intensive standard of review, and panels ought to have the ability to carefully examine the way governments have sought to justify SPS measures. Panels should not, however, conduct their own new risk assessment in relation to the measures.[46]

If the new SPS standard was positioned on a sliding scale with *de novo* review at one end and total deference at the other, it would be positioned closer to the *de novo* end of the scale. For comparison purposes, the SPS standard would be more intensive than the standard applied in trade remedy disputes but it would be less intensive than the standard applied under GATT 1994 and some other WTO Agreements. Under GATT 1994, the absence of domestic administrative processes means that a WTO panel is the reviewer at first instance and there are no restrictions on the scope of review.[47] By contrast, the

---

44 SPS Agreement, art 5.6. The least trade restrictive requirement takes into account the technical and economic feasibility of the measure.

45 SPS Agreement, arts 2.3, 5.5. See also *Australia-Apples*, First Written Submissions of Australia [186].

46 See Panel Report, *Japan-Agricultural Products II* [8.32] where the panel states: 'We are not empowered, nor are the experts advising the panel, to conduct our own risk assessment'. See also Michael M. Du, 'Standard of Review under the SPS Agreement after *EC-Hormones II*' (2010) 59(2) *International & Comparatively Law Quarterly* 448.

47 See Chapter 7, Section 7.6.3. See also for example Panel Report, *EC-Selected Customs Matters* [7.264]–[7.265], where the panel found that allegedly divergent tariff classification practices in different EC Member States did not amount to a non-uniform administration of customs regulations contrary to GATT 1994 Article X:3(a). As there had been no prior factual inquiry conducted by an EC authority the panel fully examined the claims and evidence and made its own findings.

SPS Agreement contemplates domestic administrative procedures in some provisions which define the scope and intensity of review. This general description of intensity of review does not always allow for an accurate application of a standard of review, and it is important for panels to also examine the quality of decision-making by members in carrying out their independent obligations.

There are essentially two related strands to this panel review of member obligations in SPS cases. Firstly, there is the need to ensure that the measures are a rational outcome of the evidence reviewed by the domestic authority. That is, panels will need to test the reasoning and conclusions of the authorities. Secondly, there is the requirement for panels to examine the overall credibility of domestic authorities in the manner in which they have carried out their function in reviewing and implementing SPS measures. Where a panel is reviewing the validity of a risk assessment, the panel would need to ensure that there is a rational relationship between the risk assessment and the measure that is in issue. This is consistent with the approach of the Appellate Body in *EC-Hormones*.[48]

The determination of the presence or absence of a rational relationship can only be done on a case-by-case basis, after account is taken of all considerations rationally bearing upon the issue of potential health effects.[49] Hence, it is very difficult to prescribe an exact test to determine the quality of domestic-level processes given that it will depend upon the nature of the measures and conduct of the authorities. This means that there will inevitably be some variation in the intensity of review in SPS disputes. There is also the question of whether a panel should exercise deference in assessing whether a measure is least trade restrictive in nature pursuant to Article 5.6 of the SPS Agreement. It is arguable that a more intensive standard of review should apply because of the fact that panels do have the competency to assess measures against this type of economic criteria, particularly given that panels perform a similar analysis when considering Article XX of GATT 1994.

It may also be possible to further articulate the standard of review under the SPS Agreement by reference to the regulatory context and intention of this Agreement. In the case of the SPS Agreement, the regulatory intention is evidenced by its structure in dealing with the competing objectives of free trade and regulatory autonomy in the field human, animal and plant health and safety.[50] The SPS Agreement therefore goes beyond the objective of

48 Appellate Body Report, *EC-Hormones* [193]–[194].
49 Appellate Body Report, *EC-Hormones* [194].
50 First paragraph of the Recitals to the SPS Agreement.

non-discrimination between members. This structure suggests the need for a more deferential approach to interpreting SPS provisions. However, there are factors present that do not support this proposition. In particular, there is the requirement for measures to be based on scientific principles and not maintained without sufficient scientific evidence.[51]

There is accordingly, a high degree of rigour that is required of domestic authorities in issuing measures, and of panels in reviewing such measures. Panels will be required to exercise a more intensive standard of review to determine the rationality of competing scientific arguments. This is difficult to do without redeciding a case on its merits. In other words, panels may be faced with '...an interpretation of scientific evidence that essentially eviscerates them and defers to national judgments about "science"...' or an interpretation that will be more intensive but at the expense of regulatory autonomy.[52] Ultimately the difficulty with the standard of review being heavily reliant on the regulatory intention of any of the WTO Agreements is that the regulatory intention may not be readily apparent from its text. Accordingly, this criterion may only be useful where the jurisdictional competencies are not able to be drawn from the structure and wording of the applicable WTO Agreement and the review task of panels in examining measures is otherwise unclear.[53]

The new SPS standard can be illustrated by reference to various SPS cases. In *Japan-Apples*, the panel and Appellate Body were asked to adjudicate on the science of whether mature symptomless apples exported from the United States to Japan, posed a risk for the spread of fire blight into Japan, given this disease's presence in the United States. The panel was required to carefully examine expert evidence from both parties, and it engaged its own experts. The Appellate Body rejected Japan's argument that the panel had applied a *de novo* standard of review, because it arrived at its own conclusions about the science. However, the panel did arguably apply a *de novo* standard, or at the very least a 'correctness' test, in making its objective the

---

[51] SPS Agreement, art 2.2, which is discussed in Alan O. Sykes, 'Domestic Regulation, Sovereignty and Scientific Evidence Requirements: A Pessimistic View' in George A. Bermann and Petros C. Mavroidis (eds), *Trade and Human Health and Safety* (Cambridge University Press, 2006) 260.

[52] Sykes, 'Domestic Regulation, Sovereignty and Scientific Evidence Requirements: A Pessimistic View', above n 51, 258.

[53] See below n 107. *Contra* Michael M. Du, 'Domestic Regulatory Autonomy under the TBT Agreement: From Non-discrimination to Harmonization' (2007) 6(2) *Chinese Journal of International Law* 269, 306.

need to determine the truth and accuracy of the scientific arguments.[54] Under the new standard proposed in this chapter, the role of a panel would be to focus on the strength of the linkage between the risk assessment and the resultant measure, and associated reasoning. Further, any expert commissioned by the panel would be given a narrow brief to comment on aspects of the respondent's risk assessment, rather than to determine the best science in the matter.

The issue of the role of panels in determining the best science has also arisen in the *US-Continued Suspension* decision. In that decision, the Appellate Body appears to have altered its views on the standard under the SPS Agreement. Specifically, the Appellate Body criticised the panel for seeking to determine whether the risk assessment of the EC was correct, instead of determining whether the risk assessment is supported by coherent reasoning and is supported by respectable scientific evidence.[55] Further, the Appellate Body stipulated that a panel should assess whether the reasoning articulated on the basis of the scientific evidence is objective and coherent.[56] Consistent with what I have been arguing, this decision has signalled that the standard of review is likely to be modestly more deferential in future SPS disputes. This represents a shift in approach from earlier cases where statements made by WTO Tribunals concerning the standard of review were more limited and vague.[57]

The standard of review argued for in this book in relation to the SPS Agreement may yet be articulated in future WTO disputes. There was an opportunity to identify the boundaries between WTO and domestic competencies in

---

54 See Appellate Body Report, *Japan-Apples* [240]. See Button, *The Power to Protect: Trade, Health and Uncertainty in the WTO*, above n 11, 178 where the author states: 'It is difficult to discern in the panel's consideration of these and other scientific questions any point at which the panel did not conduct a de *novo* review.' See also Jan Bohanes and Nicolas Lockhart, 'Standard of Review in WTO Law' in Daniel Bethleham, Donald McRae, Rodney Neufield and Isabelle Van Damme (eds), *The Oxford Handbook of International Trade Law* (Oxford University Press, 2009) 378.

55 Appellate Body Report, *US-Continued Suspension* [590].

56 Appellate Body Report, *US-Continued Suspension* [591]. For further discussion of this ruling see *World Trade Organization, Appellate Body Annual Report for 2008*, WTO Doc WT/AB/11 (9 February 2009) 23–5, available at www.wto.org, last accessed 31 March 2012. The United States argued that the panel had in fact applied the correct standard of review: see *US-Continued Suspension, Appellee Submission of the United States of America,* WT/D8320 (26 June 2008), available at www.ustr.gov/trade-topics/enforcement/dispute-settlement-proceedings/wto-dispute-settlement/continued-suspension-, last accessed 31 March 2012.

57 See, for example, the description of the standard of review put forward by the Appellate Body in Appellate Body Report, *EC-Hormones* [116].

the decision of *EC-Approval and Marketing of Biotech Products*.[58] Despite the importance of the subject of the use of genetically modified organisms in foods, the dispute largely dealt with the question of whether various measures concerning the approval and marketing of genetically modified organisms constituted SPS measures as defined in Annex A(1) of the SPS Agreement.[59] Measures introduced by various EC member states prohibiting the importation and marketing of specific biotech products were found by the panel to be SPS measures.[60] Risk assessments had not been carried out by any EC member states and, in the absence of evidence that the measures were based upon reputable scientific studies, the panel determined that the measures were inconsistent with SPS Article 5.1.[61] Arguably this case does not support the notion of increasing deference of the standard of review in SPS disputes, but given the focus on procedural matters in this case, it is difficult to definitively draw this conclusion.[62]

---

58 Panel Report, *EC-Approval and Marketing of Biotech Products*.

59 The subject measures comprised a de facto moratorium by the EC on approvals for importing genetically modified products, product-specific measures maintained by the EC and safeguard measures of EC member States prohibiting the importing and marketing of these products. See Panel Report, *EC-Approval and Marketing of Biotech Products* [2.1]–[2.5]

60 See Panel Report, *EC-Approval and Marketing of Biotech Products* [7.2603]–[7.2610] re Austria – T25 Maize; [7.2658]–[7.2662] re Austria – Bt176 Maize; [7.2698]–[7.2702] re Austria – MON 810 Maize; [7.2745]–[7.2749] re France – MS1/RF1 oilseed rape; [7.2770]–[7.2774] re France – Topas oilseed rape; [7.2809]–[7.2813] re Germany – Bt176 maize; [7.2850]–[7.2854] re Greece – Topas oilseed rape; [7.2886]–[7.2891] re Italy – T25 maize, MON 810 maize, MON 809 maize, Bt 11 maize; [7.2918]–[7.2922] re Luxembourg – Bt176 maize.

61 See Panel Report, *EC-Approval and Marketing of Biotech Products* [7.3056]–[7.3070] re Austria – T25 Maize; [7.3084]–[7.3087] re Austria – Bt176 Maize; [7.3105]–[7.3108] re Austria – MON 810 Maize; [7.3126]–[7.3129] re France – MS1/RF1 oilseed rape; [7.3136]–[7.3139] re France – Topas oilseed rape; [7.3156]–[7.3159] re Germany – Bt176 maize; [7.3176]–[7.3178] re Greece – Topas oilseed rape; [7.1394]–[7.3197] re Italy – T25 maize, MON 810 maize, MON 809 maize, Bt 11 maize; [7.3210]–[7.3213] re Luxembourg – Bt 176 maize. Risk assessments in the form of scientific studies did exist but the panel found that these measures were not based upon these risk assessments as required by SPS Article 5.1. The panel also rejected the argument of the EC that governments could rely on new and divergent scientific opinion to satisfy the risk assessment requirements. For a discussion on compliance with this ruling see *World Trade Organization, Dispute Settlement Body, Minutes of Meeting held on 19 February 2009*, WT/DSB/M/265 (29 April 2009) [29]–[34], available at www.wto.org, last accessed 31 March 2012.

62 The EC also failed to satisfy the requirements under SPS Article 5.7 concerning provisional measures. In this regard, the EC did not rebut the proposition that the scientific evidence concerning the effects of genetically modified organisms was insufficient to perform a risk assessment.

7.4 THE AGREEMENT ON TECHNICAL BARRIERS TO TRADE

7.4.1 Key Concepts and Obligations

The TBT Agreement regulates technical regulations, standards and assessment procedures of members. It has received relatively little scholarly attention.[63] The Agreement has a very wide scope, in that it covers border issues, such as the requirement for importers to fulfil certain bureaucratic procedures to bring goods into a country, and it also deals with technical matters concerning the goods, including product standards, process and production methods, packaging and labelling.[64] A distinction is drawn between technical regulation, which is mandatory, and standards, which are not.[65]

The central purpose of this Agreement is to delineate desirable and undesirable usages of technical regulation in the context of international trade.[66] Maintaining and improving international standards and conformity assessment procedures may have a number of social benefits.[67] For example, standards may improve the quality of exports, protect purchasers from deceptive practices and protect the health and safety of consumers. International standards may also assist developing countries to acquire technology and know-how to improve their economic situation. More generally, the use of international standards is often a mechanism to facilitate international trade given that standards are likely to reduce costs and increase commercial certainty between traders.

Despite the intended benefits, the TBT Agreement also recognizes that standards may be used as a barrier to trade. Therefore, the Agreement calls upon members not to apply technical regulations and standards in a manner that would constitute a means of arbitrary or unjustifiable discrimination between countries.[68] Article 2.2 of the Agreement stipulates that technical

---

63 Du, 'Domestic Regulatory Autonomy under the TBT Agreement: From Non-discrimination to Harmonization', above n 53, 270. This author notes that: 'This is probably because most technical barriers in international trade are prototypical examples of "low politics".'

64 The terms 'technical regulation', 'standard' and 'conformity assessment procedures' are defined in Annex 1 to the TBT Agreement.

65 *Ibid.*

66 Recitals to the TBT Agreement.

67 *Ibid.*

68 This general negative obligation can be loosely traced back to the exceptions in sub-articles XX(b) (public health), XX(d) (deceptive practices) and Article XXI (national security) of the GATT 1994, but there is no specific reference to technical regulations and standards in the GATT 1994.

regulations shall not be more trade-restrictive than would be necessary to fulfil a legitimate objective; taking into account the risks non-fulfilment would create. This article then non-exhaustively lists these objectives as including national security, prevention of deceptive practices, protection of human health or safety, animal or plant life or health, or the environment. These terms are not defined, and this Agreement, instead, places an obligation on members to assess risks in these policy areas with relevant elements of consideration being available scientific and technical information, related processing technology and intended end-use of products.[69] The Agreement, therefore, carves out large areas from the general most favoured nation and national treatment obligations in respect of technical standards.[70]

In order to generate some uniformity of outcomes, members must, where possible, base their technical regulations on international standards.[71] Members are also required to explain the justification for a technical regulation to members where such regulation may have a significant effect on the trade of members.[72] Further, where a technical regulation is not in accordance with an international standard and it may have significant trade effects, members must notify the membership of its existence, provide details of the measure and its rationale, and allow members to provide comments prior to its introduction.[73]

There have been very few disputes under the TBT Agreement, and therefore it is difficult to shed light on how WTO Tribunals are interpreting the TBT provisions.[74] The key issues to date have been the scope of the Agreement and the relationship between a member's legitimate objectives and harmonized international standards. In *EC-Asbestos*, the Appellate Body took a broad and pragmatic approach to the question of whether a measure is a technical regulation, and therefore, within the scope of the TBT Agreement.[75] In *EC-Sardines*, the panel did not accept the EC's argument that it was inappropriate to base the term 'sardine' on the international standard because consumers had

[69] TBT Agreement, art 2.2.

[70] These positive obligations are set out in TBT Agreement, art 2.1. TBT Agreement, art 5.1.1 prescribes these obligations in respect of conformity assessment procedures.

[71] TBT Agreement, art 2.4.

[72] TBT Agreement, art 2.5.

[73] TBT Agreement, art 2.9.

[74] To date the only panel decision where TBT provisions were central to the dispute is in *EC-Sardines*. However, TBT provisions have been part of complaints in other panel decisions such as *EC-Asbestos* and *EC-Approval and Marketing of Biotech Products*.

[75] Appellate Body Report, *EC-Asbestos* [69]–[72].

come to associate sardines with a narrower product range.[76] Therefore, the EC's measure was found to be inconsistent with Article 2.4, which requires technical regulations to be based on international standards. It appears that panels will place emphasis on the need for international uniformity, although it is difficult to know to what extent complainants will be able to determine what a defending member's legitimate objectives are prior to a dispute. Finally, a very significant issue that is unknown at this stage is whether any of the jurisprudence concerning the requirement in the SPS Agreement for measures to be least trade restrictive will be read into Article 2.2 of the TBT Agreement.[77]

The central issue under the TBT Agreement is to what extent panels will objectively examine the aims and objectives of a measure and determine its legitimacy, as opposed to deferring to a member's own interpretations of such matters. In *US-Tuna II (Mexico)*, when considering a claim under Article 2.2 of the TBT Agreement, the panel stated that it is not bound by a member's own characterization of its objectives and such categorization should be made in an independent and objective fashion.[78] However, in the same decision, the panel also noted that it must consider the member's description of its own objectives in order to clarify what those objectives are and to respect the right of a member to adopt measures in pursuance of certain legitimate objectives.[79] From this the tension between objective panel review and a member's own prerogative to implement measures can be seen.[80]

7.4.2 The Application of the New Standard to the TBT Agreement

In this section, I will deal with how the new standard of review may be applied in relation to TBT measures. The mode of analysis will be the same as that

---

[76] Note that the Appellate Body subsequently reversed this finding based on the panel's incorrect allocation of the burden of proof, but it confirmed that the international standard was not ineffective or inappropriate. See Appellate Body Report, *EC-Sardines* [290].

[77] See Du, 'Domestic Regulatory Autonomy under the TBT Agreement: From Non-discrimination to Harmonization', above n 53, 290–91. In *US-Tuna II (Mexico)*, [7.461] the panel does note that 'We find further support for our interpretation of the terms of Article 2.2 in the text of Article 5.6 of the SPS Agreement, which contains language very similar to that of Article 2.2 of the TBT Agreement.'

[78] Panel Report, *US-Tuna II (Mexico)* [7.405].

[79] Panel Report, *US-Tuna II (Mexico)* [7.393].

[80] There is undoubtedly a mixture of subjective and objective considerations involved with an Article 2.2 analysis. For example, the question of whether a measure is legitimate must import some subjective meaning as it cannot merely refer to whether a member's measure has met its own objectives.

undertaken for the SPS Agreement. That is, I will first answer the question of whether panels should apply the general standard of review, as opposed to a specific standard of review in TBT-related disputes. In the event that the answer is in favour of a specific standard, I will attempt to define the basic characteristics of the new TBT standard having regard to the major obligations that are conceded to members. The key aspect is that such obligations will demonstrate the level of intensity of the TBT standard. Finally, I also discuss issues that are likely to arise under the TBT Agreement that are relevant to the determination of the quality of national level decision-making. This focus on the quality of national processes should allow panels to better define the standard of review in TBT disputes.

In order to determine whether the general standard of review should apply to TBT disputes, it is necessary to consider the text of this Agreement so as to identify whether members have any direct obligations in connection with the imposition or maintenance of TBT measures. On an initial reading, it would appear that the TBT Agreement does not involve members retaining jurisdictional competencies. This is because the Agreement appears to merely prescribe basic obligations and then sets out the exceptions to these obligations. In this regard, these obligations include the provision of national treatment and most favoured nation status for technical regulations, the requirement to, where possible, base technical regulations on international standards, and to ensure that technical regulations are not more trade restrictive than necessary to fulfil legitimate objectives.[81] These obligations, whilst very general, simply set out mandatory matters for members to comply with, and they do not appear to carve out matters that members are contingently responsible for.

Despite the above, the TBT Agreement has a similar 'methodology' to the SPS Agreement, in that it subtly, and without formal procedures, does contemplate members being involved in the assessment of TBT measures to determine WTO compliance. The key provision, in this regard, is Article 2.2, which requires members to conduct some kind of risk assessment to show that technical regulations are directed to legitimate objectives and are not more trade restrictive than necessary to the achievement of these objectives. It is, however, noteworthy that a risk assessment is not expressly mandated but is implied from Article 2.2 by couching substantive obligations in language such as: 'members shall ensure that…' and 'In assessing risks…'.[82] There are also other related obligations, such as the obligation to base technical regulation on

[81] TBT Agreement, arts 2.2, 2.4.

[82] This is similar to the language in Article 5.1 of the SPS Agreement. However, there is no definition of 'Risk Assessment' in the TBT Agreement and the language is not an explicit as to a member's responsibilities. Article 2.2 is also discussed in Button, *The Power to Protect: Trade, Health and Uncertainty in the WTO*, above n 11, 86.

international standards, and the requirement to provide reasons in support of technical regulations, which evidence the retaining of competencies by members.[83] In addition, there are the various notification and other procedural requirements that members must comply with when adopting new technical measures.[84] Therefore, there is a rationale for not applying the general standard of review to the TBT Agreement, but adopting a specific standard instead.

To identify the specific standard of review that would be applied by panels, it is again necessary to focus on the major provisions that evidence the division of jurisdictional competencies. When examining Article 2.2, it is clear that the requirement to carry out a risk assessment is not a very onerous obligation.[85] Firstly, there is a lack of formality in that the TBT Agreement does not contain any procedures about how a risk assessment is to be carried out. Indeed, it is even unclear as to whether a risk assessment must occur before a TBT measure is adopted.[86] In some respects, the TBT Agreement resembles a set of guidelines rather than a robust mandatory regime. Secondly, the matters that must be taken into account in a risk assessment are vague, as is the non-exhaustive list of legitimate objectives. It is even unclear as to whether a least trade restrictive analysis must be part of a risk assessment.[87] All of this demonstrates that members are not retaining significant responsibility in the assessment of TBT measures. Accordingly, the standard of review applied by panels should be highly intensive, with only a relatively small deviation from the general standard of review.

The major difference between panel assessment in TBT cases and the general standard of review is that panels would not be simply comparing the measure against the terms of the TBT Agreement, but rather, they would be examining a member's own risk assessment to determine compliance.[88] However, given that the lack of formality and the ambiguity of substantive obligations concerning risk assessments, panels should carefully scrutinize

---

[83] TBT Agreement, arts 2.4, 2.5.

[84] TBT Agreement, art 2.9.

[85] To date, there have been no WTO disputes directly interpreting Article 2.2 of the TBT Agreement.

[86] *Ehlermann* and *Lockhart* discuss this issue and note that if Article 2.2 is more of an elective process and there are no procedural guarantees (as apply in trade remedy matters) it is difficult to know how much deference panels will accord. (See Claus-Dieter Ehlermann and Nicolas Lockhart, 'Standard of Review in WTO Law' (2004) 7(3) *Journal of International Economic Law* 514.)

[87] See Du, 'Domestic Regulatory Autonomy under the TBT Agreement: From Non-discrimination to Harmonization', above n 53, 281, where the author argues [that through Article 2.2] 'the TBT extends the least trade restrictive rule to measures that were consistent with the national treatment obligation'.

[88] It is acknowledged that whilst the general standard is different from *de novo* review, panels would have to perform their own risk assessment if the obligations in Article 2.2 were not for members to fulfil.

risk assessments by closely examining the arguments and evidence before them. Whilst it may be difficult to draw this distinction, it is again a matter of panels reviewing the quality of domestic processes to ensure that members are accountable, but without going beyond the panel review task. It is, for example, appropriate for panels to be satisfied that a measure is necessary for the fulfilment of a legitimate objective, and that the risk assessment took into account scientific and technical information. There should also be a rational relationship between the conclusions in the risk assessment and the measure. What is difficult to predict, however, is exactly how closely panels will examine these questions. It is logical that panels will carefully review the risk assessment, and any scientific evidence, but it is less likely that panels will wish to closely examine whether a policy objective is legitimate, or whether there may be other domestic processes or regulations that are less trade restrictive in nature.[89] There is also an argument that Article 2.2 of the TBT Agreement is similar to the list of exceptions contained in Article XX of GATT 1994, and therefore these provisions should be interpreted in a like manner. If this proposition was accepted, this could mean that a similar standard of review should be applied. However, the fundamental difference is that GATT 1994 Article XX contains a list of limited exceptions to the GATT rules rather than setting forth positive rules.[90] Article 2.2 of the TBT Agreement contains some positive rules guiding the members' preparation, adoption or application of technical regulations to meet certain policy objectives.[91] Accordingly, a panel should not, for instance, strictly apply the same criteria that it would apply in a case concerning whether a measure is necessary under GATT 1994 Article XX(b). Panels would need to be careful that, in weighing and balancing factors which might satisfy the requirement of necessity, they do not completely remove domestic regulatory autonomy and apply a *de novo* standard.[92]

---

[89] Regarding the use of regulatory intention as a basis of interpretation, see above n 801 and accompanying text. *Contra* Du, 'Domestic Regulatory Autonomy under the TBT Agreement: From Non-discrimination to Harmonization', above n 53, 306 where the author notes: 'My research indicates that the extent of the margin of appreciation left to WTO members under the TBT Agreement largely depends upon the value that the technical regulation purports to protect.'

[90] Appellate Body Report, *US-Wool Shirts and Blouses* [335]. See also Rudiger Wolfrum, Peter-Tobias Stoll and Anja Seibert-Fohr (eds), *Max Planck Commentaries on World Trade Law Volume 3: WTO-Technical Barriers and SPS Measures* (2007) 220. It is also noted that the respondent has the burden of proof in respect of Article XX claims, whereas the complainant has the burden of proving that it has complied with Article 2.2.

[91] *Ibid* 220.

[92] Appellate Body Report, *Korea-Various Measures on Beef* [161]. See also Wolfrum, Stoll and Seibert-Fohr, *Max Planck Commentaries on World Trade Law Volume* 3, above n 90, 218.

7.5 THE GENERAL AGREEMENT ON TARIFFS AND TRADE 1994

7.5.1 Key Concepts and Obligations

The GATT is the original document, signed on 30 October 1947, which set out the multilateral rules for trade in goods. GATT 1947 has now been incorporated into a new document, known as GATT 1994, which is part of the WTO Agreements that entered into force in 1995. GATT 1994 contains the key substantive provisions of GATT 1947 comprising Articles I to XXXVII, as amended from time to time since 1947. It also contains additional technical protocols and differs in other ways from GATT 1947. GATT 1994 is an Annex to the Marrakesh Agreement.[93] The GATT no longer functions as the sole documentary foundation of the international trading rules, and is now one of a suite of agreements that set out these rules. GATT 1994 operates as an umbrella agreement in that it identifies basic obligations and exceptions that apply across all disciplines, and it also refers to the essential commitments in several major disciplines, from which specific agreements have been drafted through successive negotiating rounds.[94] GATT 1994, therefore, does not have a specific field of regulation and its major importance is in articulating many of the general principles that the WTO applies to the international trading system. Many of these principles may be categorized as efforts to avoid discrimination between members in the context of trade liberalization.[95]

The most important provisions in GATT 1994 are Articles I and III, which state the principles of most favoured nation and national treatment, as well as Article XX, which lists the general exceptions to GATT 1994. Most favoured nation treatment is the requirement for members to accord, to all other members, any 'advantage, favour, privilege or immunity', granted in respect of a like product originating in or destined for any other country.[96] The focus of this rule is customs duties and charges, but it also applies to all rules and formalities in connection with the importation and exportation of goods. National treatment is the requirement for members to treat imported products in a manner that is no less favourable than for like products of national

---

93 Marrakesh Agreement, Annex 1A.

94 An introduction to the GATT 1947 is in Chapter 2, Section 2.2.

95 Appellate Body Report, *Korea-Various Measures on Beef* [161]. See also Wolfrum, Stoll and Seibert-Fohr, *Max Planck Commentaries on World Trade Law Volume* 3, above n 90, 5.

96 Arguably, most favoured nation has become a broader principle or norm of international trade, and goes beyond the original confines of customs duties and other border measures.

origin.[97] The object of Article III is to ensure that members do not apply internal taxes or regulations to imported or domestic goods in a manner that would afford protection to domestic production.[98] It can be seen how this Article anticipated the possible circumvention of Article I by GATT contracting parties.

Article XX of GATT 1994 has been of great ongoing significance to the WTO and its membership, because of its capacity to undermine the substantive disciplines set out in the Uruguay Round Agreements. The two major aspects of Article XX are what is known as the chapeau, and the actual list of exceptions. The chapeau is a condition precedent for the exercise of the exceptions, and requires that measures must not be applied in a manner that would constitute a means of arbitrary or unjustified discrimination between countries, nor as a disguised restriction on international trade. The exceptions themselves are very broadly worded, and cover such issues as the protection of public morals; human, animal or plant life or health; and the conservation of exhaustible natural resources, which of course may include environmental matters. The first two of the above exceptions require the measures to be 'necessary', whereas the third must simply 'relate' to the conservation of natural resources. Despite the generalized wording of Articles I and III, and the imprecise wording of Article XX, there has not been a large number of cases that deal principally with GATT provisions.[99] In many cases, the major dispute between parties has related to provisions of specific disciplines, such as the Anti-Dumping Agreement, and the violations of the GATT asserted are not central to the dispute. Therefore, it may be suggested that disputes will occur under the GATT where no other specific rules apply. The cases also suggest that this will involve questions of discrimination against certain products around questions of product likeness, customs classification and customs administrative procedures. The case of *EC-Asbestos*, by way of example, dealt with questions of likeness and the availability of the protection of human

---

[97] The key substantive provisions are GATT 1994, arts III:2 and III:4, which apply to internal taxes and regulations respectively.

[98] GATT 1994, art III:1.

[99] Major cases principally concerning GATT 1994 provisions include *US-Gasoline*, *Japan-Alcoholic Beverages II*, *Canada-Periodicals*, *Argentina-Textiles and Apparel*, *EC-Computer Equipment*, *Japan-Film*, *US-Shrimp*, *Korea-Alcoholic Beverages*, *Chile-Alcoholic Beverages*, *EC-Asbestos*, *Argentina-Hides and Leather*, *Dominican Republic-Import and Sale of Cigarettes*, *EC-Chicken Cuts (Brazil)*, *EC-Chicken Cuts (Thailand)*, *Mexico-Taxes on Soft Drinks*, *EC-Selected Customs Matters*, *Brazil-Retreaded Tyres*, *India-Additional Import Duties*, *China-Auto Parts*, *Columbia-Ports of Entry*, *China-Publications and Audiovisual Products*.

health exception in the context of Canadian exports of a particular type of asbestos to the European Union.[100]

7.5.2 The Application of the New Standard to GATT 1994

In this section, I will deal with how the new standard of review would apply to GATT 1994. The approach I will take is identical to that taken in examining the SPS and TBT Agreements; namely, I will assess whether panels should apply the general standard of review or a specific standard in GATT 1994 disputes. Based on this assessment, I will then seek to illustrate the new standard of review by reference to the major GATT 1994 provisions, and factual scenarios drawn from previous cases.

The threshold issue in determining whether the general standard will apply is to identify any jurisdictional competencies have been retained by members. It is recalled from the previous section that GATT 1994 sets out very general obligations, and there is virtually no detail in relation to how members may meet or implement these obligations. Members therefore have the complete freedom in the way they adopt these rules. Critically, the principal GATT 1994 provisions, such as Articles I, III and XX, do not contemplate any participation by members in the scrutiny of measures.[101] There is no process articulated in these provisions that requires members to justify the imposition or maintenance of measures through particular procedures, or at all. In other words, these articles govern solely the substantive aspects of the relevant national rules.[102] Accordingly, there is unlikely to have been much, if any, fact-finding at a national level that should subsequently be taken into account by panels.[103] In these circumstances, it would be inappropriate to deviate from the general standard of review, and it is not necessary to consider the formulation of a specific standard for GATT 1994 disputes. The general standard of review is a highly intensive standard, requiring panels to examine all available and sufficient evidence, and to conduct a comprehensive review of the facts of the case. In the absence of a prior national level fact-finding process, it is entirely appropriate for panels to conduct this type of review. For example, in *Chile-Alcoholic Beverages*, the panel was required to examine whether the Chilean

---

[100] Panel Report, *EC-Asbestos* [8.105]–[8.155]; Appellate Body Report, *EC-Asbestos* [84]–[132].

[101] Note that other articles, such as Article VI, dealing with anti-dumping and countervailing duties, do implicitly create obligations on the members to investigate, but in this case there are no procedures for investigation and Article VI almost exclusively deals with the conditions under which anti-dumping or countervailing duties may be imposed.

[102] Bohanes and Lockhart, 'Standard of Review in WTO Law', above n 54, 398.

[103] *Ibid.*

beverage, 'pisco' was a like product with other alcoholic beverages, such as whisky, gin and tequila, for the purposes of Article III:2.[104] The panel's role is as an arbiter of the facts in the first instance, and there should be no deference to the respondent member, on the basis of a member's previous examination of the issues at a national level.[105] The panel performed a similar task in *EC-Asbestos*, in examining whether European measures violated Article III:4 or were justified under Article XX.[106] The determination of these types of cases will therefore involve a panel simply making findings based upon the merits of a dispute.

This approach may be reinforced by reference to the regulatory intention of GATT 1994.[107] The GATT is essentially a 'negative integration contract'.[108] Subject to compliance with WTO obligations, WTO members are able to unilaterally define their policies which might affect trade, and are not constrained to follow particular policies. It is this basic structure of the GATT in setting out broad negative covenants that creates the need for a more strict interpretation of GATT provisions. This is to be contrasted with the SPS and TBT Agreements, which have extended these basic obligations, and deal with many affirmative obligations concerning matters such as standard setting and positive harmonization.[109]

There is always an intersection between the standard of review and more general methods of interpretation of WTO provisions. In this regard, it is noted that even where no deference in fact-finding and evaluation is warranted, WTO Tribunals may find other means of deferring to member measures by, for example, interpreting substantive obligations more favourably. In *EC-Asbestos*, the Appellate Body stated that 'WTO members have the right to determine the level of protection of health that they consider appropriate in a given situation.'[110] This type of interpretation has the effect of enlarging the scope of the policy choices that members may make.

---

[104] Panel Report, *Chile-Alcoholic Beverages* [7.16]–[7.88]. As with many GATT cases, there is no express reference to the standard of review being applied in the factual analysis.

[105] For example, there may have been a departmental review or litigation about the issue.

[106] Panel Report, *EC-Asbestos* [8.105]–[8.155], [8.169]–[8.222].

[107] It is contended however that the notion of regulatory intention should only be a subsidiary means of defining the standard of review: see n 53 above and accompanying text.

[108] Petros C. Mavroidis, *Trade in Goods: The GATT and Other Agreements Regulating Trade in Goods* (Oxford University Press, 2007) 36.

[109] Mitsuo Matsushita, Thomas J. Schoenbaum and Petros C. Mavroidis, *The World Trade Organization: Law, Practice and Policy* (Oxford University Press, 2nd ed, 2006) 495.

[110] Appellate Body Report, *EC-Asbestos* [168].

In parts 7.2 to 7.4 of this chapter, I have set out how the new standard of review would apply to the SPS Agreement, the TBT Agreement and GATT 1994, by reference to the major obligations contained in those Agreements. I have established that a different standard of review would be applied under each of these Agreements. In approximate terms, GATT 1994 requires the most intensive standard, followed by the TBT Agreement, and then the SPS Agreement, having the most deferential standard of the three. I have only had the opportunity to survey six WTO Agreements in this manner. However, many other WTO agreements, such as the GATS or the Agreement on Customs Valuation, are likely to involve a similar analysis to GATT 1994, with the result being reliance on the general standard of review.

7.6 COMPARISON OF THE NEW STANDARD WITH THE CURRENT STANDARD APPLIED TO NON-TRADE REMEDY DISPUTES

In this section, I will briefly examine how the new standard of review of facts compares with its treatment to date by WTO Tribunals under disputes brought under the SPS and TBT Agreements and GATT 1994. This section is intended to be a brief survey. The purpose of this comparison is to demonstrate that the new standard could lead to a more principled and consistent approach that would benefit panels and litigants in the future. It will be demonstrated that, in some instances, panels have been overly intrusive in their approach, but in others they have applied a standard that is very similar to the new standard, but without identifying what that standard actually is.

7.6.1 The SPS Agreement

Prominent disputes under the SPS Agreement provide a very good example of how the current factual standard of review has become progressively more intensive over time. This tendency may, in part, be explained by the frequent requirement for panels to examine detailed scientific evidence. However, it is also a product of there not being clear principles for applying the standard of review. In *Australia-Salmon* and *EC-Hormones*, the panels undertook a close analysis of the measures and the member risk assessments and found that the measures were not based upon a risk assessment pursuant to Article 5.1.[111] Put another way, the key finding of the panel in *EC-Hormones* was that there was

[111] Panel Report, *Australia-Salmon* [8.50]–[8.99]; Panel Report, *EC-Hormones* [8.101]–[8.162].

no conformity between the scientific conclusions in studies relied upon, and the scientific conclusions implicit in the measures.[112] The Appellate Body, in *EC-Hormones*, arguably invited an even more intensive standard when it reversed the panel's finding that the expression 'based on' in Article 5.1, involves a 'minimum procedural requirement' that a risk assessment be 'taken into account'.[113] Instead the Appellate Body defined the expression 'based upon' to refer to a certain objective relationship between the measure and the risk assessment.[114] That is, there must be rational relationship between the measure and the risk assessment, in that the risk assessment must reasonably support the measure.[115] The panel, in *Japan-Apples*, in seeking to apply the rational relationship test, arguably applied a standard of review that is indistinguishable from *de novo* review or a correctness test.[116]

The meaning of the rational relationship test was clarified by the Appellate Body in *US-Continued Suspension* when it found that the panel had applied a correctness test in itself deciding on what it considered to be the best science.[117] It was held that the panel should have determined whether the risk assessment was supported by coherent reasoning and respectable scientific evidence.[118] In refining the rational relationship test, the Appellate Body is implicitly critical of panels having 'overreached' in applying this standard.

There are aspects of the factual standard of review applied by the Appellate Body in both *EC-Hormones* and *US-Continued Suspension* that resemble the standard proposed in this book. In this regard, there is a focus on the national level review process that must be undertaken by members and confirmation that it is the role of panels to examine the integrity of such a process and the resultant measure. However, a major difference is that the new standard of review emphasises that it is the role of panels to examine the nature and overall quality of the domestic review process rather than focussing more directly on the rationality of a particular measure. This is in recognition of the fact that there will always be a degree of variance in how panels apply a standard of review. This is particularly the case in SPS disputes, where there will be pressure on panels to correctly interpret the science so that measures are not more trade restrictive than necessary.

---

112 Panel Report, *EC-Hormones* [8.140]–[8.141].

113 Appellate Body Report, *EC-Hormones* [188]–[191].

114 *Ibid.*

115 Appellate Body Report, *EC-Hormones* [193].

116 Panel Report, *Japan-Apples* [8.228]–[8.292].

117 Appellate Body Report, *US-Continued Suspension* [587]–[590].

118 *Ibid.*

7.6.2 The TBT Agreement

It is very difficult to identify the current TBT standard of review given there have been so few cases to date. Critically, there have been very few cases directly discussing Article 2.2, which refers to some kind of risk assessment by members to ensure that technical regulations are not more trade-restrictive than necessary to fulfil a legitimate objective. It is therefore difficult to determine whether the approach by panels in reviewing the formulation of TBT measures at a national level would be similar to that taken in reviewing SPS measures. The best current evidence is the approach taken in the *EC-Sardines* decision in relation to the Article 2.4 requirement to, where possible, base technical regulations on international standards.[119] In this decision, the panel found that the European measure violated Article 2.4 by applying a strict construction to the text of the international standard and by determining that the standard must be adopted and not merely referenced in formulating the national measure.[120] These findings suggest that panels will adopt a strict and close to *de novo* standard of review when interpreting TBT provisions. Despite this, it is possible that Article 2.2 would be applied differently because it contemplates a risk assessment by members, and therefore some level of discretion, rather than merely promulgating rules. However, in my view, WTO Tribunals will continue to apply a *de novo* type of review to all TBT provisions, because there is unlikely to be a high level of sensitivity by the membership to more WTO intrusion in TBT issues.[121]

The new factual standard that I would apply to disputes concerning TBT Agreement Article 2.2 and related provisions would be reasonably close to the standard applied for disputes under Article 5.1 of the SPS Agreement. This is because, despite the lack of textual detail, the TBT Agreement does contemplate members undertaking an active process to formulate TBT measures. It is acknowledged, however, that the ambiguity of the obligations in Article 2.2 should require panels to apply a standard that is marginally more intensive than that applied in respect of Article 5.1 of the SPS Agreement. There is also a teleological argument for the TBT standard of review to be more intensive and very close to the general standard of review because Article 2.2 of the TBT Agreement deals with a wide variety of policy exceptions, whereas Article 5.1 of the SPS Agreement principally concerns demonstrating scientific justification for the exception. Further, within Article 2.2 there is more of an overlapping of

119 Panel Report, *EC-Sardines* [7.63]–[7.139]

120 Panel Report, *EC-Sardines* [7.104], [7.110]–[7.111].

121 Du, 'Domestic Regulatory Autonomy under the TBT Agreement: From Non-discrimination to Harmonization', above n 53, 270.

the policy exceptions and the least trade restrictive requirements in comparison to Article 5.1.

7.6.3 GATT 1994

The standard of review issue has not arisen to date in the various decisions concerning GATT 1994 provisions. Panels have generally applied an unrestrictive standard of review to GATT 1994 cases, by examining the evidence presented about the measures and determining whether the measures do or do not violate GATT provisions. Indeed, it may even be inappropriate to classify the review task of panels as a standard of review in that the task is to determine strict compliance with WTO obligations.[122] Cases dealing with Article III of the GATT provide good examples of this. In the various alcohol cases, such as *Japan-Alcoholic Beverages II*, *Chile-Alcoholic Beverages* and *Korea-Alcoholic Beverages*, panels were required to examine whether particular traditional local alcoholic beverages were 'like products' in comparison to various imported alcoholic beverages.[123] In *Japan-Alcoholic Beverages II*, the panel (as upheld by the Appellate Body) found that likeness is to be determined on a case-by-case basis by comparing the properties of the products, consumer tastes and tariff classifications.[124] In *Brazil-Retreaded Tyres*, the panel was required to examine whether the import ban on retreaded tyres violated GATT 1994 Article XI:1.[125] In that case most of the factual analysis concerned whether the ban was justified under GATT 1994 Article XX(b), as this required the panel to assess whether the scientific argument by Brazil that waste tyres is likely to cause disease and environmental harm was valid.[126] In all of the above decisions, panels have not applied a deferential standard of review, and have instead applied a correctness standard.

In this book, the standard of review that I am advocating for GATT 1994 provisions is very similar to that applied by panels to date. Under the new test, however, the reason for applying a highly intensive standard is based upon the delineation of jurisdictional competencies, rather than on an objective assessment test, or merely giving best effect to the wording of the WTO Agreements. Further, there are some differences between the standard applied to date and the new proposed standard. In this regard, the intensity of the new standard is

---

122 Jeffrey Waincymer, *WTO Litigation: Procedural Aspects of Formal Dispute Settlement* (Cameron May, 2002) 349.

123 Panel Report, *Japan-Alcoholic Beverages II* [6.6]–[6.33]; Panel Report, *Chile-Alcoholic Beverages* [7.5]–[7.88]; Panel Report, [10.34]–[10.98].

124 Panel Report, *Japan-Alcoholic Beverages II* [6.21]–6.22].

125 Panel Report, *Brazil-Retreaded Tyres* [7.1]–[7.34].

126 *Ibid* [7.35]–[7.102].

regulated by the 'all available and sufficient evidence' and 'comprehensive review' tests discussed in Chapter 4. The present standard of review does not apply this administrative law type of standard and relies upon the minimal wording of Article 11 of the DSU and generalized principles of treaty interpretation.

7.7 CONCLUSION

This chapter has described how the new standard of review, as proposed in this book, would be applied to various non-trade remedy agreements, comprising the SPS and TBT Agreements and GATT 1994. The new standard of review is principally a product of the degree to which members have retained autonomy in formulating or maintaining measures. Where such autonomy exists (and national level authorities have some material level of responsibility to relation to measures) WTO panels should apply a factual standard of review that is more deferential than would otherwise apply. However, as with trade remedy disputes, panels must still review the quality of the domestic authority decision-making, and central to this is whether a panel is satisfied that the measure is rationally derived from the evidence that was before the domestic authority. The proposed standard of review will be quite similar for the major SPS and TBT provisions, but GATT 1994 provides an example of where a highly intensive and non-deferential standard is fully justified. A brief comparison of the way the standard has been applied to date, as against the new standard, shows that the standard is becoming more agreement-specific. This is perhaps somewhat of a response to the need to cautiously adjudicate disputes involving life or health.[127] However, there needs to be an appropriate test to regulate this issue and provide for more consistency in the approach of WTO Tribunals.

[127] Goh, 'Tipping the Apple Cart: The Limits of Science and Law in the SPS Agreement after *Japan-Apples*', above n 43, 669.

8. Conclusion

8.1 OVERVIEW OF THIS WORK

8.1.1 Critique and Contentions

In this book, it is argued that the current WTO standard of review is inadequate, and a new standard of review should be developed. The challenge is to formulate a standard that provides sufficient oversight of domestic measures in order for the WTO to ensure compliance by members with WTO obligations, but without undermining the legitimacy of the WTO as an institution.

The current standard of review is inadequate largely because it is based on Article 11 of the DSU.[1] Article 11 refers to a panel's obligation to conduct an objective assessment of the matter before it. This obligation extends both to the facts of the case, and the ultimate legal question of whether a measure is in conformity with the WTO Agreements. This standard, however, does not give any material guidance to panels about the manner and level of scrutiny of both factual and legal questions.[2] This is because Article 11 only refers to the need for objectivity and, by implication, to fulfil a minimum due process requirement when conducting cases. The current standard of review therefore has the propensity to lead to panels 'over' or 'under' scrutinizing cases. This inadequacy of the current standard of review is also evidenced by the fact that the Appellate Body has seen fit to make statements in a number of decisions, both about the nature of the standard of review generally, and how the standard may be applied in relation to specific WTO Agreements. In many instances, these statements suggest the need for a new standard of review that is consistent with the approach advocated in this book. However, the Appellate Body has not to date laid down any overall conceptual foundation for a new doctrine.

1 See Appellate Body Report, *EC-Hormones* [116] for the first reliance by the Appellate Body on Article 11 and Chapter 2, Sections 2.4.2 and 2.4.3 for discussion of its development and some of the major problems with its use.

2 See Chapter 2, Section 2.4.2. For a summary of problems with the current WTO standard of review see Catherine Button, 'The WTO's Objective Assessment Standard of Review and Panel Review of Health Measures' in Andrew D. Mitchell (ed), *Challenges and Prospects for the WTO* (Cameron May, 2005) 85, 91–7.

The problems in applying the present WTO standard of review strongly suggest the need to develop a new conceptual foundation for a standard of review. Fundamentally, a new standard of review should assist panels to understand how they are to review measures. However, more broadly, a new standard of review should satisfy three key underlying criteria: it should be faithful to the fundamental objectives of WTO dispute settlement; it should promote legitimacy of the WTO as an institution; and it should be part of the development of more advanced and user-friendly dispute settlement procedures.[3]

The guiding mechanism in the development of a new standard of review doctrine in this book is the notion of jurisdictional competencies.[4] In the context of WTO dispute settlement this refers to the division of responsibilities between members and WTO panels to carry out particular WTO obligations related to the issuing or review of measures. If a WTO Agreement does not expressly or implicitly provide for members to retain any jurisdictional competencies, then a general standard of review should be applied that is highly intensive in nature.[5] This requires panels to examine all available and sufficient evidence, and to conduct a comprehensive review of both factual and legal issues. If, however, a WTO Agreement does provide for the retaining of jurisdictional competencies by members, then the general standard of review is modified depending upon the nature and extent of these competencies.[6] This would potentially generate a specific standard of review for disputes arising under different WTO Agreements. Panels would therefore apply more or less deference when reviewing measures, depending upon the type of WTO obligations in dispute. For example, the new test would require panels to apply a significant degree of deference in trade remedy cases, and a lesser degree of deference in many SPS cases. By contrast, cases dealing principally with GATT 1994 provisions, should involve close panel scrutiny, and no deference to members. There would be some variation in the standard of review within each WTO Agreement based upon the specific obligations that are in dispute.

Within the framework of jurisdictional competencies, panels should also focus on the quality of the domestic level processes that have been undertaken to satisfy particular WTO obligations. This will usually involve some degree of formal and substantive evaluation, and may involve specific approaches that are suggested by the nature or wording of the WTO obligation under scrutiny. The rational relationship test that the Appellate Body has used to

3 These principles are discussed in Chapter 3, Section 3.3.
4 See Chapter 5, Section 5.2.1.
5 See Chapter 4, Sections 4.2.1 and 4.2.2.
6 See Chapter 5, Sections 5.2.1 and 5.2.2.

review the WTO consistency of risk assessments for SPS measures is a good example of how panels may apply a specialized test to determine the quality of domestic-level processes.[7] The central tenet of the specific standard of review is that panels must test the rationality of domestic authority findings based on evidence that was before the authority. This book does not articulate the precise contours of the standards of review that would emerge from the application of this new test. Such an endeavour is beyond what is possible in a work of this kind and, at some point, becomes a speculative exercise. It has only been possible to survey some of the major areas of application of the new standard. This book puts forward the foundations for WTO Tribunals and scholars to develop these specific standards of review in the future. The challenge will still exist in some contentious disciplines, particularly those involving matters of scientific judgment, for panels to determine how intensively they must scrutinize a measure to affirm its rationality and the overall quality of decision-making.

In summary, this new approach has several major advantages. Firstly, it would create a new theoretical grounding for the standard that is clearer and more capable of consistent application compared with the objective assessment test. Secondly, it would guard against the standard of review becoming too intensive in nature. Thirdly, it would not be difficult to adopt given that there are already precedents whereby a variable standard has been referred to based upon the obligations in issue.[8] Fourthly, it would allow for greater consistency between the anti-dumping standard of review and the standard that would apply in respect of other trade remedy disputes.[9] It may also be justified by reference to interpretive 'tools' of public international law such as the VCLT, the concept of inherent jurisdiction, and other principles.

8.1.2 Summary of Chapters

In this book, I have examined the standard of review at a conceptual level and then sought to apply this in a WTO context. In Chapter 1, I offered a definition of a standard of review, which essentially refers to the level of scrutiny

---

[7] Appellate Body Report, *EC-Hormones* [116], [193].

[8] For discussion on how the standard of review has been applied to date under various WTO Agreements see Claus-Dieter Ehlermann and Nicolas Lockhart, 'Standard of Review in WTO Law' (2004) 7(3) *Journal of International Economic Law* 491.

[9] See for example, Ministerial Declaration on Dispute Settlement Pursuant to the Agreement on Implementation of Article VI of the General Agreement on Tariffs and Trade 1994 or Part V of the Agreement on Subsidies and Countervailing Measures, which recognizes 'the need for consistent resolution of disputes arising from anti-dumping and countervailing duty measures.'

or oversight of a previous decision, or put another way, the extent to which a decision-maker is afforded any deference by a subsequent decision-maker. I then discussed the various types of standards that frequently are applied, noting their relative intensity or deference along a 'sliding scale'.[10] Facts and law have historically been treated differently, primarily because the need for consistency in the application of legal rules is often viewed as more important than any deference towards the legal findings of the original decision-maker.[11]

Standards of review are based on both constitutional and administrative law considerations.[12] From a constitutional perspective, standards of review need to take into account the constitutional structures of an institution, including any separation of functions, and the objects of the institution. Administrative law considerations are also important in that standards of review applied in judicial-type processes should, in conjunction with other procedural rules, promote a high quality of decision-making. In addition, standards of review are often based upon practical, as well as theoretical criteria. There may, for example, be limits on the level of oversight due to a dispute settlement body having inadequate funding or less than qualified decision-makers.

In Chapter 1, I briefly examined how a standard of review would be applied within various different legal systems, including Australia, the United States, France and by the ECJ.[13] I have also referred to how standards of review function in the context of the ICJ as well as NAFTA and ICSID Tribunals. This examination showed that the standard of review was different in each system and that there was consistently a high degree of deference in the scrutiny of factual issues. However, as each system has its own constitutional design and processes, it may be somewhat difficult to judge the merits of each system and derive relevant principles. Further, there is the more obvious difficulty of trying to transplant standards of review from these systems to the WTO, which has its own history and institutional objectives. At best we can seek to deduce common principles, but they must be applied cautiously in the WTO context. This suggests that basing a new standard of review directly on domestic administrative law or other international systems may be of limited value, and that the WTO needs to develop its own standard of review.

The WTO does fundamentally have a need for a standard of review because, in many international trade disciplines, panels are reviewing member state measures that result from complex administrative, judicial or quasi-judicial

10 See Chapter 1, Section 1.2.2.
11 See Chapter 1, Section 1.2.3.
12 See Chapter 1, Section 1.2.4.
13 See Chapter 1, Section 1.2.5.

processes.[14] In other words, panels are not always merely determining whether domestic legislation complies with the WTO rules. The standard of review is therefore essential to the development of a sophisticated dispute settlement system of this kind. However, formulating an appropriate standard of review is difficult in the absence of long-standing doctrines of the kind that frequently exist in domestic legal systems.

As discussed in Chapter 2, the WTO has a unique institutional history and has had more diplomatic than legalistic origins.[15] It is also a member-driven organization with 'legislation' in the form of multilateral trade agreements, the result of long and often difficult trade negotiations.[16] It is not clear whether this history has a positive or negative influence on the ability to reform the standard of review, but it does highlight the need to address legitimacy concerns in this endeavour.

The standard of review issue first surfaced as an issue of contention in the *EC-Hormones* decision in the late 1990s. This dispute concerned SPS measures in relation to United States beef exports, and raised questions about the extent to which the WTO could override domestic law and policy.[17] Whilst the standard of review applied by the WTO has little or no direct relationship to sovereignty issues, this dispute brought into focus the importance and influence of the manner in which WTO Tribunals review national decisions.[18] In subsequent disputes, WTO Tribunals have developed the standard of review,

---

14 See Sharif Bhuiyan, *National Law in WTO Law: Effectiveness and Good Governance in the World Trading System* (Cambridge University Press, 2007) 146. This makes the relationship between WTO panels and its members in reviewing member measures broadly analogous to that of domestic Courts and domestic government agencies. In a domestic law context, there is the need for specific rules about the type and level of judicial oversight of government decisions that is very common within administrative law. See also David Palmeter, 'The WTO Standard of Review in Health and Safety Disputes' in George A. Bermann and Petros C. Mavroidis (eds), *Trade and Human Health and Safety* (Cambridge University Press, 2006) 224, in which it is suggested that the most accurate analogy in a domestic law context for the role of WTO panels is that of the Federal Court in the United States reviewing a state law for conformity to the United States constitution.

15 See Chapter 2, Section 2.2.

16 *Ibid.*

17 For discussion of the factual and European regulatory background see Natalie McNelis, 'The Role of the Judge in the EU and WTO: Lessons from the BSE and Hormones Cases' *Journal of International Economic Law* (2001) 189; *UK v Commission* (C-180/96) [1998] ECR I-2265.

18 Stephen Croley and John H. Jackson, 'WTO Dispute Procedures, Standard of Review and Deference to National Governments' (1996) 90(2) *American Journal of International Law*; John H. Jackson, 'The Great 1994 Sovereignty Debate: United States Acceptance and Implementation of the Uruguay Round Results' (1997) 36 *Columbia General of Transnational Law*.

albeit in an often confusing and inconsistent manner. Further, as discussed in Chapter 2, WTO Tribunals have not as yet clarified the meaning of the unique anti-dumping standard of review, and it is difficult to justify the fact that this standard does not apply to other trade remedy agreements given the similar concepts and policy considerations.

Given this problem, in Chapter 3, I discussed a number of alternative models put forward by other authors.[19] Almost all tests put forward prescribe some degree of deference where a member State has fulfilled certain basic procedural or substantive criteria. For example, a test may be developed to refrain from overturning a decision that is reasonably made by a domestic authority, or where a member has undertaken sufficient deliberation in relation to a measure.[20] A different approach was highlighted by Ehlermann and Lockhart in identifying that the generalized objective assessment test must function with a more detailed underlying standard of review.[21] This approach bases the standard not, in the first instance, on how a decision was made, but rather on the type of WTO obligation in dispute.[22] The effect of this is to recognize that the standard of review is a combination of procedural scrutiny and the substantive obligations under review.[23] This is a fundamentally different approach in comparison with earlier proposals and one with which I agree, and I have taken these observations into account in developing the new standard of review advanced in this work.

In order to develop a theoretical framework, I examined in Chapter 3 the principles that may inform the construction of a new standard of review. The major principles that I identified are the need to promote WTO dispute settlement objectives, the need for adjudicative legitimacy, and the need to function in conjunction with appropriate procedures. The last point goes to basic practical administrative issues, such as clarity, efficiency, expertise and procedural fairness, whereas the first two are really institutional issues. A new standard of review must take these factors into account, particularly the first two, which means that the standard of review should be uniquely formulated to suit the institutional design and context of the WTO.

The new standard of review that I have proposed consists of two parts. The first part is a general standard of review that WTO panels should apply to all WTO disputes, absent the conditions discussed below that would result in its

---

19 See Chapter 3, Section 3.2.

20 See Chapter 3, Sections 3.2.2 and 3.2.3.

21 See Chapter 3, Sections 3.2.5.

22 Ehlermann and Lockhart, 'Standard of Review in WTO Law', above n 8.

23 This approach enables the standard of review to be viewed partly as an interpretation of the WTO texts and the usual methods and principles of treaty interpretation may be applied.

modification. This general standard stipulates that panels should apply an unrestricted and highly intensive standard of review to both factual and legal issues. The basic architecture of this standard, discussed in Chapter 4, is the requirement for panels to examine all available and sufficient evidence and to conduct a comprehensive review.[24] The first limb really maintains the current situation of panels basing their review on material before them, but being required to request further information should this be necessary to reach an informed decision on the merits. The second limb, which deals with the manner of substantive review, requires panels to conduct a thorough review and to publish detailed reasons of the decision. It is contended that the general standard would promote the standard of review principles identified and would be an improvement over alternative standards that have previously been put forward. However, the general standard does suffer from some deficiencies in that it may be applied inflexibly and lead to excessive intrusion in particular WTO disciplines. It may therefore detract from the goal of the WTO enhancing its legitimacy as an international organization.

Chapter 5 explores the need to modify the general standard of review in some instances to create a specific standard of review. This would potentially generate different standards of review depending upon the particular WTO disciplines and obligations that are under review. The main reason is that in some Agreements, members have retained the authority and competency to review and make decisions in relation to their own measures.[25] This is particularly the case with anti-dumping and countervailing duty measures, and to a more limited extent, with SPS and TBT measures. I have therefore advocated the use of greater deference where the WTO Agreements have provided for members to retain specific competencies, and that the degree of deference should be proportionate to scope of the competencies retained.[26] The aim of this approach is to ensure that the best overall quality of decision-making is achieved in relation to measures, by a combination of rigorous national level processes and sufficient WTO oversight. There would still be adequate WTO scrutiny to counter the possibility or perception of bias by domestic authorities in favour of local producers and interests in, for example, trade remedy investigations.

In Chapters 6 and 7, I considered how the new standard of review may apply to two groups of agreements, the trade remedy agreements and various non-trade remedy agreements. I have not dealt with all non-trade remedy agreements, but rather I have focussed on the major agreements where the

---

[24] See Chapter 4, Sections 4.2.1 and 4.2.2.
[25] See Chapter 5, Section 5.1.
[26] See Chapter 5, Section 5.2.2.

standard of review is likely to be contentious. Broadly speaking, the new standard of review would result in a higher degree of deference when applied to the trade remedy agreements, and it would result in much less deference when applied to some of the non-trade remedy agreements, such as in the case of the SPS and TBT Agreements. No deference at all would be applied in relation to disputes concerning the provisions of GATT 1994 and many other non-trade remedy agreements. It is important to recall that the standard of review would not necessarily be applied uniformly to a WTO Agreement, as each obligation or set of obligations must be considered separately. Nonetheless, it would not be difficult for panels to delineate the circumstances when the general or a specific standard of review are required, nor would it be difficult to apply an appropriate specific standard because similar WTO obligations would be treated in a like manner over time. The regulatory philosophy of each Agreement may also assist to determine the intensity of the standard of review, particularly in circumstances where the delineation of jurisdictional competencies is not clearly articulated in the text of the WTO Agreements. However, as the regulatory intention of a WTO Agreement is not always settled, caution must be exercised in using it as a method of interpretation of the standard of review, and where it is utilized, it should be applied merely as a fall-back method of interpretation.

Finally, it is contemplated that the new standard of review proposed by this book would be introduced by means of future Appellate Body and panel rulings. This would involve panels and the Appellate Body using their inherent powers to develop such a new test. It could be introduced 'legislatively' through a revision to the DSU, but this is unlikely given the ongoing

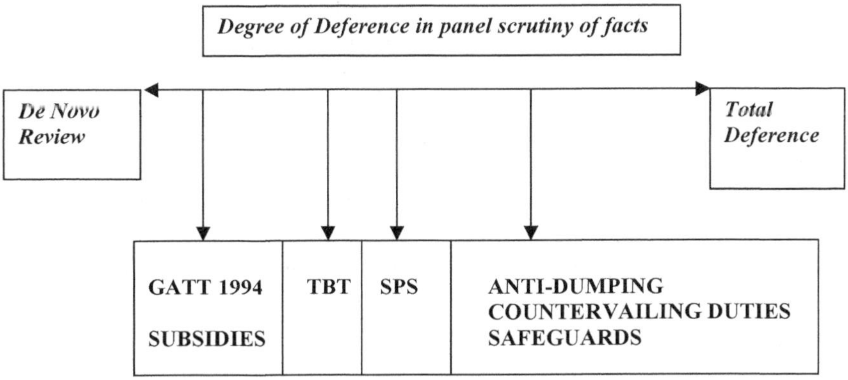

Figure 8.1 Spectrum of panel deference for selected WTO agreements

Table 8.1 Summary of the New Standard of Review

WTO Agreement	Standard of Review of Facts
General Agreement on Tariffs and Trade 1994	General Standard of Review • Highly intensive and no deference
Anti-Dumping Agreement	Specific Standard of Review • High degree of deference to factual issues • Major relevant obligations: Articles 2, 3, 5 and 6
Agreement on Subsidies and Countervailing Measures	*Countervailing Measures* Specific Standard of Review • High degree of deference to factual issues • Major relevant obligations: Articles 10 to 22 *Subsidies* General Standard of Review • Highly intensive and no deference
Safeguards Agreement	Specific Standard of Review • High degree of deference to factual issues • Major relevant obligations: Articles 2 to 7
SPS Agreement	Specific Standard of Review • Medium degree of deference for Articles 2.2, 3.3, 5.1 to 5.3 • Medium to low deference for Articles 5.4 to 5.6 • General Standard of Review – other Articles
TBT Agreement	Specific Standard of Review • Low degree of deference for Article 2.2 • General Standard of Review – other Articles

WTO Agreement	Standard of Review of Law
All WTO Agreements	General Standard of Review • Highly intensive and no deference

WTO Agreement	Mixed questions of fact and law
Agreements and obligations where the General Standard of Review applies	General Standard of Review • Highly intensive and no deference
Agreements and obligations where a Specific Standard of Review applies	Specific Standard of Review • Some deference but less than for purely factual questions

difficulties with the membership concluding the Doha Round of negotiations. Bhuiyan notes that:

> The absence of a standard of review clause should not, however, be a matter of great surprise or shock. While it may not be unreasonable to think, or expect, that some guidance should exist somewhere in the treaty, it is also true that treaty provisions on a subject such as this are most likely to be formulated at a level of considerable abstraction.[27]

The standard of review test advanced in this book may be represented, albeit in a simplified fashion, in terms of relative deference along a spectrum, as set out in Figure 8.1 on page 221.

These outcomes are broadly summarized in Table 8.1 on pages 222–3.

8.2 DIRECTIONS FOR FUTURE RESEARCH

The standard of review issue for the WTO is one aspect of the broader subject of the development of international law. In particular, many scholars are currently considering whether there ought to be a further harmonization in the legal rules, procedures, practices and principles applied by various interna-

[27] Bhuiyan, *National Law in WTO Law*, above n 14, 155.

tional institutions.[28] In the years to come, it will be interesting to observe to what extent the standard of review merely reflects the specific institutional needs of the WTO, as opposed to it being a product of trends in the development of international law. With this comment in mind, there are a number of issues related to this work, that are likely to be worthy of exploration in the future.

Firstly, and most obviously, there is scope to further develop the ideas put forward in this work. There are several aspects of the standard of review argued for that I have not sufficiently covered, and which could be expanded upon further. It would be useful to explore what a standard of review advocated in this book would look like if applied to other WTO Agreements, such as the TRIPS Agreement or GATS. Further case analysis and case studies would also be warranted to better understand how the new standard of review may have affected dispute settlement outcomes.[29] Also, given that this work focusses on the standard of review of facts carried out by panels, it would be advantageous for further research to be undertaken on other aspects of the standard of review, including in relation to the classification of issues of fact and law, the merits of a strict or undeferential legal standard, the standard applied by the Appellate Body in reviewing panel rulings, and the standard applied by Article 21.5 panels in reviewing earlier panel decisions.[30]

Secondly, there is much scope for the further exploration of the legal concepts and principles that may inform the design of a standard of review. In other words, there is certainly the need for my arguments and ideas in this work to be tested against alternative standard of review proposals, and to better appreciate the international legal context in which such proposals are applied. This is likely to involve further consideration of the impact and relevance of matters such as sovereignty, subsidiarity, human rights and treaty interpretation.[31] The view expressed in this work is that it is very difficult to

---

28 See for example, Chester Brown, *A Common Law of International Adjudication* (Oxford University Press, 2007) 225–37. There are also various works on the problems of harmonization: see International Law Commission, Report of the Study Group on Fragmentation of International Law: Difficulties arising from the Diversification and Expansion of International Law, UN Doc A/CN.4/L.682 (4 April 2006).

29 Some of the arguments in this book have been put forward in First Written Submissions of Australia, *Australia-Apples* [175]–[189].

30 Regarding Article 21.5 cases, see in particular comments and findings of the Appellate Body in *US-Continued Suspension* [585]–[592]. For an introduction into these issues see Matthias Oesch, *Standards of Review in WTO Dispute Resolution* (Oxford University Press, 2003).

31 Bhuiyan, *National Law in WTO Law*, above n 14, 202–6.

base a procedural instrument, such as a standard of review, directly on these broader considerations, but they are influential nonetheless. It will be interesting to see how the debate proceeds concerning what underlying principles are presently impacting upon the governance of institutions such as the WTO. Further, the relationship between the standard of review and other procedural rules, such as the burden of proof and relevant principles, for instance judicial economy are worthy of future research.[32]

Thirdly, and perhaps most compelling, would be to examine how the new standard of review may apply to other international organizations and international agreements. The most obvious application would be in respect of organizations and agreements that have a similar subject matter and a similar relationship with their constituent members. NAFTA, ICSID and many of the various recent bilateral and regional trade agreements may qualify in this regard.[33] At this stage, the standard of review has not been a major issue, but there may be a need to apply a specific standard of review in the future, particularly if these fora are progressively used by litigants as an alternative to WTO dispute settlement. This is a distinct possibility, but a precondition of this is a sophisticated dispute settlement system, akin to that which operates in the WTO, as well as a high volume of cases to develop these systems.

Fourthly, it would be interesting to see if the standard of review could or should be used to determine particular WTO policy outcomes. Of particular interest at the present time would be research into whether a flexible standard of review could be applied to promote the special and differential treatment objectives of the WTO Agreements, and the development agenda that is part of the Doha Round of negotiations.[34] In practical terms, consider whether it is appropriate in an anti-dumping complaint for a panel to apply a more intensive standard of review where the complainant is a developing country and the

---

[32] James Cameron and Kevin R. Gray, 'Principles of International Law in the WTO Dispute Settlement Body' (2001) 50 *International and Comparative Law Quarterly* 248, 276–83.

[33] See Chapter 1, Section 1.2.5.5. See also Bhuiyan, *National Law in WTO Law*, above n 14, 149–53.

[34] See for example, Andrew D. Mitchell, 'A Legal Principle of Special and Differential Treatment for WTO Disputes' (2006) 5(3) *World Trade Review* 445. Special and differential treatment concerns the granting of special concessions or rights in favour of developing countries. Such treatment features in most of the WTO Agreements and may take various forms such as longer time periods for implementing WTO commitments or less stringent restrictions concerning the use of safeguards and subsidies by developing country WTO members that are not available to the general WTO membership.

respondent is a developed country.[35] This sounds like a worthy proposition considering the relative resources of these WTO members. However, it may result in a major reinterpretation of the WTO Agreements that goes beyond the original meaning of the Agreements. It would also mean that a flexible standard of review would not be based on a division of jurisdictional competencies between the WTO and its members, but rather it would be based on giving preference to particular policy objectives over other objectives, which are also part of the WTO Agreements. That is, the standard would be moving further away from a textual approach and towards one that is based more directly on policy considerations. Ideally, such policy issues should be dealt with through changes to the WTO Agreements, or via broader methods of interpretation of the Agreements, rather than using the standard of review for this purpose. Still, it is an interesting proposition, particularly when many different issues such as environmental and cultural protection may be treated in this type of manner.[36]

8.3 THE SIGNIFICANCE OF THE STANDARD OF REVIEW ISSUE FOR THE WTO: CONCLUDING REMARKS

Standards of review have traditionally been developed in more complex legal systems. The rise of this issue in the WTO context is no exception. In the case of the WTO, its importance is largely a product of the relationship between the WTO as an international institution and its members, being almost exclusively sovereign states. However, it is also the result of the nature of and practices concerning specific international trade and trade-related issues that the WTO regulates. National level approaches to matters such as quarantine procedures, product standards and anti-dumping investigations are often controversial. Given the complexity of many of these issues, the standard of review is an important legal instrument for determining the amount of oversight that the WTO exercises over members in deciding whether there is compliance with the WTO Agreements. Whilst the standard of review is an aspect of procedure,

---

[35] See Seung Wha Chang, 'WTO for Trade and Development Post-Doha' in William J. Davey and John H. Jackson (eds), *The Future of International Economic Law* (Oxford University Press, 2008) 115, 130 where the author suggests that an independent body to be established to make an objective assessment of the development relevance of a developing country member's measures. The type of standard of review may be relevant in deciding upon special and differential treatment.

[36] See for example, Andrew Green and Tracey Epps, 'The WTO, Science, and the Environment: Moving Towards Consistency' (2007) 10(2) *Journal of International Economic Law* 285.

the type of standard applied to a review of a member's conduct may affect the way in which the WTO Agreements are interpreted and applied. In this way, it may have substantive legal effects. A standard of review that is not well articulated or applied may also result in varying degrees of oversight, which also goes to questions of fairness and uniformity in the treatment of litigants.

If a new standard of review is not adopted in WTO dispute settlement and the current position of 'drifting along' is maintained, then members are likely to continue to raise this issue in many future appeals to the Appellate Body. It may also lead to dissatisfaction amongst different segments of the membership. Major developed nations who are frequent users of the dispute settlement system may become frustrated by the lack of certainty, and developing nations may become cynical that their rights and interests are not being adequately protected. It is therefore important for the WTO, and in particular the WTO Secretariat and the Appellate body, to take leadership over this issue. At the present time, reforming the standard of review is not a high priority in the DSU negotiations in comparison to other procedural issues such as the Appellate Body remand powers and sequencing of member compliance.[37] It is acknowledged that the standard of review is not an institutional panacea, in which all mischief and deficiencies may be cured. It is nonetheless a very important instrument of accountability and governance that, if properly addressed, the WTO and the international trading community would benefit from significantly.

[37] The DSU reform negotiations are not tied to the Doha Round of negotiations. These negotiations are generally conducted within the Special Sessions of the DSB, which forms part of the Trade Negotiations Committee.

Bibliography

ARTICLES/BOOKS/REPORTS

Akakwam, Philip, 'The Standard of Review in the 1994 Antidumping Code: Circumscribing the Role of GATT Panels in Reviewing National Antidumping Determinations' (1996) 5 *Minnesota Journal of Global Trade* 277

Amar, Akhil Reed, 'Intertextualism' (1999) 112 *Harvard Law Review* 747

Aronson, Mark, 'Unreasonableness and Error of Law' (2001) 26 *University of New South Wales Law Journal* 1

Aronson, Mark, Bruce Dyer and Matthew Groves, *Judicial Review of Administrative Action* (Law Book Company, 3rd ed, 2004)

Australian Department of Foreign Affairs and Trade (ed), *Ten Years of WTO Dispute Settlement: Australian Perspectives* (Commonwealth of Australia, 2006)

Bartels, Lorand, 'Applicable Law in WTO Dispute Settlement Proceedings' (2001) 35(3) *Journal of World Trade* 499

Becroft, Ross S., 'The Standard of Review Strikes Back: The US-Korea DRAMS Appeal' (2006) 9(1) *Journal of International Economic Law* 207

Beetham, David, *The Legitimation of Power* (MacMillan, 1991)

Bermann, George A. and Petros C. Mavroidis (eds), *Trade and Human Health and Safety* (Cambridge University Press, 2006)

Bhala, Raj, *Modern GATT Law: A Treatise on the General Agreement on Tariffs and Trade* (Sweet & Maxwell, 2005)

Bhuiyan, Sharif, *National Law in WTO Law: Effectiveness and Good Governance in the World Trading System* (Cambridge University Press, 2007)

Bohanes, Jan and Nicolas Lockhart, 'Standard of Review in WTO Law' in Daniel Bethlehem (ed), *The Oxford Handbook of International Trade Law* (Oxford University Press, 2009)

Borght, Kim Van der (ed), *Essays on the Future of the WTO: Finding a New Balance* (Cameron May, 2003)

Broude, Tomer, 'Genetically Modified Rules: The Awkward Rule-Exception-Right Distinction in EC-Biotech' (2007) 6 *World Trade Review* 215

Broude, Tomer, 'Principles of Normative Integration and the Allocation of

International Authority: The WTO, the Vienna Convention on the Law of Treaties and the Rio Declaration' (2008) 6 *Loy UChi International Review*

Brown, Chester, *A Common Law of International Adjudication* (Oxford University Press, 2007)

Brown, L. Neville and John S. Bell, *French Administrative Law* (Clarendon Press, 5th ed, 1998)

Brown, L. Neville and Tom Kennedy, *The Court of Justice of the European Communities* (Sweet & Maxwell, 4th ed, 1994)

Brownlie, Ian, *Principles of Public International Law* (Oxford University Press, 7th ed, 2008)

Burca, Grainne De and Joanne Scott (eds), *The EU and the WTO Legal and Constitutional Issues* (Hart Publishing, 2001)

Burke-White William W. and Andreas von Staden, 'Private Litigation in a Public Law Sphere: The Standard of Review in Investor-State Arbitrations' (2010) 35(2) *Yale Journal of International Law*

Butterworths Australian Legal Dictionary (Butterworths, 1997)

Button, Catherine, *The Power to Protect – Trade, Health and Uncertainty in the WTO* (Hart Publishing, 2004)

Button, Catherine, 'The WTO's Objective Assessment Standard of Review and Panel Review of Health Measures' in Andrew D. Mitchell (ed), *Challenges and Prospects for the WTO* (Cameron May, 2005) 85

Cameron, James and Kevin R. Gray, 'Principles of International Law in the WTO Dispute Settlement Body' (2001) 50 *International and Comparative Law Quarterly* 248

Cane, Peter and Leighton McDonald, *Principles of Administrative Law: Legal Regulation of Governance* (Oxford University Press, 2008)

Capps, Patrick, Malcolm Evans and Stratos Konstadinidis (eds), *Asserting Jurisdiction: International and European Legal Perspectives* (Hart Publishing, 2003)

Cass, Deborah, 'The 'Constitutionalization' of International Trade Law: Judicial Norm-Generation as the Engine of Constitutional Development in International Trade' (2001) 12(1) *European Journal of International Law* 39

Cass, Deborah, *The Constitutionalization of the World Trade Organization: Legitimacy, Democracy, and Community in the International Trading System,* International Economic Law Series (Oxford University Press, 2005)

Cassese, Sabino, 'Administrative Law Without the State? The Challenge of Global Regulation' (2005) 37 *New York University Journal of International Law and Politics* 663

Chapus, Rene, *Droit du Contentieux Administratif* (Montchrestien, 12th ed, 2006)

Colares, Juscelino F., 'A Theory of WTO Adjudication: From Empirical Analysis to Biased Rule Development' (2009) 42(2) *Vanderbilt Journal of Transnational Law* 383

Cottier, Thomas, 'Preparing for Structural Reform in the WTO' (2007) 10(3) *Journal of International Economic Law* 497

Cottier, Thomas and Petros Mavroidis (eds), *The Role of the Judge in International Trade Regulation – Experience and Lessons for the WTO* (University of Michigan Press, 2003)

Croley, Steven and John H. Jackson, 'WTO Dispute Procedures, Standard of Review, and Deference to National Governments' (1996) 90 *The American Journal of International Law* 193

Cunningham, Richard, 'Part II: Review of Key Substantive Agreements: Panel II E: Antidumping Agreement (AD) and Agreement on Subsidies and Countervailing Measures (SCM): Commentary on the First Five Years of the WTO Antidumping Agreement and Agreement on Subsidies and Countervailing Measures' (2000) 31 *Law and Policy in International Business* 897

Cunningham, Richard and Troy Cribb, 'Dispute Settlement through the lens of "Free Flow of Trade" – A Review of WTO Dispute Settlement of US Anti-dumping and Countervailing Duty Measures' (2003) 6(1) *Journal of International Economic Law* 155

Davey, William J., 'Has the WTO Dispute Settlement System Exceeded its Authority?' (2001) 4(1) *Journal of International Economic Law* 79

Davey, William J., 'The WTO: Looking Forwards' (2006) 9(1) *Journal of International Economic Law* 3

Davey, William J. and John H. Jackson (eds), *The Future of International Economic Law* (Oxford University Press, 2008)

David, Rene, *French Law: Its Structure, Sources and Methodology* (Louisiana State University Press, 1972)

Davies, Arwel, 'Connecting or Compartmentalizing the WTO and the United States Legal Systems? The role of the Charming Betsy Canon' (2007) 10(1) *Journal of International Economic Law* 117

Dehousse, Renaud, *The European Court of Justice: The Politics of Judicial Integration* (Macmillan Press, 1998)

Desmedt, Axel, 'Hormones: "Objective Assessment" and (or as) Standard of Review' (1998) 1(4) *Journal of International Economic Law* 695

Desmedt, Axel, 'Proportionality in WTO Law' (2001) *Journal of International Economic Law* 441

Dordi, Claudio, 'Comment: Mexico Anti-Dumping Measures on Rice' (2008) 7 *World Trade Review* 325

Douglas, Roger, *Administrative Law* (Lexis Nexus Butterworths, 2nd ed, 2004)

Douglas, Roger, *Douglas and Jones's Administrative Law* (Federation Press, 6th ed, 2009)

Du, Michael M., 'Domestic Regulatory Autonomy under the TBT Agreement: From Non-discrimination to Harmonization' (2007) 6(2) *Chinese Journal of International Law* 269

Du, Michael M., 'Standard of Review under the SPS Agreement after EC-Hormones II' (2010) 59(2) *International and Comparative Law Quarterly* 441

Durling, James, 'Deference But Only When Due: WTO Review of Anti-Dumping Measures' (2003) 6(1) *Journal of International Economic Law* 125

Ehlermann, Claus-Dieter and Nicolas Lockhart, 'Standard of Review in WTO Law' (2004) 7(3) *Journal of International Economic Law* 491

Enright, Christopher, *Federal Administrative Law* (Federation Press, 2001)

Epps, Tracey, 'Reconciling Public Opinion and WTO Rules under the SPS Agreement' (2008) 7(2) *World Trade Review* 359

Esty, Daniel, 'Good Governance at the World Trade Organization: Building a Foundation of Administrative Law' (2007) 10(3) *Journal of International Economic Law* 509

Falk, Richard A., *The Role of Domestic Courts in the International Legal Order* (Syracuse University Press, 1964)

Footer, Mary E., *An Institutional and Normative Analysis of the World Trade Organization* (Martinus Nijhoff, 2006)

Franck, Thomas M., *The Power of Legitimacy Amongst Nations* (Oxford University Press, 1990)

Franck, Thomas M., *The Empowered Self: Law and Society in the Age of Individualism* (Oxford University Press, 1999)

Franck, Thomas M., *Recourse to Force: State Action against Threats and Armed Attacks* (Cambridge University Press, 2002)

Frier, Pierre Laurent and Jacques Petit, *Précis de Droit Administratif Mis a Jour, Précis Domat* (Montcrestien, 5th ed, 2008)

Gardiner, Richard K., *Treaty Interpretation* (Oxford University Press, 2008)

Goh, Gavin and Trudy Witbreuk, 'An Introduction to the WTO Dispute Settlement System' (2001) 30(1) *University of Western Australia Law Review* 51

Goh, Gavin, 'Tipping the Apple Cart: The Limits of Science and Law in the SPS Agreement after *Japan-Apples*' (2006) 40(4) *Journal of World Trade* 655

Grando, Michelle T., *Evidence, Proof, and Fact-Finding in WTO Dispute Settlement* (Oxford University Press, 2010)

Green, Andrew and Tracey Epps, 'The WTO, Science and the Environment: Moving Towards Consistency' (2007) 10(2) *Journal of International Economic Law* 285

Greenwald, John, 'WTO Dispute Settlement: An Exercise in Trade Law Legislation?' (2003) 6(1) *Journal of International Economic Law* 113

Groves, Matthew and H.P. Lee, *Australian Administrative Law: Fundamentals, Principles and Doctrines* (Cambridge University Press, 2007)

Guzman, Andrew T., 'WTO Dispute Resolution in Health and Safety Cases' (2007) *UC Berkeley Public Law Research Paper No. 989371*, available at SSRN: http://ssrn.com/abstract=989371, last accessed 31 March 2012

Guzman, Andrew T., 'Determining the Appropriate Standard of Review in WTO Disputes' (2009) 42(1) *Cornell International Law Journal* 45

Hamilton, Lee, 'US Antidumping Decisions and the WTO Standard of Review; Deference or Disregard?' (2003) 4 *Chicago Journal of International Law* 265

Harlow, Carol, 'Global Administrative Law: The Quest for Principles and Values' (2006) 17(1) *European Journal of International Law* 187

Hay, Peter, 'International and Supranational Organizations: Some Problems of Conceptualization' in Wayne R. LaFave and Peter Hay (eds), *International Trade, Investment and Organization* (University of Illinois Press, 1967)

Heiskanen, Veijo, 'The Regulatory Philosophy of International Trade Law' (2004) 38(1) *Journal of World Trade* 1

Helfer, Laurence and Anne-Marie Slaughter, 'The Effectiveness of the Council of Europe's Human Rights Regime', in Bob Reinalda and Bertjak Verbeek (eds), *Autonomous Policymaking By International Organizations* (Routledge, 1998) 141

Helfer, Lawrence and Anne-Marie Slaughter, 'Towards a Theory of Effective Supranational Adjudication' (1998) 107 *Yale Law Journal* 273

Hilf, Meinhard, 'Power, Rules and Principles – Which Orientation for WTO/GATT Law' (2001) *Journal of International Economic Law* 111

Hirsch, Moshe, *The Arbitration Mechanism of the International Centre for the Settlement of Investment Disputes* (Martinus Nijhoff, 1993)

Hockin, Thomas A., *The American Nightmare – Politics and the Fragile World Trade Organization* (Lexington Books, 2003)

Horlick, Gary, 'Antidumping at the Seattle Ministerial: With Tear Gas in My Eyes' (2000) 3(1) *Journal of International Economic Law* 178

Horlick, Gary and Peggy Clarke, 'Standards for Panels Reviewing Antidumping Determinations under the GATT and WTO' in Ernst-Ulrich Petersmann (ed), *International Trade Law and the GATT and WTO Dispute Settlement System* (Kluwer Law International, 1997)

Howse, Robert, 'Democracy, Science and Free Trade: Risk Regulation on Trial at the World Trade Organization' (2000) 98 *Michigan Law Review* 2329

Howse, Robert and Kalypso Nicolaidis, 'Enhancing WTO Legitimacy: Constitutionization or Global Subsidiarity' (2003) 16(1) *Governance* 73

Hudec, Robert E, 'Broadening the Scope of Remedies in WTO Dispute Settlement' in Freidl Weis and Jochem Weirs (eds), *Improving WTO Dispute Settlement Procedures* (Cameron May, 2000) 345

Hudec, Robert E., *Enforcing International Trade Law – the Evolution of the Modern GATT Legal System* (Butterworths, 1993)

Hudec, Robert E., 'Broadening the Scope of Remedies in WTO Dispute Settlement' in Freidl Weiss and Jochem Weirs (eds), *Improving WTO Dispute Settlement Procedures* (Cameron May, 2000)

International Law Commission, *Report of the Study Group on Fragmentation of International Law: Difficulties Arising from the Diversification and Expansion of International Law*, UN Doc A/CN.4/L.682 (4 April 2006)

Jackson, John H., *World Trade and the Law of the GATT* (Bobbs-Merrill Company, 1969)

Jackson, John H., 'Editorial Comment: The WTO Dispute Settlement Understanding-Misunderstandings on the Nature of Legal Obligation' (1997) 91 *American Journal of International Law* 60

Jackson, John H., 'The Great 1994 Sovereignty Debate: United States Acceptance and Implementation of the Uruguay Round Results' (1997) 36 *Columbia Journal of Transnational Law* 157

Jackson, John H., *The World Trading System – Law and Policy of International Economic Relations* (MIT Press, 2nd ed, 1997)

Jackson, John H., *The World Trade Organization Constitution and Jurisprudence,* Chatham House Papers (The Royal Institute of International Affairs, 1998)

Jackson, John H., 'The Changing Fundamentals of International Law and Ten Years of the WTO' (2005) 8(1) *Journal of International Economic Law* 3

Joerges, Christian and Ernst-Ulrich Petersmann (eds), *Constitutionalism, Multilevel Trade Governance and Social Regulation (Studies in International Trade Law Vol. 9)* (Hart Publishing, 2006)

Kaikobad, Kaiyan, *The International Court of Justice and Judicial Review: A study of the Court's powers with respect to judgments of the ILO and UN administrative tribunals* (Kluwer Law International, 2000)

Knight, Dean R., 'A Murky Methodology: Standards of Review in Administrative Law' (2008) 6 *New Zealand Journal of Public and International Law* 117

Kumm, Mattias, 'Constitutionalising Subsidiarity in Integrated Markets: The Case of Tobacco Regulation in the European Union' (2006) 12(4) *European Law Journal* 503

Lane, W.B. and Simon Young, *Administrative Law in Australia* (Law Book Company, 2007)

Lang, Andrew, 'Reconstructing Embedded Liberalism: John Gerard Ruggie and Constructivist Approaches to the Study of the International Trade Regime' (2006) 9(1) *Journal of International Economic Law* 81

Layton, Duane and Jorge Miranda, 'Advocacy before World Trade Organization Dispute Settlement Panels in Trade Remedy Cases' (2003) 37(1) *Journal of World Trade* 69

Leitner, Kara and Simon Lester, 'WTO Dispute Settlement 1995–2004: A Statistical Analysis' (2005) 8(1) *Journal of International Economic Law* 231

Li, Catherine, 'In Quest of the Proper Standard of Review in WTO Trade Remedy Cases' in Mitsuo Matsushita, Dukgeun Ahn and Tain-Jy Chen (eds), *The WTO Trade Remedy System: East Asian Perspectives* (Cameron May, 2006)

Loeb, Hamilton and Michael Owen (eds), *North American Free Trade Agreement: Summary and Analysis* (Matthew Bender, 1993)

Maki, Peter, 'Interpreting GATT Using the Vienna Convention on the Law of Treaties: A Method to Increase the Legitimacy of the Dispute Settlement System' (2000) 9(1) *Minnesota Journal of Global Trade* 343

Marks, Susan, 'Naming Administrative Law' (2005) 37 *Journal of International Law and Politics* 995

Marquez, Pablo, 'Standardization and Capture: The rise of standardization in international industrial regulation and global administrative law' (2007) 7(3) *Global Jurist*, article 5, available at http://www.bepress.com/gj/vol7/iss3/art5, last accessed 31 March 2012

Matsushita, Mitsuo, Thomas J. Schoenbaum and Petros C. Mavroidis, *The World Trade Organization: Law, Practice and Policy* (Oxford University Press, 2004)

Matsushita, Mitsuo, Thomas J. Schoenbaum and Petros C. Mavroidis, *The World Trade Organization: Law Policy and Practice* (Oxford University Press, 2nd ed, 2006)

Mavroidis, Petros C., *Trade in Goods: The GATT and the Other Agreements Regulating Trade in Goods* (Oxford University Press, 2007)

Mavroidis, Petros C., Patrick A. Messerlin and Jasper M. Wauters, *The Law and Economics of Contingent Protection* (Elgar International Economic Law, 2008)

McCormack, Timothy L.H. and Sue Robertson, 'Jurisdictional Aspects of the Rome Statute for the New International Criminal Court' (1999) 25 *Melbourne University Law Review* 47

McNelis, Natalie, 'The Role of the Judge in the EU and WTO – Lessons from the BSE and Hormones Case' (2001) 4(1) *Journal of International Economic Law* 189

Mitchell, Andrew D. (ed), *Challenges and Prospects for the WTO* (Cameron May, 2005)

Mitchell, Andrew D., 'A Legal Principle of Special and Differential Treatment for WTO Disputes' (2006) 5(3) *World Trade Review* 445

Mitchell, Andrew D., *Legal Principles in WTO Disputes* (Cambridge University Press, 2008)

Mitchell, Andrew D. and David Heaton, 'The Inherent Jurisdiction of WTO Tribunals: The Select Application of Public International Law Required by Judicial Function (2010) 31 *Michigan Journal of International Law* 561

Neugebauer, Regine, 'Fine Tuning WTO Jurisprudence and the SPS Agreement: Lessons from the Beef Hormone Case' (2000) 31(4) *Law and Policy in International Business* 1255

Oesch, Matthias, 'Standards of Review in WTO Dispute Resolution' (2003) 6(3) *Journal of International Economic Law* 635

Oesch, Matthias, *Standards of Review in WTO Dispute Resolution* (Oxford University Press, 2003)

Orakhelashvili, Alexander, *The Interpretation of Acts and Rules in Public International Law* (Oxford University Press, 2008)

Ortino, Federico, *Basic Legal Instruments for the Liberalization of Trade: A Comparative Analysis of EC and WTO Law* (Hart Publishing, 2004)

Ortino, Federico, 'Treaty Interpretation and the WTO Appellate Body Report in US-Gambling: A Critique' (2006) 9(1) *Journal of International Economic Law* 117

Ortino, Federico and Ernst-Ulrich Petersmann (eds), *The WTO Dispute Settlement System 1995–2003* (Kluwer Law International, 2004)

Oxman, Bernard H., *Jurisdiction of States*, Max Planck Encyclopedia of Public International Law, available at http://www.mpepil.com, last accessed 31 March 2012

Palmeter, David and Petros C. Mavroidis, *Dispute Settlement in the World Trade Organization: Practice and Procedure* (Cambridge University Press, 2nd ed, 2004)

Paulwelyn, Joost, *Conflict of Norms in Public International Law* (Cambridge University Press, 2003)

Petersmann, Ernst-Ulrich, *The GATT/WTO Dispute Settlement System: International Law, International Organizations and Dispute Settlement* (Kluwer Law International, 1997)

Pillay, Anashri, 'Courts, Variable Standard of Review and Resource Allocation: Developing a Model for the Enforcement of Social and Economic Rights' (2007) (6) *European Human Rights Law Journal* 616

Presley, Mari, 'Sovereignty and Delegation Issues regarding US Commitment to the World Trade Organization's Dispute Settlement Process' (1998) 8 *Journal of Transnational Law and Policy* 173

Princen, Sebastiaan, 'EC Compliance with WTO Law: The Interplay of Law and Politics' (2004) 15(3) *European Journal of International Law* 555

Prusa, Thomas, 'Comment: US-Countervailing Duty Investigation of DRAMS' (2008) 7(1) *World Trade Review* 231

Prusa, Thomas J., 'Comments on "Antidumping: Overview of the Agreement"' in Kyle W. Bagwell, George A. Bermann and Petros C. Mavroidis (eds), *Law and Economics of Contingent Protection in International Trade* (Cambridge University Press, 2010) 257

Pryles, Michael, 'The Basis of Adjudicatory Competence in Private International Law' (1972) 21 *International and Comparative Law Quarterly* 61

Qureshi, Asif H., *Interpreting WTO Agreements: Problems and Perspectives* (Cambridge University Press, 2006)

Reeves, Tony and Ninette Dodoo, 'Standards of Proof and Standards of Judicial Review in European Commission Merger Law' (2006) 29 *Fordham International Law Journal* 1034

Regimbald, Guy, 'Correctness, Reasonableness, and Proportionality: A New Standard of Judicial Review' (2005) 31 *Manitoba Law Journal* 239

Rosenne, Shabtai, *The World Court: What It Is and How It Works* (Martinus Nijhoff, 5th ed, 1995)

Rosenthal, Paul and Robert Vermylen, 'Part II: Review of Key Substantive Agreements: Panel II E: Antidumping Agreement (AD) and Agreement on Subsidies and Countervailing Measures (SCM): The WTO Antidumping and Subsidies Agreements: Did the United States achieve its objectives during the Uruguay Round?' (2000) 31 *Law and Policy in International Business* 871

Sampson, Gary P. (ed), *The Role of the World Trade Organization in Global Governance* (United Nations University Press, 2001)

Sands, Philippe (ed), *Manual on International Courts and Tribunals* (Butterworths, 1999)

Sapir, Andre and Petros C. Mavoidis, 'Mexico – Anti-Dumping Measures on Rice: "Don't ask me no questions and I won't tell you no lies"' (2008) 7 *World Trade Review* 305

Schaffer, Ellen G. and Randall J. Snyder (eds), *Contemporary Practice of Public International Law* (Oceania Publications, 1997)

Schneider, Andrea, 'Getting Along: The Evolution of Dispute Resolution Regimes in International Trade Organizations' (1999) 20(4) *Michigan Journal of International Law* 697

Schott, Jeffrey J. (ed), *Completing the Uruguay Round: A results orientated approach to the GATT trade negotiations* (Institute for International Economics, 1990)

Schwarze, Jurgen, 'The Future of the European Union Legal and Political Order' in Patrick J. Birkinshaw and Mike Varney (eds), *The European Union Legal Order after Lisbon* (Kluwer Law International, 2010)

Scott, Joanne, *The WTO Agreement on Sanitary and Phytosanitary Measures* (Oxford University Press, 2007)

Shaffer, Gregory, 'A Structural Theory of WTO Dispute Settlement: Why

Institutional Choice Lies at the Centre of the GMO Case' (2008) 41 *New York University Journal of International Law and Politics* 1

Shany, Yuval, *Regulating Jurisdictional Relations between National and International Courts* (Oxford University Press, 2007)

Slaughter, Anne-Marie, Alec Sweet and Joseph Weiler (eds), *The European Court and National Courts – Doctrine and Jurisprudence: Legal Change in its Social Context* (Oxford University Press, 1998)

Spamann, Holger, 'Standard of Review for World Trade Organization Panels in Trade Remedy Cases: A Critical Analysis' (2004) 38(3) *Journal of World Trade* 509

Steger, Debra, *Peace Through Trade: Building the World Trade Organization* (Cameron May, 2004)

Stephan, Paul, 'American Hegemony and International Law: Sheriff or Prisoner? The United States and the World Trade Organization' (2000) 1 *Chicago Journal of International Law* 49

Stewart, Terence P. (ed), *The GATT Uruguay Round: A Negotiating History (1986–1992) Volume 1: Commentary* (Kluwer, 1993)

Stewart, Terence P. and Amy S. Dwyer, *Handbook on WTO Trade Remedy Disputes – The First Six Years (1995–2000)* (Transnational Publishers, 2001)

Stoler, Andrew, 'The WTO Dispute Settlement Process: Did we get what negotiators wanted?' (2004) 3(1) *World Trade Review* 99

Strauss, Peter L., *An Introduction to Administrative Justice in the United States* (Carolina Academic Press, 1989)

Sykes, Alan, 'Comparative Advantage and the Normative Economics of International Trade Policy' (1998) 1(1) *Journal of International Economic Law* 49

Szafarz, Renata, *The Compulsory Jurisdiction of the International Court of Justice* (Kluwer Academic Publishers, 1993)

Tallberg, Jonas, 'Delegation to Supranational Institutions: Why, How and with What Consequences' (2002) 25(1) *West European Politics* 23

Tamberlin, Brian and Lucas Bastin, 'Australia and the World Trade Organization Decision Enforcement' (2007) 81 *Australian Law Journal* 802

Tarullo, Daniel, 'The Hidden Costs of International Dispute Settlement: WTO Review of Domestic Anti-Dumping Decisions' (2002) 34 *Law and Policy in International Business* 109

The Macquarie Dictionary (Macquarie, 5th ed, 2009)

The Oxford English Dictionary (Oxford University Press, 2nd ed, 1989)

Trachtman, Joel P., 'Regulatory Jurisdiction and the WTO' (2007) 10(3) *Journal of International Economic Law* 631

Trebilcock, Michael J. and Robert Howse, *The Regulation of International Trade* (Routledge, 3rd ed, 2005)

Trujillo, Elizabeth, 'Mission Possible: Reciprocal Deference between Domestic Regulatory Structures and the WTO' (2007) 40(1) *Cornell International Law Journal* 201

United States General Accounting Office, 'Report to the Ranking Minority Member, Committee on Finance, US Senate – World Trade Organization Standard of Review and Impact of Trade Remedy Rulings' (GAO-03-824, 2003)

Van Damme, Isabella, *Treaty Interpretation by the WTO Appellate Body* (Oxford University Press, 2009)

Van den Bossche, Peter, *The Law and Policy of the World Trade Organization: Text, Cases and Materials* (Cambridge University Press, 2005)

Voon, Tania and Alan Yanovich, 'The Facts Aside: The Limitation of WTO Appeals to Issues of Law' (2006) 40(2) *Journal of World Trade* 239

Wade, Sir William and Christopher Forsyth, *Administrative Law* (Oxford University Press, 10th ed, 2009)

Wagner, David M., 'Gonzales v Oregon: The Assisted Suicide of Chevron Deference' (2007) *Michigan State Law Review* 435

Waincymer, Jeff, *WTO Litigation: Procedural Aspects of Formal Dispute Settlement* (Cameron May, 2002) Warren, Kenneth F., *Administrative Law in the Political System* (Prentice Hall, 3rd ed, 1997)

Weber, Max, *Economy and Society* (University of California Press, 1968)

Weiler, Joseph (ed), *The EU, the WTO and the NAFTA: towards a common law of international trade* (Oxford University Press, 2000)

Weiss, Friedl, *Improving WTO Dispute Settlement Procedures: Issues and Lessons from the Practice of Other International Courts and Tribunals* (Cameron May, 2000)

Windsor, Matthew, 'A Fine Balance?: Delegation, Standards of Review, and Subsidiarity in WTO Dispute Settlement' (2008) 14 *Auckland University Law Review* 41

Wolfrum, Rudiger, Peter-Tobias Stoll and Anja Seibert-Fohr (eds), *Max Planck Commentaries on World Trade Law Volume 3: WTO – Technical Barriers and SPS Measures* (Martinus Nijhoff Publishers, 2007)

Woodley, Mick, *Osborn's Concise Law Dictionary* (Sweet & Maxwell, 11th ed, 2009)

World Trade Organization, *The Future of the WTO: Addressing institutional challenges in the new Millennium: Report by the Consultative Board to the Director-General Supachai Panitchpakdi* (World Trade Organization, 2004)

WTO Secretariat, *Guide to the Uruguay Round Agreements* (Kluwer Law International, 1999)

WTO Secretariat, *A Handbook on the WTO Dispute Settlement System* (Cambridge University Press, 2004)

Yanovich, Alan and Tania Voon, 'What is the Measure at Issue?' in Andrew D. Mitchell (ed), *Challenges and Prospects for the WTO* (Cameron May, 2005) 115

Yardley, D.C.M., *Principles of Administrative Law* (Butterworths, 1986)

Yu, Lei, 'Rule of Law or Rule of Protectionism: Anti-Dumping Practices Toward China and the WTO Dispute Settlement System' (2002) 15(2) *Columbia Journal of Asian Law* 295

Zahrnt, Valentin, 'Domestic Constituents and the Formulation of WTO Negotiating Positions: What the Delegates Say' (2008) 7(2) *World Trade Review* 393

Zimmermann, Thomas A., 'The DSU Review (1998–2004) Negotiations, Problems and Perspectives', in Dencho Georgiev and Kim Van der Borght (eds), *Reform and Development to the Dispute Settlement System* (Cameron May, 2006) 451

Zleptnig, Stefan, 'The Standard of Review in WTO Law: An Analysis of Law, Legitimacy and the Distribution of Legal and Political Authority' (2002) 6(17) *European Integration Online Papers* 1, available at http://eiop.or.at/eiop/texte/2002-017.htm, last accessed 31 March 2012

CASE LAW

Arizona v Thomas 824 F 2d 745, 748 (9th Cir, 1987)

Associated Provincial Picture Houses Ltd v Wednesbury Corpn [1948] 1 KB 223

Chevron USA Inc v Natural Resources Defense Council 467 US 837, 104 (1984)

Citizens to Preserve Overton Park Inc v Volpe 401 US 402 (1971)

Commission v Tetra Laval (C-39/03) [2005] ECR I-987

Consolidated Edison Co. v NLRB, 305 US 197 (1938)

Consolo v Federal Maritime Commission, 383 US 607 (1966)

Delcourt v Belgium (1970) 11 Eur Court HR (ser A)

Drake v Minister for Immigration and Ethnic Affairs (1979) 2 ALD 60

Industrial Union Department, AFL-CIO v American Petroleum Institute 448 US 607, 100 (1980)

Italy v Council (C-166/78) [1979] ECR 2575

La Grange, Conseil d'Etat 15 February 1961

NLRB v Columbian Enameling and Stamping Co., 306 US 292 (1939)

Pacific Coast Federation of Fishermen's Associations v National Maritime Fisheries Service 265 F 3d 1028 (9th Cir, 2001)

Rougemont Conseil d'Etat 7 July 1967

SA Roquette Freres v Council (C-179/80) [1980] ECR 3333

SAM Schiffahrt GmbH and Heinz Stapf v Bundesrupblik Deutschland (C-248/95) [1997] ECR I-4475

Société Anonyme Librairie Francois Maspero, Conseil d'Etat 2 November 1973

Sociéte dé Lotissement de la Plage de Pampelonne, Conseil d'Etat 29 March 1968

UK v Commission (C-180/96) [1998] ECR I-2265

Universal Camera Corp. v National Labor Relations Board, 340 US 474 (1951)

LEGISLATION

Administrative Appeals Act 1975 (Cth)
Administrative Appeals Tribunal Act 1975 (Cth)
Administrative Decisions (Judicial Review) Act 1977 (Cth)
Administrative Procedure Act 5 USC § 559 (1946)
Tariff Act 19 USC § 1654 (1930)
Trade Act 1974 19 USC Ch 12

TREATIES

Final Act Embodying the Results of the Uruguay Round of Multilateral Trade Negotiations 15 April 1994 33 ILM 1140 (1994)

General Agreement on Tariffs and Trade, opened for signature 30 October 1947, 55 UNTS 187 (entered into force 29 July 1948)

International Convention on the Settlement of Investment Disputes between States and Nationals of Other States, opened for signature 18 March 1965, 575 UNTS 159 (entered into force 14 October 1966)

Marrakesh Agreement Establishing the World Trade Organization, opened for signature 15 April 1994, 1867 UNTS 3 (entered into force 1 January 1995) and Annexes 1 to 4

North American Free Trade Agreement, signed 17 December 1992, [1994] CTS 2 (entered into force 1 January 1994)

Treaty on European Union, opened for signature 7 February 1992 OJ C 191 (entered into force 1 November 1993)

Vienna Convention on the Law of Treaties, opened for signature on 23 May 1969, 1155 UNTS 331 (entered into force 27 January 1980)

OTHER SOURCES

Accession of the People's Republic of China, WTO Doc WT/L/432 (2001)

Agreement on Implementation of Article VI of the General Agreement on Tariffs and Trade BISD 26S/171

Agreement on Interpretation and Application of Articles VI, XVI and XXIII of the General Agreement on Tariffs and Trade BISD 26S/56

Australia-Measures affecting the importation of apples from New Zealand (WT/DS367), First Written Submissions of Australia, available at www.dfat.gov.au/trade/negotiations/disputes/index, last accessed 31 March 2012

Australia-Measures affecting the importation of apples from New Zealand (WT/DS367), Executive Summary of the Second Written Submission of New Zealand, available at www.mfat.gov.nz/Treaties-and-International-Law/02-Trade-law-and-free-trade-agreements/index.php, last accessed 31 March 2012

Australia-Measures Affecting the Importation of Apples from New Zealand (WT/DS367) Third Party Submission of the United States of America (1 August 2008), available at www.ustr.gov/trade-topics/enforcement/dispute-settlement-proceedings/wto-dispute-settlement/Australia-apples, last accessed 31 March 2012

Charter for an International Trade Organization, UN Doc. E/Conf. 2/78 (24 March 1948)

New Draft Consolidated Chair Texts of the AD and SCM Agreements, World Trade Organization, Negotiating Group on Rules, WTO doc TN/RL/W/236 (19 December 2008)

Shaffer, Greg, 'Administrative Law Tools and the "Mood" of the Appellate Body decision in the United States – Continued Suspension of Obligations in the EC-Hormones Dispute' (6 November 2008), available at www.//world tradelaw.typepad.com/ielpblog/2008/11/page/2, last accessed 31 March 2012

Statement of Administrative Action for the Uruguay Round Agreements Act, Pub.L. 103-465 Stat. 4809 (1994), 19 USC 3501

Statute of the International Court of Justice

Understanding Regarding Notification, Consultation, Dispute Settlement and Surveillance, L/4907, adopted 28 November 1979, BISD 26S/210

United States-Measures Affecting the Importation of Certain Passenger Motor Vehicle and Light Vehicle Tyres, WTO Doc WT/DS299/1 (2009) (Request for Consultations)

US-Continued Suspension (WT/D8320), Appellee Submission of the United States of America (26 June 2008), available at www.ustr.gov/trade topics/enforcement/dispute-settlement-proceedings/wto-dispute-settlement/continued-suspension-, last accessed 31 March 2012

US-Continued Suspension (WT/DS320), Oral Statement of the United States of America to the Appellate Body (28 July 2008), available at www.ustr.gov/trade-topics/enforcement/dispute-settlement-proceedings/wto-disputesettlement/continued-suspension-, last accessed 31 March 2012

US-Countervailing Duty Investigation on DRAMS (WT/DS296), Appellant Submission of the United States of America (5 April 2005), available at www.ustr.gov/trade-topics/enforcement/dispute-settlement-proceedings/wto-dispute-settlement/countervailing-duty-, last accessed 31 March 2012

Van den Bossche, Peter, 'The Doha Development Round Negotiations on the Dispute Settlement Understanding' (Paper presented at the WTO Conference New Agendas in the 21st Century, Taipei, 28–9 November 2003)

Waincymer, Jeff, 'An Australia United States Free Trade Agreement – Implications for anti-dumping and countervailing' (Paper presented at the An Australia United States Free Trade Agreement Opportunities and Challenges, Hyatt Hotel, Canberra, 21 June 2001)

World Trade Organization, Dispute Settlement Body, Minutes of Meeting held on 5 November 2001, WTO Doc WT/DSB/M/112 (4 December 2001), available at www.wto.org, last accessed 31 March 2012

World Trade Organization, Dispute Settlement Body, Minutes of Meeting held on 9 May 2006, WTO Doc WT/DSB/M/211 (12 June 2006), available at www.wto.org, last accessed 31 March 2012

World Trade Organization, Appellate Body Annual Report for 2008, WTO Doc WT/AB/11 (9 February 2009), available at www.wto.org, last accessed 31 March 2012

World Trade Organization, Dispute Settlement Body, Minutes of Meeting held on 19 February 2009, WTO Doc WT/DSB/M/265 (29 April 2009), available at www.wto.org, last accessed 31 March 2012

Index